Eunny P. Lee
The Vitality of Enjoyment in Qohelet's Theological Rhetoric

Beihefte zur Zeitschrift für die alttestamentliche Wissenschaft

Herausgegeben von
John Barton · Reinhard G. Kratz
Choon-Leong Seow · Markus Witte

Band 353

W
DE
G

Walter de Gruyter · Berlin · New York

Eunny P. Lee

The Vitality of Enjoyment
in Qohelet's Theological Rhetoric

W
DE
G

Walter de Gruyter · Berlin · New York

♾ Printed on acid-free paper which falls within
the guidelines of the ANSI to ensure permanence and durability.

ISBN-13: 978-3-11-018441-9
ISBN-10: 3-11-018441-9

Bibliographic information published by Die Deutsche Bibliothek

Die Deutsche Bibliothek lists this publication in the Deutsche Nationalbibliografie; detailed
bibliographic data is available in the Internet at < http://dnb.ddb.de >.

For my parents

Acknowledgements

This monograph is a slightly revised version of a doctoral dissertation presented to the Biblical studies department of Princeton Theological Seminary in the fall of 2003. I wish, first of all, to thank my dissertation committee: Jacqueline Lapsley who pushed me early on to consider the social implications of this study, and Dennis Olson who in the final stages helped to clarify its theological categories. The quickness with which they reviewed the final draft and offered constructive feedback helped me greatly. I am most deeply indebted to Choon-Leong Seow, my thesis advisor and mentor. It was he who first inspired in me a love for the earthy wisdom of Ecclesiastes, and guided this project from start to finish. His genuine enjoyment of scholarship, commitment to his students, and generosity of spirit are qualities that I will ever seek to emulate.

I am also grateful to Princeton Theological Seminary, especially the Biblical Studies department, which graciously granted me relief from various departmental responsibilities while I worked to complete the dissertation. Patrick Miller, Katharine Sakenfeld and J.J.M. Roberts, my first Old Testament teachers from my M. Div. days, warmly welcomed me as a colleague and happily allowed me to grow into my own. Other members of the department also provided a truly supportive and collegial environment in which I could do—and enjoy—my work. I am thankful to my students at PTS, whose joy in learning and commitment to the church energized and gave meaning to my research and writing. My research assistant, Laura Wright, provided invaluable assistance in preparing the manuscript for publication.

My heartfelt appreciation goes also to my pastors Timothy and Angella Son, and their daughter Grace. Their friendship, wise counsel, and encouragement buoyed my spirit whenever I tired or faltered.

And then there is my family. Shinna and Don Alava, and my nieces Gabrielle and Anna reminded me of the rejuvenating value of "eating, drinking, being glad"... and playing. In my sister Bo I had a tireless cheerleader and understanding friend. Finally, my parents Jong Hyeong and Nam Sun Lee have supported and inspired me all my life by their own example of faithful service to Christ, their loving care, their ceaseless prayers. With love and gratitude, I dedicate this work to them.

Eunny P. Lee, June 2005

Table of Contents

Acknowledgements vii

Table of Contents ix

Abbreviations xi

Introduction 1

Chapter One: Integrity of the Book.. 11

    1.1 Introduction 11
    1.2 Broad Framework... 15
    1.3 Catchwords and Linking Devices 18
    1.4 Genre, Rhetoric, and Subversion.. 23
        1.4.1 Multivalence.. 25
        1.4.2 Irony and the Rhetoric of Subversion.................................... 26
    1.5 Integrity and *Hebel* 30
    1.6 Summary 31

Chapter Two: The Vitality of Enjoyment in Qohelet's Theological
Rhetoric.. 32

    2.1 Introduction 32
    2.2 In the Hand of God (Eccl 2:24 – 26)... 35
    2.3 The Human Portion (Eccl 3:12 – 13, 22)..................................... 40
    2.4 The Divine – and Human – "Answer" (Eccl 5:17 – 19) 44
    2.5 The Paradox of Joy (7:14)... 50
    2.6 By the Sweat of One's Brow (8:15) 58
    2.7 To Life! (9:7 – 10) 62
    2.8 Farewell to Joy (11:7 – 12:7)... 72
    2.9 Conclusion.. 80

Chapter Three: The Fear of God: The Dialogics of Piety 83

3.1 Introduction 83
3.2 The Inscrutable Work of God (3:14) 86
3.3 In the Presence of the Wholly Other (5:6) 91
3.4 A Morality of "Both" (7:18) 99
3.5 To Believe or Not to Believe (8:12b — 13) 105
3.6 The End of the Matter (12:13b) 110
3.7 Conclusion 118

Conclusion: Qohelet's Theology of Enjoyment 123

4.1 Introduction 123
4.2 The Normativity of Enjoyment 125
4.3 The Ethic of Joy and Social Responsibility 129
4.4 Enjoyment and Double Agency 135

Bibliography 141

Index of Ancient Texts 159

Abbreviations

ÄAT   Ägypten und Altes Testament

AB   Anchor Bible Commentary

ABR   *Australian Biblical Review*

AEL   M. Lichtheim, ed. *Ancient Egyptian Literature*. 3 vols. Berkeley: University of California, 1971–80.

AJBI   Annual of the Japanese Biblical Institute, Tokyo

AnBib   Analecta Biblica

ArbT   *Arbeiten zur Theologie*, Stuttgart

ASTI   *Annual of the Swedish Theological Institute*

ATD   Das Alte Testament Deutsch

BBB   Bonner biblische Beiträge

BETL   Bibliotheca ephemeridum theologicarum lovaniensium

Bib   *Biblica*, Rome

BK   *Bibel und Kirche*, Stuttgart

BKAT   Biblischer Kommentar: Altes Testament

BSac   *Bibliotheca Sacra*

BTB   *Biblical Theology Bulletin*

BV   Biblical Viewpoint

BWL   W. G. Lambert, ed. *Babylonian Wisdom Literature*. Oxford: Clarendon, 1960.

BZAW   Beihefte zur Zeitschrift für die alttestamentliche Wissenschaft

CBQ   *Catholic Biblical Quarterly*, Washington, D. C.

CBQMS   Catholic Biblical Quarterly Monograph Series

CBSC   Cambridge Bible for Schools and Colleges

CD   Karl Barth, *Church Dogmatics*. 4 vols. Edinburgh: T. & T. Clark, 1936–1977.

CJT   *Canadian Journal of Theology*

CTM   *Concordia Theological Monthly*

DJD   Discoveries in the Judean Desert

EBib   Études bibliques

ERT   *Evangelical Review of Theology*

ETL   *Ephemerides Theologicae Lovanienses*, Louvain

EvT   *Evangelische Theologie*

FO   *Folia Orientalia*

GKC   E. Kautzsch, ed. *Gesenius' Hebrew Grammar*. Translated by A. E. Cowley. 2d ed. Oxford: Clarendon, 1980.

HAR	*Hebrew Annual Review*
HAT	Handbuch zum Alten Testament
HKAT	Handkommentar zum Alten Testament
HR	*History of Religions*, Chicago
HSM	Harvard Semitic Monographs
HUCA	*Hebrew Union College Annual*, Cincinnati
IBC	Interpretation: A Bible Commentary for Teaching and Preaching.
ICC	International Critical Commentary
IDB	*Interpreter's Dictionary of the Bible*
IEJ	*Israel Exploration Journal*, Jerusalem
Int	*Interpretation*, Richmond, VA
IRT	Issues in Religion and Theology
ISBL	Indiana Studies in Biblical Literature
ITC	International Theological Commentary
ITQ	*Irish Theological Quarterly*, Maynooth
JAAR	*Journal of the American Academy of Religion*
JBL	*Journal of Biblical Literature*
JNES	*Journal of Near Eastern Studies*, Chicago
JQR	*Jewish Quarterly Review*
JRE	*Journal of Religious Ethics*
JSOT	*Journal for the Study of the Old Testament*, Sheffield
JSOTSup	Journal for the Study of the Old Testament: Supplement Series
JSS	*Journal of Semitic Studies*, Manchester
KAT	Kommentar zum Alten Testament
KTU	M. Dietrich, O. Loretz, and J. Sanmartin. *The Cuneiform Alphabetic Texts from Ugarit, Ras Ibn Hani and Other Places* (KTU, 2d ed.).
LBH	Late Biblical Hebrew
LD	Lectio divina
LXX	Septuagint
NCBC	New Century Bible Commentary
NEchtB	Die Neue Echter Bibel
NICOT	New International Commentary on the Old Testament
OBO	Orbis biblicus et orientalis
OLA	Orientalia Lovaniensia Analecta
OLP	*Orientalia lovaniensia periodica*
Or	*Orientalia*
OTE	*Old Testament Essays*
OTL	Old Testament Library
PSB	*Princeton Seminary Bulletin*, Princeton, NJ

RB	*Revue biblique*, Paris
RevExp	*Review and Expositor*, Louisville, KY
RHPR	*Revue d'histoire et de philosophie religieuses*
SBLDS	Society of Biblical Literature Dissertation Series
SBTh	Studia Biblica et Theologica
SJT	*Scottish Journal of Theology*, Edinburgh
SubBi	Subsidia Biblica
TAD	B. Porten and A. Yardeni. *Textbook of Aramaic Documents from Ancient Egypt*. Jerusalem, 1986.
TDOT	*Theological Dictionary of the Old Testament*
ThQ	*Theologische Quartalschrift*
ThViat	*Theologia Viatorum*, Berlin
TTZ	*Trierer theologische Zeitschrift*
TynBul	*Tyndale Bulletin*
TZ	*Theologische Zeitschrift*, Basel, Switzerland
VS	Verbum Salutis
VT	*Vetus Testamentum*, Leiden
VTSup	Supplements to Vetus Testamentum
WBC	Word Biblical Commentary
WTJ	*Westminster Theological Journal*, Philadelphia
WW	*Word & World*, Fort Lee, NJ
ZAW	*Zeitschrift für die alttestamentliche Wissenschaft*, Berlin
ZTK	*Zeitschrift für Theologie und Kirche*

Introduction

Ecclesiastes is a book of contradictions. That is a truism as far as its content is concerned; Ecclesiastes seems to hold at once contradictory perspectives on life. Indeed, it was in no small part because of its apparent contradictions that the early rabbis considered consigning the book to oblivion: "The sages sought to suppress the book of Qohelet because its words are mutually contradictory" (*b. Shab.* 30b). At the same time, Ecclesiastes may be called a book of contradictions for the polar positions it has generated among interpreters from antiquity to the present. Today, a majority of commentators regard the author as a consummate pessimist who relentlessly announces that "all is vanity," while others herald him as an indefatigable optimist, even a "preacher of joy," who maintains that "there is nothing better for people under the sun than to eat and drink and enjoy themselves" (8:15). But that is, of course, only the most obvious instance of interpretive disagreement. Indeed, on virtually every critical issue, one may readily cite scholars holding not just variant positions but diametrically opposite ones. Even where one might reasonably expect near unanimity, one finds only contradictions.

The thematic word *hebel* is a case in point in this regard. No one disputes the importance of this *leitmotif* for the interpretation of the book. Not only does the term recur throughout the book and at key junctures, it occurs in the memorable epigram that frames Qohelet's reflections (1:2; 12:8). Yet, while all agree on the importance of the term, the question of its precise translation, meaning, and function in the book continues to be disputed vigorously. The traditional understanding of *hebel* is still the dominant one, as is evident in the prevalence of the rendering "vanity" or some equivalent term in the standard English translations.[1] The negative overtones associated with this ubiquitous refrain have undergirded the pessimistic reading of the book. Others who highlight the positive dimensions of the book, however, have proposed alternative ways of understanding this key word. The term *hebel*, they contend, connotes not "vanity," "futility," or

---

1   Note "vanity" in NRSV, NAB, and NJB; "futility" in NJPS and REB; "emptiness" in NEB; and "meaninglessness" in NIV.

"meaninglessness," but that which is "transient,"[2] "enigmatic,"[3] "incomprehensible,"[4] or "ironic."[5] In disagreement with all of these, Fox maintains that *hebel* signifies something like Camus's notion of the "absurd."[6] Yet, Lohfink would return to the question again, claiming that the term approximates its literal meaning of "vapor" or "breath."[7] Even within the same school of thought, there is often a divergence of opinion concerning the meaning of *hebel*. Seow, for example, contends that the term in Ecclesiastes functions as metaphor for that which is, like the literal referent of *hebel* ("vapor" or "breath"), "beyond mortal grasp."[8] His student Douglas Miller shares his methodology but takes his interpretation in a more negative direction by arguing that "foulness," in addition to insubstantiality and transience, is a key trait of *hebel*.[9] To that argument Seow demurs, maintaining that "foulness" is not really a trait of *hebel*, for "[w]hereas *hebel* is always transient and always substantial, it is not always foul."[10] The term *hebel* itself, it seems, is like a breath—eluding scholarly attempts to grasp and fix its meaning determinately.

Apart from the meaning of *hebel*, interpretive antinomies are evident in scholarly discussions of two of the most prominent motifs in the book: the enjoyment of life and fear of God. As in the case of *hebel*, these two themes are widely recognized to be critical to the book's

---

2   D. C. Fredericks, *Coping with Transience: Ecclesiastes on Brevity in Life* (The Biblical Seminar 18; Sheffield: JSOT Press, 1993); Kathleen A. Farmer, *Who Knows What is Good? A Commentary on the Books of Proverbs and Ecclesiastes* (ITC; Grand Rapids: Eerdmans, 1991); D. B. Macdonald, *The Hebrew Philosophical Genius: A Vindication* (Princeton: Princeton University Press, 1936), 70–85.

3   Graham Ogden, *Qoheleth: Readings—A New Bible Commentary* (Sheffield: JSOT, 1987); idem, "'Vanity' It Certainly is Not," *TBT* 38 (1987): 301–307.

4   William Ewart Staples, "The 'Vanity' of Ecclesiastes," *JNES* 4 (1943): 95–104; idem, "Vanity of Vanities," *Canadian Journal of Theology* 1 (1955): 141–56.

5   Edwin M. Good, *Irony in the Old Testament* (London: SPCK, 1965; repr. Sheffield: Almond, 1981), 176–83; Timothy K. Polk, "The Wisdom of Irony: A Study of *Hebel* and Its Relation to Joy and Fear of God in Ecclesiastes," *SBTh* 6, no. 1 (1976): 3–17.

6   Michael V. Fox, "The Meaning of HEBEL for Qohelet," *JBL* 105, no. 3 (1986): 409–27.

7   Norbert Lohfink, "Koh 1,2 'alles ist Windhauch'—universale oder anthropologische Aussage?" in *Der Weg zum Menschen* (ed. R. Mosis and L. Ruppert; Freiberg: Herder, 1989), 201–16.

8   Choon Leong Seow, *Ecclesiastes: A New Translation with Introduction and Commentary* (AB 18C; New York: Doubleday, 1997), 102; idem, "Beyond Mortal Grasp: The Usage of *Hebel* in Ecclesiastes," *ABR* 48 (2000): 1–16.

9   Douglas B. Miller, "Qohelet's Symbolic Use of *lbh*," *JBL* 117 (1998): 437–54; idem, *Symbol and Rhetoric in Ecclesiastes: The Place of Hebel in Qohelet's Work* (Leiden/Boston: Brill, 2002).

10   Seow, "Beyond Mortal Grasp," 13.

teachings. Yet, again, there are conflicting views on the meaning and function of these motifs in Qohelet's discourse. The proponents of optimism handle them in one way, the proponents of pessimism in an entirely different way.

The more prominent of the two is the commendation of enjoyment. Eight times in his discourse, Qohelet counsels the enjoyment of life (2:24—26; 3:12—13, 22; 5:17—19; 7:14; 8:15; 9:7—10; 11:7—12:1).[11] These "joy passages" are remarkable for the commonality of their language, and the persistent and emphatic quality of the exhortation. This is all the more so when one moves beyond the explicit language of joy (śimḥâ and śāmēᵃḥ) to other metaphors and idioms for joy: eating, drinking, donning bright garments, anointing one's head with oil, and being with one's beloved, as well as the expressions "see good" (2:1, 24; 3:13; 5:17), "do well" (3:12), "be in good" (7:14), and "see life" (9:9). Joy appears in virtually every literary unit of the book—with other sobering elements, to be sure, but nonetheless present everywhere. It is notable also that this repetition does not occur at random, but in strategic places in the movement of the book, often marking the climactic moment of a literary unit where Qohelet engages in explicit and sustained theological reflections. Accordingly, many have commented on the pivotal role of the joy passages in Qohelet's rhetoric,[12] some even opting for this refrain over against the more prevalent *hebel* refrain, as the primary structuring principle of the book.[13] Their analysis demonstrates how emphatically the refrain functions for many readers.

Advocates of the optimistic view find here the most compelling support for their sanguine assessment of the book's message. According to these scholars, this unrelenting counsel conveys the book's central message, demonstrating unequivocally that "Qohelet's focus is upon an affirmative rather than a negative view of human

---

11 Most scholars do not include 7:14 in this category. However, this study will contend that the author employs not only the explicit vocabulary of śmḥ but also various other metaphors and idioms to communicate his commendation of enjoyment. The expression "be in good" in 7:14 functions precisely in this manner; it therefore appropriately qualifies as a "joy passage."

12 Martin A. Klopfenstein, "Die Skepsis des Qoheleth," *TZ* 28 (1972): 97—109; R. K. Johnston, "Confession of a Workaholic: A Reappraisal of Qoheleth," *CBQ* 38 (1976): 14—28; T. Polk, "The Wisdom of Irony," 3—17; R. N. Whybray, "Qoheleth Preacher of Joy," *JSOT* 23 (1982): 87—98; N. Lohfink, "Qoheleth 5:17—19—Revelation by Joy," *CBQ* 52 (1990): 625—635.

13 F. Rousseau, "Structure de Qohélet I 4—11 et plan du livre," *VT* 31 (1981): 200—17. See also J. F. Genung, *The Words of Qoheleth* (Boston: Houghton Mifflin, 1904); A. F. Rainey, "A Study of Ecclesiastes," *CTM* 35 (1964): 148—57.

life."[14] All other observations in the book pale in comparison, serving only as a backdrop against which he teaches the preeminent value of joy. Indeed, the calls to enjoyment are said to be "theological statements of faith in a just and loving God, despite many signs which might appear contrary."[15] For Whybray, the "Preacher" proclaims the gospel of joy: enjoyment is what enables a person to transcend the troublesome realities of human existence.[16] Lohfink makes an even more daring theological claim when he asserts that joy is nothing less than "revelation," the means by which God "answers" humanity.[17]

This approach to the joy texts, however, has not carried the day. The majority of scholars highlight instead the book's thoroughgoing pessimism, insisting that Qohelet's probing skepticism is what characterizes the book from start to finish. Hence, Crenshaw introduces his commentary to Ecclesiastes with this overview of the book's message: "Life is profitless; totally absurd ... Enjoy life if you can ... And even as you enjoy, know that the world is meaningless."[18] According to his reading of the book, *hebel* ultimately trumps joy. In a similar vein, W. H. U. Anderson states even more explicitly that the joy passages are ultimately "invalidated" by the decisive pronouncement of *hebel*.[19] For these interpreters, Qohelet's commendation of enjoyment is merely a concession to the absurd circumstances of life, communicating an attitude of jaded resignation, not resilient faith. Fox likens the persistent endorsement of enjoyment to the "gesticulations of a lunatic," a senseless activity that is meaningful only in a crazed person's private world.[20] Another scholar suggests that the counsels of joy are a reflex of the author's conflicted psychological make-up that arose as a result of his troubled childhood and marital experiences.[21] Qohelet's notion of enjoyment, at best, points to "little pleasures to

---

14   Ogden, *Qoheleth*, 14, 22. See also Robert Gordis, *Koheleth — the Man and His World* (3rd ed.; New York: Schocken, 1968), 131; E. Good, *Irony in the Old Testament*, 176 – 83; Hagia Hildegard Witzenrath, *Süss ist das Licht: eine literaturwissenschaftliche Untersuchung zu Koh 11,7 – 12,7* (St. Ottiliten: EOS Verlag, 1979); Whybray, "Qoheleth, Preacher of Joy," 87 – 98.

15   Ogden, *Qoheleth*, 22.

16   Whybray, "Qoheleth, Preacher of Joy," 91.

17   Lohfink, "Qoheleth 5:17 – 19 – Revelation by Joy," 625 – 635.

18   James Crenshaw, *Ecclesiastes: A Commentary* (OTL; Philadelphia: Westminster, 1987), 23.

19   W. H. U. Anderson, *Qoheleth and Its Pessimistic Theology: Hermeneutical Struggles in Wisdom Literature* (Lewiston/Queenston/Lampeter: Mellen Biblical Press, 1997), 74.

20   Michael V. Fox, *A Time to Tear Down and A Time to Build Up: A Rereading of Ecclesiastes* (Grand Rapids, Mich.: Eerdmans, 1999), 130.

21   Frank Zimmermann, *The Inner World of Qohelet* (New York: KTAV, 1973).

soothe the troubled spirit,"[22] or "wishful thinking" that provides "psychological relief."[23] In one way or another, then, the joy texts are dismissed as a peripheral strain in the book, a far cry from the lofty "revelation of joy" envisioned by Lohfink.

The other prominent theme in the book is the fear of God. Despite the fact that there are only seven references to the fear of God in the book, virtually all interpreters of Ecclesiastes acknowledge its importance.[24] Indeed, it has been argued that "the interpretation of this phrase in Ecclesiastes is of the greatest importance for the assessment of Qohelet's thought."[25] This consensus is due in part, no doubt, to the recognition that the fear of God is a well-established wisdom principle; indeed, one may say that it is the critical starting place for the wisdom enterprise (see Prov 1:7; 2:5; 9:10; 15:33; Job 28:28; cf. Ps 111:10). The theme plays a key role in both Proverbs and Job, appearing prominently in the important introductory verses of those books (Prov 1:7; Job 1:1, 8−9). Interpreters, therefore, are compelled to attend to the way it is featured in Ecclesiastes as well, all the more so because Ecclesiastes ends by calling attention once more to this important theme: "The end of the matter; all has been heard. Fear God …" (12:13). Whether or not one believes this to be a legitimate conclusion to Qohelet's discourse,[26] the final form of the book reserves the privileged position at the very end for this counsel; it is the last word with which the reader is left. Some have therefore argued on this basis that the closing admonition to fear God functions as an important hermeneutical key for reading the book.[27]

Here, again, scholarly opinion concerning the meaning and function of this theme is sharply divided. For Franz Delitzsch, this subject matter is so important that the book is characterized by it— Ecclesiastes is the "supreme song of the fear of God," and by virtue of

---

22   Crenshaw, *Ecclesiastes*, 27. See also Fox, *A Time to Tear Down*, 129−131, 239−241; Tremper Longman, *The Book of Ecclesiastes* (NICOT; Grand Rapids: Eerdmans, 1998), 35, 121−22, 168.

23   W. H. U. Anderson, *Qoheleth and Its Pessimistic Theology*, 73.

24   See especially Toshiaki Nishimura, "Quelques Reflexions Semiologiques A Propos de 'La Crainte de Deiu' de Qohelet," in *AJBI* 5 (1979): 67−87.

25   Whybray, *Ecclesiastes*, 25.

26   To be discussed in chapter 3.

27   Gerald T. Sheppard, "The Epilogue to Qoheleth as Theological Commentary," *CBQ* 39 (1977): 182−89; Brevard S. Childs, *Introduction to the Old Testament as Scpriture* (Philadelphia: Fortress, 1979), 585−588; Longman, *Book of Ecclesiastes*.

this association, the "quintessence of biblical piety."[28] Delitzsch represents a long line of interpreters (both Christian and Jewish) who have appealed to this theme to argue for the book's rightful place in the canon. Scholars today are less inclined to make such an interpretive move; nevertheless, some continue to underscore the orthodox orientation of this theme in Ecclesiastes in order to temper, if not offset, its radical skepticism. According to Ogden, although Qohelet repeatedly observes the perplexing realities of life, the sage, in the end, "throws his full support behind the tradition" and affirms that fearing God is "the only way to success."[29] Others, to one degree or another, second that positive assessment. For Whybray, Qohelet's notion of the fear of God is no different from what is found in the rest of the Old Testament: "in short, the reverence for, and worship of God, characteristic of sincere Yahwists."[30] Brown is more nuanced in pointing out Qohelet's unique development of this motif, but declares that fear of God is, after all, the book's "chief virtue," the thing that "most comprehensively shapes the contours of right character."[31]

The majority of scholars, however, approach the fear of God in Ecclesiastes very differently. On the one hand, the references to this "orthodox" theme are dismissed altogether as the product of editorial tampering, an interpretive strategy that was especially prevalent in the heyday of source criticism. Although not as widespread today, commentators continue to downplay the final injunction in the epilogue and at least some of the internal references to fearing God (especially 7:18; 8:12—13) as largely irrelevant to the meaning of the book. On the other hand, if these references are granted to be integral to the book, interpreters offer a radically different construal of this concept, one that is in keeping with the pessimistic interpretation of the book. The fear of God in Ecclesiastes is said to depart from its general meaning elsewhere in the Old Testament and connote a literal feeling of terror before an arbitrary and potentially menacing deity. Zimmerli, for instance, reckons that fearing God, for Qohelet, means living with the possibility that a mysterious and capricious deity God might strike at any moment, like a sudden bolt of lightning, and inflict terror on the

---

28   Franz Delitzsch, *Commentary on the Song of Songs and Ecclesiastes* (trans. M. G. Easton; Edinburgh: T. & T. Clark, 1891), 183; trans. of *Hoheslied und Koheleth* (Leipzig: Dörffling und Franke, 1875).

29   Ogden, *Qoheleth*, 137.

30   R. N. Whybray, "Qohelet as a Theologian," in *Qohelet in the Context of Wisdom* (ed. A. Schoors; Leuven: Leuven University Press, 1998), 264—66.

31   William P. Brown, *Character in Crisis: A Fresh Approach to the Wisdom Literature of the Old Testament* (Grand Rapids, Mich.: Eerdmans, 1996), 143.

hapless mortal.[32] Or, as another critic puts it, the traditional precept to fear God comes to mean "to be on guard *against* Elohim." [33] According to such interpretations, Qohelet's notion of fearing God highlights only the dark chasm between God and humanity, and humanity's complete alienation from the deity. Entirely absent are the positive aspects that are typically associated with it in traditional wisdom. Crenshaw plainly articulates this view when he singles out Ecclesiastes as the "one book in the Old Testament where the fear of God seems to stand alone without any hint of divine compassion."[34]

So the two main approaches to Ecclesiastes continue to debate the meaning of joy and fear of God in Ecclesiastes. The polarization in scholarly opinion is perhaps inevitable to some degree. As Murphy has noted, the contradictive nature of the book, combined with the subjectivity of the interpreter, makes Ecclesiasts particularly susceptible to a "selective emphasis."[35] However, the continued division among interpreters only perpetuates the propensity for accentuating one aspect of the book at the expense of another. Furthermore, as one reading is pitted against and subverts other readings, it becomes increasingly difficult to appropriate the message of the book theologically with any measure of confidence. Given this state of affairs, one must now consider whether a rapprochement is possible between these opposing readings that can push past the current impasse, and offer readings that are able to hold the tension fruitfully

---

32   Walther Zimmerli, "Das Buch des Predigers Salomo," *Sprüche/Prediger* (ATD 16/1; Göttingen: Vandenhoeck & Ruprecht, 1962), 174.

33   Elias J. Bickerman, *Four Strange Books of the Bible: Jonah, Daniel, Koheleth, Esther* (New York: Schocken Books, 1967), 149.

34   James L. Crenshaw, "The Eternal Gospel (Eccl. 3:11)," in *Essays in Old Testament Ethics* (ed. J. L. Crenshaw and J. T. Willis; New York: KTAV, 1974), 25. See also Egon Pfeiffer, "Die Gottesfurcht im Buche Kohelet," in *Gottes Wort und Gottes Land* (ed. H. Reventlow; Göttingen: Vandenhoeck & Ruprecht, 1965), 133–35; Johannes Fichtner, *Die altorientalische Weisheit in ihrer israelitisch-jüdischen Ausprägung* (BZAW 62; Giessen: A. Töpelmann, 1933), 52–53; Gordis, *Koheleth*, 223; Loader, *Ecclesiastes*, 41; Bernhard Lang, "Ist der Mensch Hilflos? Das biblische Buch Kohelet, neu und kritisch gelesen," *ThQ* 159 (1979): 45.

35   Roland E. Murphy, *Ecclesiastes* (WBC 23A; Dallas: Word Books, 1992), lv. See also Johannes Pedersen, *Scepticisme Israélite* (Paris: Alcan, 1931), 20. Pedersen observes that very different types have found their own image in Ecclesiastes, and, remarkably, none of the various interpretations is completely without some basis. Different interpreters have highlighted the aspect of the book that was most fitting for themselves and their age. Yet all interpreters confronted one difficulty—that there were also other aspects that could not be harmonized with their preferred view.

within themselves, and thereby do justice to both the subversive *and* constructive value of the book.[36]

Ecclesiastes is, indeed, a book of contradictions. It confronts the contradictions inherent to the human condition and speaks about them with brutal candor. Moreover, it effectively conveys those contradictions through forms of discourse that seem to revel in ambiguity and indeterminacy. Perhaps, in the end, one is left to return to the Preacher's claim that everything is like mist and mortals cannot lay a definitive claim to anything. However, that is not the only word proffered by the sage. He also insists that human beings, despite their inability to grab and hold on to anything, may go forth in this life and engage the given times and moments constructively. This, after all, is what it means to fear God according to the worldview of the ancient sages: to recognize both the tragic limitations and the joyous possibilities of human existence. One may therefore set to rest the debate about whether the book ought to be characterized as either optimistic or pessimistic in its outlook. Qohelet's stance toward life may more appropriately be described as *faithful realism*. The sage confronts the reality of human existence, with both its tragic and the joyous dimensions, and calls his audience to respond faithfully to the mysterious activity of God by living life to the full.

This study begins with a chapter that makes a case for the integrity of the book. As noted above, the contradictions in Ecclesiastes led to the expedient of historical criticism that the current form of the text must be the result of a complex compositional-redactional history. This approach allows readers to dismiss certain aspects of the book — including the themes of enjoyment and fear of God — as the product of editorial activity, and thus tangential to the message of the book. I argue, however, that the contradictory strains in Ecclesiastes are integral to Qohelet's discourse; they are part and parcel of the author's observations concerning the human condition. If the text is read as a unified composition, then neither the commendations of enjoyment nor the injunction to fear God may be dismissed as a secondary or peripheral concern. Instead, the interplay between these two important motifs must be interpreted anew.

Indeed, current scholarship is increasingly granting the possibility of the book's unity. Highly influential in this regard are the works of Michael Fox and C. L. Seow, who argue on form-critical grounds that the book (with the possible exception of the "colophon" in 12:13b—14)

---

36   Note Fox's recent re-reading of the book, which makes the constructive dimension a more intentional and explicit part of his program (Fox, *A Time to Tear Down and A Time to Build Up*).

must be read as a unified literary composition.[37] Beyond their form-critical arguments, I catalogue other features of the text that further support the theory of a unified composition: (1) hints of organization on a macro level that point to a broadly coherent design; (2) the use of numerous catchwords and linking devices that effectively connect various aspects of the author's thoughts into a meaningful whole; and finally, (3) the use of rhetorical strategies that intentionally exploit contradictions in order to demonstrate that uncertainties and contingencies are an inevitable reality of human existence. Taken together, these features of the text further confirm that Ecclesiastes is indeed a unified and meaningful composition. This assessment undergirds my contention that the commendations of joy and the fear of God are indeed critical to the book's theological claims, and must be interpreted in light of the whole work and in relationship to one another

Chapter 2 then examines the place and function of the so-called "joy passages" (2:24—26; 3:12—13, 22; 5:17—19; 7:14; 8:15; 9:7—10; 11:7—12:7) in Qohelet's discourse. I demonstrate, first, that these commendations of enjoyment are *essential* to the author's overall rhetorical strategy and theological argumentation, and may not be dismissed as a tangential strain. These texts are placed strategically within the book and are crafted to interact with and build upon one another as the author develops his argument from beginning to end. Second, I argue that the commendations of enjoyment are the vehicle through which the sage most emphatically communicates his vision of piety and the moral life. What he offers is not "a counsel of despair," or "wishful thinking," or a hedonistic call to maximize pleasure and avoid pain. Neither does he espouse a spiritualized joy by which a person may become impervious to the troublesome realities of earthly existence. Qohelet plainly acknowledges that enjoyment, like everything else has its limitations, because life forever retains its tragic dimension, its mortal boundaries. His notion of enjoyment, shaped by his faithful realism, requires the human agent to confront life with all its contradictions and contingencies, and to appropriate each moment—whether good or bad—as the grant of a mysterious God. In short, enjoyment, for Qohelet, has to do with *living life* to the full, with a

---

37   Michael V. Fox, "Frame-Narrative and Composition in the Book of Qohelet," *HUCA* 48 (1977): 83—106; Choon Leong Seow, "Qohelet's Autobiography," in *Fortunate the Eyes that See: Essays in Honor of David Noel Freedman* (ed. A. B. Beck et al.; Grand Rapids, Mich.: Eerdmans, 1995), 275—87; idem, "The Epilogue of Qohelet Revisited," in *Wisdom, You Are My Sister* (ed. M. L. Barré; CBQM 29; Washington, D.C.: Catholic Biblical Association, 1997), 125—41.

sober recognition of its travails and a grateful acceptance of its possibilities.

An exposition of Qohelet's understanding of the fear of God follows in chapter 3. The analysis includes two components. First, to counter the contention that the references to the fear of God are a secondary accretion that is largely irrelevant to the book's message, a close study of the pertinent texts in Ecclesiastes (3:14; 5:6; 7:18; 8:12f; 12:13b) shows that the sage's remarks concerning the fear of God are integral—indeed indispensable—to Qohelet's discourse. The analysis then explicates the meaning of fearing God in these texts. In short, Qohelet does not dispute the view that is basic to the wisdom tradition. Fear of God in Ecclesiastes does *not* convey a notion of disabling terror, as many have argued, but of overwhelming awe in the presence of an utterly transcendent God. For Qohelet, the recognition of the deity's essential Otherness provokes a profound awareness of humanity's proper place in the world—a place that comes with *both* its tragic limitations and its joyous potentialities for human flourishing. This understanding emerges as a result of his rigorous engagement with the realities of human experience on the one hand, and with traditional wisdom on the other hand. In the end, what is most distinctive about his conception of religious duty is its association with life-centered enjoyment. Neither austere nor sentimental in his vision of piety, the sage suggests that religious duty is concretely demonstrated in the daily practice of joy.

Finally, the concluding chapter pulls together the various findings and then explores some further ethical implications of Qohelet's theology of enjoyment. For Qohelet, the moral life is grounded in the responsible practice of enjoyment, that is, enjoyment that promotes not only the flourishing of the individual, but also the life of the larger human community.

Chapter One

Integrity of the Book

1.1 Introduction

Ecclesiastes is a book of contradictions, and the contradictions have preoccupied interpreters of the book from its inception. Troubled by the tensions and inconsistencies therein, interpreters throughout the ages sought various means for resolving them or otherwise explaining their presence. With the rise of historical-criticism in the modern era, the contradictions inevitably led to questions concerning the book's integrity. Indeed, it is fair to say that for much of the twentieth century, the integrity of the book was the essential question in Qohelet studies.[38] During this period, the prevailing view was that the book in its present form was the result of a complex compositional-redactional history, wherein radical tradents of pessimistic philosophies and orthodox glossators are engaged in lively debate. Proponents of this method found evidence of editorial activity, first, in the preservation of two distinct voices in the book: while the body of the book is presented as the first-person reflections of "Qohelet," the book's frame speaks of this persona in a detached third-person voice (1:1; 12:9—14; cf. 7:27). The "epilogue" (12:9—14), moreover, looks back on the teachings of Qohelet and offers evaluative comments on his work. Hence, there emerged a widespread consensus that the book's final verses must have been appended secondarily by one or more redactor(s), in order to ameliorate the radical views of the original author.

Furthermore, the conflicting perspectives *within* the book were also attributed to different hands at work at different stages of transmission. According to one elaborate theory, a philosophical Jew with a skeptical

---

1   James L. Crenshaw, "Qoheleth in Current Research," *HAR* 7 (1983): 43. See also Carol Newsom, "Job and Ecclesiastes," in *Old Testament Interpretation: Past, Present, and Future* (eds. J. L. Mays et al.; Nashville: Abingdon, 1995), 187—90; Franz J. Backhaus, "Widersprüche und Spannungen im Buch Qohelet: zu einem neueren Versuch, Spannungen und Widersprüche literarkritisch zu lösen," in *Das Buch Kohelet: Studien zur Struktur, Geschichte, Rezeption und Theologie* (ed. Ludger Schwienhorst-Schönberger; Berlin: de Gruyter, 1997), 123—154.

orientation composed the original work, to which as many as eight other hands added various interpolations.[39] This approach held sway at the beginning of the twentieth century, and the leading commentaries adopted variations of this method, albeit in more moderate forms.[40] Their interpretive strategies focused on the contradictions in the text and sought to filter out the alleged glosses and interpolations in favor of an unadulterated "original" Qohelet. The texts most often marked for excision were those that affirm divine judgment (3:17; 8:12b—13; 11:9) or expound on the fear of God (5:6b; 7:18b; 8:12b—13). The commendations of enjoyment were also dismissed as secondary accretions, albeit to a lesser degree. If these approaches are persuasive, then the contradictions in the book can be accounted for as the result of compositional processes and not the rhetorical strategy of the author.

Recent scholarship, however, has questioned the viability of such *ad hoc* approaches, pointing to some critical methodological problems. First, a fundamental difficulty with this approach is the dilemma of where to locate Qohelet's thought over against that of the purported editors. In other words, how does one determine which side of the contradiction belongs to the original work? It becomes all too easy to impose an *a priori* judgment concerning which of the contradictory statements constitutes Qohelet's words. Indeed, the history of the book's interpretation bears out the subjective nature of this approach. In "pre-critical" interpretation, the inclination was to dismiss the "heretical" views in favor of a consistently orthodox Qohelet. Today, the trend is reversed; Qohelet is deemed to be consistently skeptical, and the orthodox voices are seen to represent the intrusions that obscure the book's true message.

---

2   Carl G. A. Siegfried discerned the work of four glossators: a Sadducean Epicurean added the admonitions to enjoy life; a sage (*ḥākām*) the sayings concerning the advantages of wisdom; a pietist (*ḥāsîd*) the assertions concerning divine judgment; and finally, a catchall group of others who were responsible for miscellaneous insertions. Additionally, Siegfried identified two epilogists and two editors. See *Prediger und Hoheslied* (Göttingen: Vandenhoeck & Ruprecht, 1898), 2–12.

3   See, for example, A. H. McNeile, *An Introduction to Ecclesiastes* (Cambridge: Cambridge University Press, 1904); George Barton, *A Critical and Exegetical Commentary on the Book of Ecclesiastes* (ICC; Edinburgh: T. & T. Clark, 1908); Emmanuel Podechard, *L'Ecclésiastes* (EBib; Paris: Gabalda, 1912). Even into the 1970's, many commentators continued to take frequent recourse to glosses. So Hans Wilhelm Hertzberg, *Der Prediger* (KAT 17/4; Gütersloh: Mohn, 1963); F. Ellermeier, *Qohelet I/1. Untersuchungen zum Buche Qohelet* (Herzberg: Jungfer, 1967); Kurt Galling, "Der Prediger," in *Die fünf Megilloth* (2d ed.; HAT 18; Tübingen: Mohr, 1969); and Aarre Lauha, *Kohelet* (BKAT 19; Neukirchen-Vluyn: Neukirchener, 1978).

There are other difficulties as well, as Fox has aptly observed.[41] The putative glosses often do not fulfill their supposed purpose—they do not ameliorate the subversive edge of Qohelet's thoughts. Indeed, despite the "orthodox" additions, the skepticism remains blatant in the text. Moreover, expunging the alleged glosses does not result in consistency, as one would expect. In fact, more often than not, it leaves syntactical and logical gaps in the flow of thought. Others have noted, furthermore, that in some instances, the dissonance is unduly exaggerated by the particular reading imposed upon a text. In other words, the contradiction may be "more in the interpretation given to the text than in the text itself."[42] To cite just one example, the statement regarding divine judgment in 3:17 is often understood in an eschatological sense—unnecessarily so—and the eschatological emphasis is then deemed to be incompatible with Qohelet's theological perspective.

Michael Fox's work marked a significant departure from this widespread approach. Although others had advocated for a final-form reading, Fox argued for an intentional and unified composition of the whole. According to his analysis, the contradictions in the book do not derive from external intrusions or from an internal dialogue with various other perspectives, but from a single intellect. Both sides of the contradiction, he insisted, belong to "Qohelet." The contradictions, in fact, constitute the essence of the book's message and must neither be resolved nor polarized in a facile manner. Fox's proposal challenged even the long-standing assumption concerning the compositional history of the epilogue. Pointing to similar framing techniques in other biblical and ancient Near Eastern texts, he asserted that the third-person retrospective voice of the epilogue does not automatically represent the work of an editor. Instead, Ecclesiastes ought to be read as a unified literary composition from beginning to end, as "the product not of editorship but of authorship."[43] Fox's conclusions were carried further by C. L. Seow, who argued on form-critical and thematic grounds that the epilogue (with the possible exception of the

---

4   Fox, *A Time to Tear Down & a Time to Build Up: A Rereading of Ecclesiastes*, 18—20.

5   Murphy, *Ecclesiastes*, xxxiii—xxxiv.

6   Fox, "Frame-Narrative and Composition in the Book of Qohelet," 83—106; idem, *A Time to Tear Down*, 1—14, 363—375. See also Tremper Longman, *Fictional Akkadian Autobiography: A Generic and Comparative Study* (Winona Lake, Ind.: Eisenbrauns, 1991).

"colophon" in 12:13b—14) should indeed be considered a part of the author's original work.[44]

Today, theories of multiple redactions have largely been set aside in favor of reading the book as a unified work.[45] There is a sense that attending to the overall shape of the book will enable a fresh appropriation of the book's message. Some interpreters, however, would return to the old theory of multiple redactions.[46] Even among those who readily see the book as generally of one piece, the epilogue, judged to be at odds with the body of the book, remains an "obvious exception."[47] Moreover, the references to the fear of God within the body of the book (especially 7:18; 8:12b—13) continue to be downplayed as orthodox interpolations. Such a dismissal undercuts an important aspect of Qohelet's theological ethic, which is articulated through the interplay of joy and fear in his discourse. It also fails to attend to the dialogical mode of theological inquiry in the book.

An argument for the authenticity of the disputed passages pertaining to the fear of God is presented in chapter 3, along with a detailed exegetical analysis of those texts. Here, I wish only to outline in broad compass the various features of the text that support the theory of a unified literary composition: (1) the presence of a broadly coherent structure; (2) the copious use of catchwords and other linking devices that connect the author's thoughts into a meaningful whole; and finally, (3) the use of rhetorical strategies that exploit ambiguity and tension in order to underscore the limits of human existence.

---

7   Seow, "Qohelet's Autobiography," 275—87; idem, "The Epilogue of Qohelet Revisited," 125—41.

8   See, for example, Eric Christianson, A Time to Tell: Narrative Strategies in Ecclesiastes (JSOTSup 280; Sheffield: Sheffield Academic Press, 1997); Gary D. Salyer, Vain Rhetoric: Private Insight and Public Debate in Ecclesiastes (JSOTSup 327; Sheffield: Sheffield Academic Press, 2001), 17, 126—166.

9   Among recent scholars, Martin Rose, identifies glosses throughout the book in his recent monograph (Rien de nouveau: Nouvelles approches du livre de Qohéleth [OBO 168; Göttingen: Vandenhoeck & Ruprecht, 1999]).

10   Murphy, Ecclesiastes, xxxiv. See also Crenshaw, Ecclesiastes; Norbert Lohfink, Qoheleth: A Continental Commentary (trans. Sean McEvenue; Minneapolis: Fortress, 2003), 11—13, 142—44; trans. of Kohelet (NechtB; Würzburg: Echter, 1980); R. N. Whybray, Ecclesiastes (NCBC; Grand Rapids, Mich.: Eerdmans, 1989), 169—74; W. Sibley Towner, "The Book of Ecclesiastes," in NIB (Nashville: Abingdon, 1994), 5:265—360; Longman, The Book of Ecclesiastes; Thomas Krüger, Kohelet (Prediger) (BKAT; Neukirchener-Vluyn: Neukirchener, 2000), 364—76; William P. Brown, Ecclesiastes: A Bible Commentary for Teaching and Preaching (IBC; Louisville: John Knox, 2000), 116.

1.2 Broad Framework

Discussions concerning the book's integrity invariably lead to some consideration of its elusive structure. Characterized as the "riddle of the sphinx,"[11] this perennial problem, like so many issues in the study of Ecclesiastes, has polarized scholarly opinion. On the one hand, some scholars argue for an overarching architectonic design, whether in the form of a palindrome,[12] polar structures,[13] or elaborate structures governed by refrains and numerological patterns.[14] In the end, however, these intricate proposals have failed to be persuasive. The convoluted diagrams and outlines that accompany such proposals are often difficult to follow and are overly dependent on the particular rubrics assigned to the discrete units. Even multiple readings do not allow such intricate structures to emerge naturally.

On the other hand, others declare that there is no discernible organization to the book whatsoever. One scholar opines that Qohelet's thoughts must have been written originally on loose pages that later became hopelessly scrambled.[15] For others, the lack of organization is a function of the nature of Qohelet's discourse. Fox, for example, compares Ecclesiastes to the meandering reflections in Wittgenstein's *Philosophical Investigations*, in which the author makes little effort to structure his thoughts systematically.[16] Qohelet's discourse is meant to be "a report of a journey of a consciousness over the landscape of experience (1:13), a landscape generally lacking highways and signposts, order and progression." Expectations of structure are therefore ultimately frustrated by the "haphazard arrangement" of his observations.

To be sure, Ecclesiastes is by no means a systematic treatise with a clearly recognizable structure. But neither is it a random assortment of

---

11   Addison G. Wright, "The Riddle of the Sphinx: The Structure of the Book of Qoheleth," *CBQ* 30 (1968): 313–34. This language was apparently first coined by E. Plumptre in *Ecclesiastes, or the Preacher* (BC 23; Cambridge: Cambridge University Press, 1898), 7; and later adopted by B. Pick, "Ecclesiastes or the Sphinx of Hebrew Literature," *Open Court* 17 (1903): 361–71.

12   Norbert Lohfink, *Kohelet* (NechtB; Würzburg: Echter, 1980), 10.

13   J. A. Loader, *Polar Structures in the Book of Qohelet* (BZAW 152; Berlin/New York: de Gruyter, 1979).

14   Addison G. Wright, "The Riddle of the Sphinx," 313–34; idem, "The Riddle of the Sphinx Revisited: Numerical Patterns in the Book of Qoheleth," *CBQ* 42 (1980): 38–51; idem, "Additional Numerical Patterns in Qoheleth," *CBQ* 45 (1983): 32–43; see also Rousseau, "Structure de Qohélet I 4–11 et plan du livre," 200–217.

15   Gustav Bickell, *Der Prediger über den Wert des Daseins: Wiederherstellung des Bisher zerstückelten Textes* (Innsbruck: Wagner, 1884), 1–45.

16   Fox, *A Time to Tear Down*, 149–152.

unrelated sayings. Even Fox recognizes a fair amount of coherence—a
thematic and stylistic coherence that derives from the book's pursuit of
a single idea from start to finish.[54] There are, however, other significant
clues that suggest not only a thematic coherence but a purposeful
organization of thought. First, there are hints of a broad framework that
are readily recognized by all readers. As many have noted, the
beginning and end of the book are memorably framed by the *hebel* (or
"vanity") epigram in nearly verbatim formulation (1:2; 12:8). In
addition, the introductory poem (1:3—11) that immediately follows the
opening *hebel* statement is matched by the final poem (12:3—7) that
immediately precedes the closing epigram.

Beyond these widely accepted hints of organization, there are clues
of a deliberate design that divides the book into two halves. The
Masoretic notations explicitly designate the midpoint of the book at
6:10, yielding 111 verses in each half.[55] Moreover, each of the two
halves is further marked by distinct refrains that function as "sections
enders" for discrete literary units. As noted by Wright, the first half of
the book contains eight sections, each concluding with the *hebel* refrain
and/or the phrase "a pursuit of wind" (1:14; 2:11, 17, 25; 4:4, 16; 6:9).
Similarly, the second half contains eight sections marked off by the
phrase "not find"/"who can find" or "not know."[56] Although these
terms are not contained exclusively in one half or the other, particular
emphases and general trends are discernible. The cadenced repetition
of these refrains creates a sense of coherence and movement.[57]

There is also a noticeable change in voice from the first to the
second half of the book, which reinforces the progression of thought.
The language of first-person reflective speech gives way to speech that

---

17   Michael V. Fox, *Qohelet and His Contradictions* (JSOTSup 71; Sheffield: Almod, 1989),
      158.
18   Freedman identifies 6:9b as the precise center of the book, with 1491 words in each
      half (cited by Seow, *Ecclesiastes*, 45).
19   Wright, "The Riddle of the Sphinx," 50.
20   Although most scholars have expressed skepticism about Wright's numerological
      analysis, many have substantially adopted his general schema with some
      modifications. See Murphy, *Ecclesiastes*, xxxv—xli; J. S. M. Mulder, "Qoheleth's
      Divison and Also Its Main Points," in *Von Kanaan bis Kerala* (ed. W. C. Delsman et al.;
      Neukirchen-Vluyn: Kevelaer/Neukirchener, 1982), 341—65; R. Rendtorff, *The Old
      Testament: An Introduction* (trans. John Bowden; Philadelphia: Fortress, 1986), 265;
      Robert Johnston, "The Rhetorical Question as a Literary Device in Ecclesiastes"
      (Ph.D. diss.; Louisville, Ky.: Southern Baptist Theological Seminary, 1986); Antoon
      Schoors, "La structure littéraire de Qoheleth," *OLP* 13 (1982): 91—116; S. G. Brown,
      "The Structure of Ecclesiastes," *ERT* 14 (1990): 195—208; Salyer, *Vain Rhetoric,*
      especially 159—60.

is increasingly weighted toward imperatives and admonitions,[21] until it culminates in the formal address to a "youth" in 11:9. The progression is distinctively theological and pedagogical in its thrust. Indeed, it is difficult to escape the impression of such a purposive movement.[22]

This movement is particularly evident in the recurring commendation of enjoyment. It has been noted that the joy passages, with their redundant quality, "constitute the book's refrain as much as his *hebel* indictment ... serves as its motto and rhetorical frame."[23] These counsels of joy appear to have a special place and function in the larger literary work, so that some have in fact appealed to these texts as the primary structuring principle for the book.[24] There are clues that these passages were designed to interact with and build upon one another. First, certain terms and ideas appear exclusively in Qohelet's discourse on joy (e.g. *yāpeh* and *mattat*). Second, it is also precisely in these places that Qohelet employs explicitly theological language in a sustained fashion. Moreover, as Whybray has noted, these passages follow one another with a gradual modulation of tone so as to express their theme with increasing emphasis and urgency.[25] Qohelet's initial commendation of enjoyment has the quality of a concession ("there is nothing better," 2:24); with each reiteration, however, the enthusiasm and urgency with which he presents his counsel of joy is heightened, until he breaks out into an effusive command to enjoy life at every possible moment (9:7−10), before the demise of human life makes such possibilities no more (11:7−12:7). The modulation of tone in these joy texts, in turn, governs the tone of the book as a whole.

In sum, although it is impossible to disclose a precise schema for the book, there is nevertheless a general impression of a structure, and one may delineate its contours and progression of thought in broad

---

21 Christianson visually plots this shift in voice in *A Time to Tell*, 244.

22 The division of the book into two broad sections ("Doctrinal" and "Admonitory") was proposed as early as 1612, by Piscator, one of the first interpreters to propose a structure for Ecclesiastes (according to C. D. Ginsburg's survey). Christian D. Ginsburg, *The Song of Songs and Coheleth, Commonly Called the Book of Ecclesiastes: Translated from the Original Hebrew, with a Commentary, Historical and Critical* (London: Longman, 1861; repr., New York: KTAV, 1970), 123.

23 William P. Brown, "'Whatever Your Hand Finds to Do' Qohelet's Work Ethic," *Int* 55, no. 3 (July 2001): 279.

24 Rousseau, "Structure de Qohelet I 4−11 et plan du livre," 200−17. Many others recognize the importance of this refrain in the movement of the book, but without giving it the pride of place that Rousseau does. See, for example, Leo G. Perdue, *Wisdom and Creation: The Theology of Wisdom Literature* (Nashville: Abingdon, 1994), 203−5; Whybray, "Qoheleth, Preacher of Joy," 87−89; Salyer, *Vain Rhetoric*, 162−65.

25 Whybray, "Qoheleth, Preacher of Joy," 87−89.

strokes. In other words, Qohelet has an argument that he wants to make, and he makes it coherently and effectively.

1.3 Catchwords and Linking Devices

Another literary strategy that connects and builds the sage's thoughts into a complex yet unified whole is the prevalent use of catchwords and linking devices. Scholars have long noted the luxurious use of keywords and refrains as a trademark of the book's literary style. Loretz, for example, catalogues twenty-eight "favorite words," and calculates that they constitute over twenty percent of the text.[26] Murphy, too, detects the presence of numerous "catch phrases" throughout the book and repeatedly appeals to them as an important criterion for determining the extent of individual literary units.[27] One may note, furthermore, that the repetition of these keywords is not haphazard but purposive, occurring at critical junctures to connect the author's thoughts and advance his argument. When the repetition of a particular word or phrase appears at the outer edges of adjacent units, they form a series of "hinges" that effectively link together various facets of Qohelet's reflections. There is a significant amount of linguistic and thematic overlap at the boundaries, so that the conclusion of one unit simultaneously segues into the subsequent unit and functions effectively as its introduction. Hence, it is not surprising that while one exegete will group a verse (or set of verses) with one unit, another will include it (them) with the adjacent unit. This, one may argue, is evidence *for*, not against, the effective concatenation of arguments. Furthermore, the concatenation is reinforced through the copious use of connective words (*gam*, *ʿôd*, *wĕšabtî*, etc.) at these boundaries; one observation builds upon another and moves the reflections into a related but divergent direction.

This strategy is evident from the start. The book opens with a superscription that describes the book as the "words of Qohelet, son of David, king in Jerusalem" (1:1). Before the author turns to the royal autobiography of Qohelet, however, he presents a poem concerning the toil that characterizes all activity under the sun (1:3—11). The "intrusive" quality of this poem has led some commentators to regard it as a later insertion.[28] But there are literary features that nicely connect

---

26   Oswald Loretz, *Qohelet und der alte Orient: Untersuchungen zu Stil und theologischer Thematik des Buches Qohelet* (Freiburg/Basel/Wien: Herder, 1964).

27   Murphy, *Ecclesiastes*, ad loc.

28   See, for example, Lauha, *Kohelet*, 32.

the poem to its immediate context and the opening epigram.[29] The reference to "everything" in the book's motto (*hakkōl hābel*, 1:2) is taken up in the poem, at both its beginning (*kol-ʿāmālô*, v. 3) and end (*kol-hannĕḥālîm*, v. 7; *kol-haddĕbārîm*, v. 8; *ʾên kol-ḥādāš*, v. 9). This catchword binds the unit together, and communicates the central thrust of the poem: despite all the routine activity and all the toil that takes place under the sun, there is nothing new. The *hebel* epigram in v. 2, then, serves a dual purpose: it forms a frame for the book (together with 12:8), and also appropriately sets the stage for the opening poem (1:3—11).

In the subsequent literary unit (1:12—2:26), the author continues to use catchphrases to connect his thoughts. The unit may be divided into five sub-sections (1:13—2:3; 2:4—11; 2:12—17; 2:18—2:23; 2:24—26),[30] which are tied together, most notably, by the first-person speech of Qohelet's autobiography. In particular, the author adds one thought to another by reiterating the introductory phrases "I set my heart" (*nātattî ʾet-libbî*, 1:13; *wāʾettĕnâ libbî*, 1:17) and "I spoke with my heart" (*dibbartî ʾānî ʿim-libbî*, 1:16; *ʾāmartî ʾānî bĕlibbî*, 2:1; cf. *tartî bĕlibbî*, 2:3). In addition, the sub-sections are linked to one another by the strategic use of anaphora (a repetition of the same word or phrase at the beginning of successive lines), which creates a "hinge" between contiguous units. The pivotal segment 2:12—17 is linked to the preceding section by the repetition of the phrase *ûpānîtî* "I turned" at the beginning of v. 12 and v. 11. Similarly, it is joined to the subsequent section by the repetition of the phrase *wĕśānēʾtî* "I hated" at the beginning v. 17 and v. 18.

Many commentators take 3:1—15 to be a coherent unit. The Catalogue of Times (3:1—8) and the subsequent prose commentary (3:9—15) are bound together by their common concern with the determination of all times and events.[31] Then, a new unit seems to be signaled at 3:16 with the introduction of a new subject matter, that of social injustice. Yet the introductory statement in 3:16 *wĕʿôd rāʾîtî*

---

29 The poem also functions as a frame for the entire book. As noted above, the book is not only bracketed by the *hebel* refrain (1:2; 12:8), but also by the prefatory poem that follows the initial *hebel* epigram (1:3—11) and the concluding poem that immediately precedes the final *hebel* epigram (12:1—7).

30 For a delimitation of the unit and its sub-divisions, see the discussion in Seow, *Ecclesiastes*, 142—43.

31 The Catalogue of Times may have been a separate poem that existed on its own. So, Addison G. Wright, "'For Everything There Is a Season': The Structure and Meaning of the Fourteen Opposites (Ecclesiastes 3,2—8)," in *De la Tôrah au Messie: Mélanges Henri Cazelles* (ed. J. Dore et al.; Paris: Desclée, 1981), 321—28. Even if that were true, the poem has been incorporated into the present context to flow fluidly and meaningfully within the movement of the book.

"furthermore I saw" suggests an association with the preceding remarks, specifically harking back to rāʾîtî "I saw" in 3:10. The particle wĕʿôd "furthermore" suggests a shift in focus, but all the while maintaining a connection with the previous reflections. One may argue that 3:16—22, then, is an extended elaboration of the observations registered in 3:10—15, in which the notion of God's sovereign determination of the times is connected to the problem of human injustice. The relationship is subsequently made explicit in 3:17, where the rationale for divine judgment is couched in terms of "a time for every matter." 3:22 then appropriately brings the unit to a close with yet another reiteration of the phrase: "So I saw that there is nothing better" than the enjoyment of the moment, for "who can bring them to see what will be after them?"

Another "hinge" is evident at 4:1. The phrase wĕšabtî ʾănî wāʾerʾeh (literally, "I turned and saw") signals a further turn in the author's argument, and marks the beginning of a new unit (4:1—16). At the same time, the expression builds upon the occurrence of the phrase "I saw" in the preceding verse (3:22; 3:10, 16). There is a thematic association as well, with the observations of "all the oppressions that take place under the sun" (4:1—3) picking up on the topic of injustice from the preceding unit.[32] To this is appended additional remarks on the problem of toil, again with the connective phrase "then I saw" (4:4). 4:7 then introduces yet another observation with the expression wĕšabtî ʾănî wāʾerʾeh. The sayings in chapter 4 are bound together thematically and formally as well. Formally, the chapter consists of a sequence of "better than" sayings (vv. 3, 6, 9, 13). Coming at the heels of the ʾên ṭôb statement in 3:22, the notion of "what is good" joins this chapter to the preceding material. Moreover, as noted by Murphy, the motif of "second" or "two" unifies the various sayings (vv. 3, 8, 9, 10, 11, 12, 15).[33] Thus, even in 4:1—16, which has been judged by many to be a collection of random sayings, there are stylistic and topical associations throughout the unit and at its borders.

As noted above, 6:9 is arguably the precise midpoint of the book. Hence, 6:10—12 functions as a "bridge" between its two halves. On the one hand, it is possible to see these verses as the continuation of 6:1—9, with the rhetorical question mah-yōtēr lāʾādām in 6:11 harking back to

---

32 Not surprisingly, some commentators group 4:1—3 with the previous unit. Gordis, *Koheleth—the Man and His World*, 148—49; 223—229; Crenshaw, *Ecclesiastes*, 101—107.

33 Murphy groups together 4:7—16. However, the reference to "two" begins earlier, at 4:3. The idea of a "second" is also communicated by other terms that designate "another" (rēʿēhû, v. 4; ḥābērô, v. 10).

mah-yôtēr lehākām in 6:8. On the other hand, these verses may be taken to be the introduction to the second half of the book, with its emphasis on what people cannot know, cannot tell, cannot grasp. Furthermore, this "bridge" is joined to the subsequent proverbial sayings (7:1—12)[34] by the repetition of the word *ṭôb*. The repetition of this catchword (eleven times) recalls the rhetorical question concerning *mah-ṭôb* "what is good" in 6:12, suggesting that the aphoristic material in 7:1—12 ought to be read in light of that leading question. Hence, just as the *hebel* epigram in 1:2 functions as the introduction to the preface as well as the book in its entirety, so also 6:10—12 serves as a kind of preamble not only to the second half of the book, but also to its opening literary unit.

Another "hinge" is present at 8:1. Many commentators designate this verse (or at least 8:1a) as the conclusion of the preceding unit, and not entirely without warrant. The rhetorical question "who is so wise"[35] in 8:1a alludes to the unattainability of wisdom—the precise point just made in 7:23—29. But it is also possible to group 8:1 with the following material. The reference to *dābār* "a thing/word" in 8:1a is picked up again in 8:3—5 (three times). The word *pānāyw* is as another catchword that joins 8:1 to 8:2. Finally, a broader structural connection is established through the repetition of the thematic word "to know." The rhetorical question "who knows?" at the beginning of the unit (8:1a) anticipates the claim that "no one knows" what is to be (8:7), as well as the closing reference to the wise "who claim to know" but ultimately fail to make sense of all that happens on earth (8:17).[36]

Within this complex, 8:9 may be highlighted as another transitional verse between two sub-sections. First, the reference to "a time when

---

34 Older commentaries tended to regard many of the sayings as interpolations from various hands. More recent studies have suggested that this compilation of proverbs features a dialogue of sorts between differing viewpoints. Wright, for example, contends that vv. 1—6 portrays a "grim" view of life, which is rejected by the *hebel* verdict in v. 6b and Qohelet's genuine views in vv. 7—12. Similarly, Diethelm Michel, *Untersuchungen zur Eigenart des Buches Qohelet* (BZAW 183; Berlin: de Gruyter, 1989), 126—37. Murphy, following Lohfink, avers that Qohelet is here dialoguing with traditional wisdom and modifying it (Murphy, *Ecclesiastes*, 61—63).

35 Reading *my kh ḥkm* instead of MT's *my khḥkm* "who is like the wise." This reading seems to be supported by the Greek traditions. As argued by Euringer, the expression *tis oiden sophous* "who knows the wise" in LXX is probably the result of an inner Greek corruption from *tis hōde sophos* "who is so wise" (as in Aq; cf. Symm, *tis houōs sophos*; also SyrH, OL). The error may have been prompted in part by the following rhetorical questions: *kai tis oiden lysine rhēmatos* "who knows the solution of a saying?" See S. Euringer, *Der Masorahtext des Koheleth* (Leipzig: Hinrich's, 1890), 93—94).

36 One may further note that the preceding unit seems to conclude tellingly with the thematic word *mṣ'* in the expression "this alone I found" (7:29).

people exercise authority (*šālaṭ*) over one another" recalls what was just said concerning the lack of authority (*šilṭôn, šallîṭ,* 8:8) over matters of life and death, and the issue of royal authority (*šilṭôn,* 8:4; see also the repetition of the cathword *'ēt* "time" in 8:9, 5—6). One may legitimately take 8:9 to be the logical conclusion of a unit that begins at 8:1b, as some commentators do.[37] At the same time, the verse is also a fitting introduction to the imminent discussion concerning inequities in this world. The phrase *'et-kol-zeh rā'îtî*[38] at the beginning of v. 9 is echoed in the expression *ûbĕkēn rā'îtî* in v. 10. The use of the expression *ûbĕkēn* "thereupon," which typically denotes something that is "next" in a series (cf. Esth 4:16; Sir 13:7) only strengthens the association. Moreover, the two-fold occurrence of the root *'śh* in 8:9 signals a concern with the various activities that take place on earth, a theme which is explored with greater scrutiny in 8:10—17 (with a twelve-fold occurrence of the root). Taken together, these various connections suggest that v. 10 and following should not be divorced from v. 9. Hence, 8:9 can be seen as the conclusion of one unit, and the introduction to the subsequent one.

There is another "hinge" at 9:1, another verse that straddles two contiguous units.[39] On the one hand, it is possible to take 9:1 as the beginning of a new unit, with the particle *kî* at the beginning of the verse functioning as an asseverative.[40] But one cannot entirely rule out the possibility of a causal nuance in *kî,* which would establish an intentional connection with the previous unit.[41] Furthermore, the verse exhibits an instance of anastrophe, where the direct object has been placed before the verb: *'et-kol-zeh nātattî 'el-libbî* "all this I set on my heart." In such cases, the object (*'et-kol*) may be anticipatory and introduce the topic that will be taken up in the following verses, but it may also refer back to the preceding observations (cf. 7:15; 8:9). Indeed,

---

37 See, for example, Fox, *A Time to Tear Down,* 273—82.

38 Note that a similar use of anastrophe (disrupted word order in which the direct object precedes the verb) functioned connectively in 7:15 as well.

39 According to Wright's schema, the second part of the second half of the book begins precisely at this point, with its characteristic repetition of the phrase "know/not know." Wright, "The Riddle of the Sphinx: The Structure of the Book of Qoheleth," 331.

40 So, JB: "Yes, I have applied myself." Similarly, A. Schoors, *The Preacher Sought to Find Pleasing Words: A Study of the Language of Qoheleth* (OLA 41; Leuven: Peeters, 1992), 107—08; Murphy, *Ecclesiastes,* 88; Longman, *The Book of Ecclesiastes,* 224; Seow, *Ecclesiastes,* 296—97.

41 So, NASB: "For I have taken all this to heart." Similarly, Fox, *A Time to Tear Down,* 290. Note also that some exegetes prefer to group 8:16—17 verses with 9:1 and following. See, for example, Fox, *A Time to Tear Down,* 287—290; Lohfink, *Kohelet,* 63—66; Barton, *Ecclesiastes,* 156—59.

the expression distantly recalls the notice *ka'ăšer nātattî 'et-libbî* "when I set my heart," which begins 8:16.[42] In addition, 8:17 maintains that even the wise, who religiously pursue and claim "to know" (*da'at*), cannot understand the work of God. 9:1 continues the thought: no one "knows" (*yôdēa'*) what is before them for all human deeds are in the mysterious "hand of God."

In sum, the author repeatedly uses catchwords and connective devices to link together various thoughts in succession, creating a series of "hinges" between adjacent units. The effective concatenation of arguments supports the argument that the book ought to be read as an integral whole.

1.4 Genre, Rhetoric, and Subversion

In addition to the theories concerning the redactional history of the book discussed above, scholars have often appealed to the presence of various rhetorical strategies to account for the contradictions in Ecclesiastes. One common approach proposes that Qohelet is engaged in a disputation with one or more opposing perspective(s). Some claim that the book contains actual dialogues between Qohelet and an unnamed interlocutor.[43] Or, as suggested by others, Qohelet periodically quotes the views of an opponent for the sake of refuting or reinterpreting them.[44] In a variation of the quotation hypothesis, Hertzberg posits the use of *zwar-aber Aussage* ("yes, but" argumentation), in which the sage juxtaposes a proposition that is assumed to be true (*zwar*) with an exception to the rule (*aber*), in order to relativize the initial proposition and expose its inadequacy.[45] These reading strategies, more often than not, are intent on resolving or otherwise dissipating the tensive nature of Qohelet's discourse.

---

42 Following Codex Leningrad, which is supported by the ancient versions (LXX, Vulg, Targ). Many Hebrew MSS, however, read *'t lby*, which may be a harmonization with the more common idiom in 1:13, 17; 8:9, 16.

43 A. Miller, "Aufbau und Grundproblem des Predigers," *Miscellanea Biblica* 2 (1934): 104–22; T. A. Perry, *Dialogues with Kohelet* (University Park, Pa.: Pennsylvania State University Press, 1993).

44 This approach was common in traditional Jewish commentaries, such as that of Ibn Ezra. Among more contemporary exegetes, see Gordis, *Koheleth—the Man and His World*, 95–108; idem, "Quotations in Wisdom Literature," *JQR* 30 (1939/40): 123–47; idem, "Quotations as a Literary Usage in Biblical, Oriental and Rabbinic Literature," *HUCA* 22 (1949): 157–219; Michel, *Eigenart*, passim; R. N. Whybray, "The Identification and Use of Quotations in Ecclesiastes," in *Congress Volume, Vienna, 1980* (VTSup 32; ed. J. A. Emerton; Leiden: Brill, 1981), 435–51.

45 Hertzberg, *Prediger*, 30–31.

However, given the absence of explicit markers of quotation or dialogue, they are vulnerable to the subjectivism that plagued the redaction hypotheses. Whenever a statement seems to be disharmonious with one's particular interpretation of Qohelet, it can easily be passed off as the views of another disputed by Qohelet.

Yet it must be emphasized that Qohelet repeatedly speaks of conversing *with his own heart* (1:16; 2:1; 3:17, 18; cf. 1:16).[46] Whatever dialogue exists in the text takes place internally, in the mind of this single persona. The sage affirms many of the normative truths taught by conventional wisdom; at the same time, he observes the many violations of the norm. He registers these inexplicable contradictions, refusing to let go of either the "truth" or the exception. As Fox puts it, what Hertzberg regards as the *zwar*-element is as much Qohelet's personal conviction as anyone else's, and the *aber*-element, the recognition of anomalies, "imposes itself on Qohelet, who would prefer to retain the rule."[47] The sage wrestles inwardly with these contradictions, and bares his conflicted mind to the reader. The resulting cognitive dissonance, therefore, cannot and must not be dissipated by recourse to an outside conversation partner.

One may note that reflective wisdom literature of other ancient Near Eastern cultures similarly exploits dialogues and contradictions in order to examine a subject matter from various angles. The Mesopotamian *Dialogue of Pessimism*, for example, is a conversation between a master and his slave, in which the two consider the merits of engaging in one activity after another, alternating back and forth between an enthusiastic endorsement and an equally adamant rejection of each of the activities.[48] At the end of this farcical exchange, the conversation reaches the terrible conclusion that all things in this life are futile and that life is therefore not worth living. Similarly, the *Babylonian Theodicy* explores multiple points of view through the vehicle of various individuals engaged in cycles of speeches.[49] In Ecclesiastes, different characters are not at work, but multiple perspectives are evoked in two ways: first, by the different voices in the frame and body of the book; and second, by the conversations that

---

46 Reflective wisdom literature of other ancient Near Eastern cultures likewise exploits dialogues (including internal dialogues) to explore contradictory realities and viewpoints. Egyptian wisdom material offers the most pertinent parallels. *The Dispute Between a Man and His Ba* (*AEL* I, 13—69) and *The Complaints of Khakheppere-Sonb* (*AEL* I, 145—49), for example, record a man's conversation with his inner self.

47 Fox, *A Time to Tear Down*, 17; similarly, Seow, *Ecclesiastes*, 42.

48 See W. G. Lambert, ed., *Babylonian Wisdom Literature* (Oxford: Clarendon, 1960), 139—50.

49 See Lambert, *BWL*, 63—92.

Qohelet takes up with his "heart" (1:16; 2:1, 15; 3:17, 18) throughout his discourse. In similar fashion, the Egyptian wisdom text known as *The Dispute Between a Man and His Ba*, presents conflicting viewpoints in the form of a dialogue between a man and his inner-self.[50] *The Complaints of Khakheperre-Sonb* also features a man who has conversations with his heart.[51] Much like Qohelet, who frequently "speaks to his heart," the personas in these Egyptian texts are engaged in a kind of debate with the self. All of these wisdom texts attest to the literary practice of exploring various, even conflicting points of view in order wrestle with and give voice to the complexity and incongruity of human experience.

If the epilogue's characterization of Qohelet as a skilled teacher and rhetorician (12:9–11) has any merit, it should hardly be surprising that the sage would use literary devices and rhetorical strategies adeptly to communicate his teachings. Indeed, one detects the abundant use of literary devices that play on contradictions and indeterminacy of meaning, such as irony, ambiguity, and double-entendre.[52] This study will not present an exhaustive catalogue of the various strategies employed by the author. It will only give a representative sampling, in order to demonstrate that the incongruities in the text serve a rhetorical purpose.

1.4.1 Multivalence

In some cases, the author exploits the ambiguity that exists on a lexical level. The multivalent root ʿnh, which may mean "to answer," "to preoccupy" (exclusively in Ecclesiastes), or "to oppress," is a case in point. In 10:19, the saying *hakkesep yaʿăneh ʾet-hakkōl* is typically taken to mean that money "answers everything" or "meets every need." Yet, in a subtle criticism of the rich and powerful, the author may be employing double-entendre to suggest that "money preoccupies everyone." Similarly, the word *maʿăneh* in 5:19 evokes the notion of God keeping humanity preoccupied with enjoyment. The precise lexical form, however, suggests that the author may also have in mind the idea that enjoyment is the divine answer to the terrible

---

50   See Lichtheim, *AEL* I, 163–69.

51   See Lichtheim, *AEL* I, 145–49.

52   See Good, *Irony in the Old Testament*, 176–83; Salyer, *Vain Rhetoric*; Harold Fisch, "Qohelet: A Hebrew Ironist," in *Poetry with a Purpose* (ISBL. Bloomington: Indiana University Press, 1988), 158–78; I. J. J. Spangenberg, "Irony in the Book of Qohelet," *JSOT* 72 (1996): 57–69.

preoccupations that absorb (and possibly "oppress") humanity (cf. 3:10; 1:13).[53]

In 12:1, the possibility of word play is enhanced by the particular orthography of a given word. The unusual plural form *bôrĕʾêkā* "your creator" has opened up questions concerning its meaning, and yielded various alternative readings, including *bĕrûʾêkā* "your well-being,"[54] *boryāk* "your vigor,"[55] *bĕʾērêkā* or *bôrĕkā* "your well," as a metaphor for wife,[56] and *bôrĕkā* "your pit," an allusion to the grave.[57] The multivalence is suggested as early as the first century by Rabbi Akabya ben Mahallalel who is reported to have said: "Know whence you came [*bʾrk*, 'your source'], whither you are going" [*bwrk*, 'your grave'], and before whom you are destined to give an accounting [*bwrʾyk*, 'your creator']" (m. *ʾAbot* 3:1; Qoh. Rabb. on 12:1; *Lev. Rabb.* section 18). Indeed, these various levels of meaning point forward to different aspects of the subsequent poem in 12:1−7.[58]

Similarly, the reference to *hāʿōlām* "eternity" in 3:11 is a well-known interpretive crux, and scholars have suggested emending it to *hāʿ elem* "darkness"[59] or *heʿāmāl* "toil."[60] The defective spelling of the word makes it amenable to such proposals (cf. *lĕʿôlām* in 3:14, where the word is written with a *mater*), and the author may have intended, at least on a graphic level, to evoke multiple levels of meaning.

1.4.2 Irony and the Rhetoric of Subversion

Another rhetorical strategy commonly employed in the book has to do with the subversive logic of Qohelet's discourse. The author employs deliberate miscues and a strategy of "indirection" to lead his readers to an altogether unexpected conclusion.[61]

---

53   These texts will be discussed in greater detail in chapter 2.
54   A. B. Ehrlich, *Randglossen zur hebräischen Bibel* (Leipzig: Hinrich's, 1914), 7:103.
55   Zimmermann, *The Inner World of Qohelet*, 160.
56   Heinrich Graetz, *Kohelet* (Leipzig: Winter, 1871), 133−34; followed by Crenshaw, *Ecclesiastes*, 184−85.
57   Galling, "Prediger," 120−22.
58   To be discussed further in chapter 2.
59   Barton, *The Book of Ecclesiastes*, 98, 101; Crenshaw, *Ecclesiastes*, ad loc.
60   MacDonald, *The Hebrew Philosophical Genius*, ad loc.; H. L. Ginsberg, *Kohelet* (Jerusalem, 1961), ad loc; Fox, *A Time to Tear Down*, 192.
61   See Ellen Spolsky, *The Uses of Adversity: Failure and Accomodation in Reader Response* (London: Associated University Press, 1990), 17−35, where she observes that for ambiguous texts, misreading is a precondition for reading, and failure is often a prerequisite for success. See also Salyer, *Vain Rhetoric*, 126−27.

This literary technique is evident in the opening poem that depicts the unending activities that fill the cosmos (1:3—11). Through the deliberate repetition of vocabulary and the copious use of active participles (no less than 15 occurrences in vv. 3—7), the poet creates the impression of incessant and frenetic activity,[62] and leads the reader to believe that there are noteworthy activities taking place in the universe. The subsequent commentary, however, makes the unanticipated conclusion that despite all the busy commotion, despite the unending drama of natural (vv. 5—7) and human activities (vv. 3—4), "there is nothing new under the sun" (v. 9). The impression of meaningful activities is exposed as a mere illusion. Seow observes that "[i]t is as if one experiences *hebel* itself. One's initial impression quickly dissipates like mist."[63]

A similar effect is achieved in the following literary unit, as the author moves from a consideration of universal activities to the activities of his Solomonic persona (1:12—2:26). This time, the author adopts the ancient Near Eastern genre of the fictional royal autobiography—but with an ironic and subversive twist. As expected for this genre, the narrator in his royal guise meticulously documents his quest for wisdom, wealth, and pleasure. However, after heightening the anticipation that some exceptional people may succeed in such grand undertakings, even this consummate wise king is made to concede time and again that everything is in fact "*hebel* and a pursuit of wind" (see 1:14, 17; 2:1, 11, 15, 17, 19, 21, 23, 26). When all is said and done, no mortal—not even Solomon, the archetypical gatherer of wisdom, wealth, and pleasure—is able to grasp and hold on to these things.[64] Again, the illusion of the king's extraordinary accomplishments only evaporates like *hebel*.

The author again employs this rhetoric of subversion with the Catalogue of Times (3:1—8). The poem is popularly understood to be about the felicitous moment for any given activity, and the human discernment of those times. Indeed, the poem may at one time have functioned that way.[65] The author carefully generates the impression of a deliberate structure through the rhythmic series of various activities, arranged in broadly antithetical pairs. So tantalizing is its semblance of

---

62 See G. Fecht, *Metrik des Hebräischen und Phönizischen* (ÄAT 19; Wiesbaden: Harrassowitz, 1991), 162—69; Luis Alonso Schökel, *A Manual of Hebrew Poetics* (Subsidia Biblica 11; Rome: Pontifico Istituto Biblico, 1988), 71, 198; Seow, *Ecclesiastes*, 111—12.

63 Seow, *Ecclesiastes*, 43.

64 See Seow, "Qohelet's Autobiography," 257—82.

65 See Lang, "Ist der Mensch hilflos?" 109—24.

order that interpreters have repeatedly attempted to uncover the poem's underlying structure.[66] None has been entirely persuasive, however, and one is left to conclude that no clear pattern or progression is discernible that can adequately account for the whole. Indeed, that is the unexpected conclusion reached at the end of the poem: finite beings cannot grasp the work of God (v. 11). Although the human agent is described enticingly as "the actor/doer" (*hā'ôšeh*, v. 9), it soon becomes clear that the real issue is the activity of a sovereign deity who determines everything. Try as they may, people are unable to discern or predict an order to the times and seasons, because they are simply beyond human control. They can live life only in the moment at hand. Beyond that, there are no guarantees, because all is *hebel* (v. 19).

In 7:1—12, the author presents a collection of seemingly disparate yet loosely cohesive sayings. Closely resembling the didactic material in the book of Proverbs, these aphorisms purport to teach what is "good" or "better." Eight times, in an extended sequence, the sage boldly declares one thing or another to be good. Yet, these sayings are introduced by the rhetorical question in 6:12 that suggests that people cannot really know "what is good" and ends with the theological claim that, in the inscrutable economy of God, what is good is inescapably mingled with what is bad (7:13—14). The overall presentation thereby subverts the reliability of the featured instructions. Ironically, the sayings demonstrate the tenuous nature of the wisdom enterprise and its findings.[67] For Qohelet, who is ever cognizant of the vagaries of life, there is no wisdom that will enable a person to take hold of an absolute good or completely escape adversity. People can only recognize and accept each moment for what it is worth, whether it be good or bad.[68]

Finally, the final poem (12:1—7) masterfully employs enigmatic imagery to create a dramatic and powerful conclusion to his discourse. The ambiguities and uncertainties that abound in this text are probably intended by the author.[69] Indeed, this evocative poem, with its obscure imagery, has long resisted interpretation.[70] The interpreters of antiquity –followed by many even today—widely read the poem as an allegory about the travails of old age. According to this reading, various images

---

66   See especially Wright, "For Everything There Is a Season" 321—28; J. A. Loader, "Qohelet 3:2—8—A 'Sonnet' in the Old Testament," *ZAW* 81 (1969): 240—42.

67   Similarly, Murphy, *Ecclesiastes*, 62; Seow, *Ecclesiastes*, 241.

68   The series of "better-than" sayings in 4:1—16 functions similarly.

69   So also Fox, *A Time to Tear Down*, 344.

70   For a more detailed discussion, see chapter 2.

in the poem are associated with different parts of an aging body.[71] Moreover, coming at the heels of Qohelet's admonitions to rejoice and remember one's Creator in the days of youth before the loss of such possibilities (11:9—10; 12:1a), such a reading seems entirely appropriate. In fact, the rhetorical movement of the overall unit, coupled with the deliberately enigmatic imagery, forcefully nudges the reader in that direction. However, the poet begins to introduce language with distinctly eschatological overtones. And at the climax of the poem, one sees a vision of a funerary procession, and startlingly realizes that it is all of humanity that is proceeding to the grave.[72] The issue is elevated to a cosmic level, and the focus of the poem is broadened from that of an individual's demise to that of humanity in general. With that cataclysmic and decisive end, "the dust will return to the earth as it was, and the life-breath will return to God who gave it" (12:7). Thus, the poet poignantly arrives at the astonishing conclusion that nothing—not even creation—is permanent. The poem then appropriately closes with *hebel*.

Through the use of rhetorical strategies that revel in indeterminacy, the author creates the illusion of *hebel* on a literary level.[73] He deliberately entices the reader to make a particular conclusion, only to frustrate and dismantle that initial conclusion. The unexpected and contradictory turns in Qohelet's argumentation, then, need not be seen as evidence of editorial tampering, or even the citation of another's views. Qohelet employs ambiguity, irony, and a rhetoric of subversion deliberately to create the experience of anomie, in order to unsettle the reader and challenge false assumptions concerning human abilities. In other words, the effect of disorientation is intended to serve a pedagogical purpose: to demonstrate that humans are granted only a fragile and tenuous existence, but are, at the same time, called to confront and take up what they are granted to the full.

---

71 It may be that the author drew upon an existing piece concerning the travails of old age in order to compose his own poem. See Choon Leong Seow, "Qohelet's Eschatological Poem," *JBL* 118, no. 2 (1999): 209—34.

72 Fox notes another rhetorical effect of this poem at this point. "What do all these people see that terrifies and afflicts them so? For whom are they mourning so intensely? The answer is inevitable: they see your death and mourn for *you*, you to whom Qohelet addressed his advice and warnings, the 'you' of v. 1 ... Your death is eclipsing their world, and you are present at the terrible scene. The bell tolls for you, and for everyone" (Fox, *A Time to Tear Down*, 338).

73 Salyer makes a similar observation in *Vain Rhetoric*, especially 17—18, 127—32.

1.5 Integrity and *Hebel*

Every interpretation of Ecclesiastes must at some point grapple with the meaning and function of *hebel*, its most notorious leitmotif. Its prominence and prevalence in the book demand that exegetes give serious attention to this key word. And the way one understands *hebel* significantly impacts how one understands the overall work. If *hebel* is understood in the traditional sense of "vanity," it may present a legitimate challenge to viewing the book as a coherent whole. The verdict that "all is vanity" flies in the face of Qohelet's insistence on the goodness of enjoying life and its simple pleasures. It also may seem to be expressly at odds with the sage's positive affirmation of divine justice and the virtues of fearing God. One would be hard-pressed to reconcile the stark negativity of the sage's thoughts with the life-affirming dimensions in the book.

Yet, it is possible that this dissonance has been unduly exaggerated by a venerable *mis*reading of *hebel*. While "vanity," "futility," and other such synonyms are appropriate translations of *hebel* in many contexts, they fail to convey the manifold nuances of the Hebrew and are not appropriate for every occurrence of the word in the book. As noted in the introduction to this study, scholars have rightly become dissatisfied with this traditional rendering, and have revisited the issue of what *hebel* means in the context of Ecclesiastes. In his trenchant study of this word, Seow makes the case that *hebel* points to that which is "beyond mortal grasp."[74] In other words, *hebel* denotes both things and situations that humans are incapable of grasping—either physically, experientially, or intellectually. In some cases, the impossibility of taking hold of a thing is due to the transient and ephemeral nature of the object under consideration, whether it be youth, material goods, the opportunities of joy, or even life itself. By extension, the futile efforts to hold on to such illusory things are also *hebel*, that is, incomprehensible (or ironic, or absurd) to the human mind. *Hebel* thus functions in tandem with Qohelet's other refrain concerning what humans cannot know and cannot find/grasp.[75]

Understood thus, there is no need to interpret the book according to the binary categories of pessimistic or optimistic, skeptical or pious. *Hebel* may encompass both perspectives. This reading of *hebel* is not

---

[74] Seow, "Beyond Mortal Grasp," 1—16.

[75] On the usage of *mṣ'* in Ecclesiastes to mean both "to find" and "to grasp," see A. R. Ceresko, "The Function of Antanaclasis (*mṣ'* "to find" // *mṣ'* "to reach, overtake, grasp') in Hebrew Poetry, Especially in the Book of Qoheleth," *CBQ* 44 (1982): 551—69.

meant to "tame" the word or the book's message. In numerous places, *hebel* maintains the connotation of the incomprehensible and absurd. Qohelet is brutally honest in acknowledging the radical limitations that are imposed upon mortals. He recognizes the vagaries of human existence before an inscrutable God, and deliberately evokes the experience of cognitive dissonance through the juxtaposition of contradictions in his discourse. Yet, the verdict of *hebel* need not preclude life-affirming possibilities. The enjoyment of life is simultaneously extolled as a good thing, fleeting though it may be. The joy refrains need not be pitted against the repeated verdict of *hebel*. As I will argue in the following chapters, both of these sentiments are part and parcel of the ancient Near Eastern conception of religion, or as the ancients themselves put it, the "fear of God." The word *hebel* can appropriately be reclaimed as Qohelet's thematic word. *Hebel*—that which is beyond mortal grasp—holds everything together.

1.6 Summary

To summarize, despite its troublesome contradictions, Ecclesiastes may in fact be read as a unified composition. Other scholars have already presented persuasive arguments for the book's integrity on the basis of form-critical and thematic considerations. However, there are other significant features of the text that support this assessment, as I have catalogued in this chapter. First, the book displays a broad framework that indicates a purposive movement in its theological argumentation. Secondly, the author employs numerous catchwords and connective devices to effectively link together and develop his multifaceted thoughts. Finally, the author employs rhetorical strategies that play on ambiguity and indeterminacy of meaning to subvert traditional expectations.

If Ecclesiastes is indeed a unitary and meaningful composition, then interpreters must not dismiss its various counterpoints as irrelevant or tangential to the book's message. The subsequent chapters will turn to two of the book's central themes—enjoyment and fear of God—and argue that they are indeed indispensable to Qohelet's discourse.

Chapter Two

The Vitality of Enjoyment in Qohelet's Theological Rhetoric

2.1 Introduction

As noted in the introduction of this study, scholars have continued to debate the significance of the so-called "joy passages" in Ecclesiastes. Because the book is more often than not read as pessimistic literature, the theme of enjoyment is typically subordinated to the message of "vanity," if not altogether dismissed. Thus W. H. U. Anderson goes as far as to say that Qohelet's commendations of joy are ultimately *invalidated* by the final and decisive verdict of *hebel*.[1] Yet the recurrent theme of spontaneity and enjoyment can hardly be ignored, and proponents of an entirely pessimistic view of Ecclesiastes are hard-pressed to account for this discordant counterpoint. The theme is simply too persistent and ubiquitous.

The proposals to discount this motif have been diverse, ranging from psychologistic explanations (i.e., Qohelet's views on enjoyment arise from a disturbed and fragmented psyche)[2] to those that are philosophically oriented (i.e. the reflections on pleasure are a reflex of Epicureanism or the like).[3] Accordingly, Anderson submits that the sage's repeated admonitions to enjoy life represent nothing more than "wishful thinking" that provides "psychological relief."[4] Or, as Michael Fox would have it, they are merely parenthetical concessions—that human beings should relish the meager and fleeting pleasures they can

---

1   W. H. U. Anderson, *Qoheleth and Its Pessimistic Theology*, 74.

2   Zimmermann, *The Inner World of Qohelet*.

3   See R. Braun, *Kohelet und die frühhellenistische Popularphilosophie* (BZAW 130; Berlin/New York: de Gruyter, 1973); John G. Gammie, "Stoicism and anti-Stoicism in Qoheleth," *HAR* 9 (1985), 169—87; L. Schwienhorst-Schönberger, "Nicht im Menschen gründet das Glück" (Herders Biblische Studien 2; Freiberg: Herder, 1996), 251—332.

4   W. H. U. Anderson, *Qoheleth and Its Pessimistic Theology*, 72—73, 109, 166.

find in an absurd world, because these can act as a narcotic of sorts that dulls the pain of existence.[5] In such ways, then, the enjoyment passages are rejected as a contradictory strain or a peripheral concern, a constant irritant within the book that obscures its real message.

Yet a closer look at the enjoyment passages within the structure of the book reveals that these passages occur in strategic places, and most often in the context of larger theological reflections. This is all the more so when one moves beyond the explicit language of joy (śimḥâ and śāmēᵃḥ) to consider the metaphors for enjoyment, such as eating, drinking, donning bright garments, anointing one's head with oil, and being with one's beloved. There are also expressions that are either synonymous with or that explicate the meaning of enjoyment in Ecclesiastes: "look into good" (2:1), "see good" (2:24), "do good" (3:12), "be in good" (7:14), and "see life" (9:9). The commendation of enjoyment, whether explicitly expressed through the familiar terms (śimḥâ, śāmēᵃḥ) or through parallel expressions and metaphors, appears in virtually every literary unit of the book—often with other sobering elements but nonetheless present everywhere. All these metaphors and idioms indicate that the theme is much more prominent than it appears at first blush, and cannot be ignored or dismissed as random musings or parenthetical digressions. Indeed, for Qohelet, they are *vital*—as basic to *life* as eating and drinking and companionship. Without enjoyment in this sense, life would simply not be *good*.

In recognition of the theme's prominence in Qohelet's theological rhetoric, a number of scholars have asserted that the recurrent commendations of joy contain the book's central message.[6] Whybray, who has famously dubbed Qohelet as a "preacher of joy," argues that the whole-hearted pursuit of joy is the governing *leitmotif* of Ecclesiastes. Qohelet identifies seven problems of human life, and in each case, recommends joy as the positive response to the stated problems. Joy thus becomes the means by which one may transcend the evils present in the world.[7] Ogden heartily seconds this view, arguing

---

5   Fox, *A Time to Tear Down and a Time to Build Up*, 129—31, 186, 239—40, 287. Similarly, Crenshaw, *Ecclesiastes*, 27; Tremper Longman, *The Book of Ecclesiastes*, 35, 121—22, 168.

6   Whybray, "Qoheleth, Preacher of Joy," 87—98; Ogden, *Qoheleth*, 13—15; Philip P. Y. Chia, "The Thought of Qoheleth: Its Structure, Its Sequential Unfolding, and Its Position in Israel's Theology" (Ph.D. diss., Sheffield University, 1988); Gordis, *Koheleth—the Man and His World*, 13; Norbert Lohfink, *Christian Meaning of the Old Testament* (trans. R. A. Wilson; Milwaukee: Bruce, 1968), 154—55; trans. of *Das Siegeslied am Schilfmeer* (Frankfurt am Main: Knecht, 1965); idem, "Qoheleth 5:17—19—Revelation by Joy," 625—35.

7   Whybray, "Qoheleth, Preacher of Joy," 91.

that "[t]hese calls to enjoyment are actually theological statements of faith in a just and loving God, despite many signs which might appear contrary."[8]

As with every attempt to single out *the essential* message of the book, however, the contradictions that are part and parcel of Qohelet's reflections on the plight of humanity are too quickly harmonized or otherwise resolved in this optimistic approach. So, for Whybray, the negative assessment of enjoyment in 2:1–2 is portrayed as the misguided views of the fictional young Solomon, as opposed to the author's more mature and decisive viewpoint (2:24–26).[9] In a similar vein, Ogden posits that Qohelet's thoughts here are merely provisional, and are later corrected and nuanced throughout the book.[10] Yet, these reflections on enjoyment in 2:1–2 are the very first comments that one encounters on the theme, and they come as a part of what may be viewed as an extended introduction, namely, chapters 1–3. Moreover, such readings overlook the place of these verses in the structure of the larger literary unit, 1:12–2:26. Thus, it seems odd that Whybray, who sees 2:24–26 as the concluding words of "Solomon's Testimony,"[11] should view 2:24–26 positively but isolate 2:1–2 as coming from a different perspective!

The difficulty with this text, for Whybray and Ogden, stems from their particular view of enjoyment, which is perhaps closer to Greek and modern notions than ancient Semitic. Accordingly, enjoyment is understood as "pleasure," "happiness," "bliss," or the like. As such, it would be antithetical to a sober recognition of the limitations of human life with all its contradictory realities. My contention, however, is that Qohelet's notion of enjoyment entails an authentic experience of the world that recognizes both its tragic limitations and its joyous possibilities of good. To characterize the commendation of enjoyment as a reflection of a hedonistic or Epicurean ideal is to misconstrue the book's perspective on enjoyment. Qohelet is not endorsing a "pleasure principle" that is intent on avoiding pain and maximizing pleasure. Nowhere does he encourage pursuit of pleasure. No, enjoyment, for Qohelet, is much more profound. It has to do with *living life* to the full—with full recognition of life's travails and woes—and making the most of every God-given opportunity. One may even argue, as Johnston has done, that Ecclesiastes is in fact calling us back to "the

---

8   Ogden, *Qoheleth*, 22.
9   Whybray, "Qoheleth, Preacher of Joy," 88–89.
10   Ogden, *Qoheleth*, 48.
11   R. N. Whybray, *Ecclesiastes* (NCBC; Grand Rapids, Mich.: Eerdmans, 1989), 46–65.

central focus of wisdom itself and its chief referent—life."[12] Enjoyment is indeed a vital notion in Qohelet's theological rhetoric.

This chapter explores the theme of enjoyment in Ecclesiastes, focusing on the key passages in which Qohelet counsels the enjoyment of life (2:24—26; 3:12—13, 22; 5:17—19; 7:14; 8:15; 9:7—10; 11:7—12:1). One must, however, also take seriously the occurrences of śimḥâ that lie outside of these positive exhortations—that is, the passages where Qohelet appears to give a conflicting assessment of the value of enjoyment (2:1—2, 10—11; 7:2—4). Through the investigation in this chapter, I seek to determine the place of enjoyment in Qohelet's thought, explicate the meaning of enjoyment (what it is and what it is not), and reflect on its theological significance and, where relevant, its ethical implications.

2.2 In the Hand of God (Eccl 2:24—26)

It has been argued that the reflections on enjoyment in 2:24—26 constitute the denouement of the larger literary unit 1:12—2:26, with its predominant concerns with the ungraspability of human life.[13] The vocabulary of this final section appears to echo that of the introductory section of the unit (1:13—2:3), and the two sections share a common set of concerns: the problem of the terrible preoccupation (ʿinyān)[14] which is given by God (1:13; 2:26), and the place of wisdom, knowledge, enjoyment (śimḥâ), and "seeing" (r'h) what is good (ṭôb). Most notably, the word ʾĕlōhîm appears exclusively in these outermost sections of the unit (1:13; 2:24, 26), giving them a singular theological accent. What we have is no ordinary inclusio, however. We do not have the mere repetition of expressions; rather, there is a significant development of the author's view of the deity at the end. Whereas God appears only briefly at the beginning of the unit (in 1:13, for the first time in the book), now, at the end of the unit, there is sustained theological reflection. And inextricably present in this theological reflection is Qohelet's perspective on what is "good," the Hebrew word for "good"

---

12   Johnston, "Confession of a Workaholic," 15.

13   For a delimitation of the unit, see the discussion in Seow, *Ecclesiastes*, 142—43.

14   In the Hebrew Bible, the noun ʿinyān is peculiar to Ecclesiastes, occurring eight times (1:13; 2:23, 26; 3:10; 4:8; 5:2, 13; 8:16), twice in conjunction with the verbal form laʿănôt (1:13; 3:10). The word is attested in Postbiblical Hebrew, with the meaning of "subject, business, case" (see Jastrow, *Dictionary*, 1095). In Ecclesiastes, it is associated with restlessness, obsession, vexation, and the human inability to find enjoyment.

(ṭôb) appearing four times within these verses.[15] Hence, one may view
Qohelet's remarks in 2:24—26 as a direct response to the question
explicitly raised in 2:3, "where, really, is good?" (ʾê-zeh ṭôb).

Qohelet offers an answer to that question: "there is no good for/in
humanity" (ʾên-ṭôb bāʾādām, 2:24).[16] Yet he immediately qualifies that
negative judgment, adding the exception to the rule: humans ought to
make themselves see "good" (wĕherʾâ ʾet-napšô ṭôb). The dialectic is
starkly posed, even illogically so. There is no good for mortals, but
there is the possibility of good that one may yet "see." Good is a
possible impossibility! As the author explicates this curious dialectic, it
becomes clear, too, that this "good" is neither entirely of one's own
making, nor is it available to everyone. Rather, it is possible only to
those who are already "good" before God (šeṭṭôb lĕpānāyw, ṭôb lipnê
hāʾĕlōhîm). Such is Qohelet's exposition of where "good" really lies. On
the one hand, it is possible for mortals, who are enjoined to "eat, drink,
and cause themselves to see good." On the other hand, despite the
causative with humanity as the subject (herʾâ ʾet-napšô), the possibility
finally resides in God, before whom one is either ṭôb or hôṭeʾ (v. 26): "it
is from the hand of God" (kî miyyad hāʾĕlōhîm hîʾ, v. 24).

For Qohelet, those who are "good before God" are those who are
"already favored" by the deity (cf. 9:7), while the hôṭeʾ (7:26; 8:12; 9:2,
18; cf. 5:5; 7:20; 10:4), the one who misses out, refers to one who is—for
whatever reason, or even no reason at all—not so favored.[17] As Seow
has suggested, the author may be drawing an analogy from the Persian
sociopolitical context, where those who were pleasing to the king
received royal grants, while others—those who missed out on the
king's largesse because they have somehow offended the sovereign—

---

15   The word ṭôb(â) is an important word for Qohelet, occurring a remarkable 52 times
     in the book (the most frequent word in the book, apart from particles). As noted by
     Antoon Schoors, its most striking connotation is that of "enjoyable," in connection
     with the sage's repeated advice to enjoy the good things of life. The word is often
     used as a substantive, with the meaning "the good things of life" (2:3, 24; 3:13; 4:8;
     5:17; 6:6; 7:14; 8:15; 9:18b). See his discussion in "Words Typical of Qohelet," in
     Qohelet in the Context of Wisdom (BETL 136; ed. A. Schoors; Leuven: Leuven
     University Press, 1998), 33—40.

16   On the use of the ʾên-ṭôb formula, see Graham Ogden, "Qoheleth's Use of the
     'Nothing is Better' Form," *JBL* 98 (1979): 339—50. Ogden makes the case that the ʾên-
     ṭôb clauses (see also 3:12, 22; 8:15) are the medium most frequently used by the
     author to convey his most fundamental advice.

17   Ginsberg is right when he remarks that these terms "mean respectively (as is
     generally recognized) 'pleasing to God' and 'displeasing,' or 'lucky' and 'unlucky'—
     not 'righteous' and 'wicked.'" See Ginsberg, *Koheleth*, 139. This point is adopted by
     many commentators, and those who attribute a moral connotation to these terms are
     forced to identify a gloss in v. 26a. Podechard, for example, assigns it to a "ḥāsîd."
     See Podechard, *L'Ecclésiaste*, 283—84.

were simply left out.[18] When all is said and done, the possibility of good ultimately comes from the hand of the divine Sovereign. Like the Persian emperor who exercised unquestionable authority over all things in the empire, the sovereign deity has the power of disposal over everything in the cosmos. A similar sentiment is communicated in 9:1, where Qohelet observes that all the deeds of the righteous and the wise are "in the hand of God" (*běyad hā'ĕlōhîm*), that is, subject to God's free and inscrutable will. God may enable a person to enjoy life; yet, the very same God may also withhold the possibility, and instead give an unpleasant preoccupation (1:13; 2:26; cf. 5:17—6:2). Like Job, who asks, "Shall we receive the good at the hand of God, and not receive the bad" (Job 2:10), Qohelet recognizes that God doles out both the good and the bad, and human recipients have no knowledge of and no control over the logic behind the divine decision. The best that humans can do is to accept and enjoy God's gift whenever it is offered. Enjoyment, thus, is not something that one seeks. Rather, it is what one may, by the will of God, have. Just as wisdom and knowledge are gifts of God, so too is *śimḥâ* (v. 26).[19]

Yet, the realization of that possibility for mortals—presumably for those who are already "good before God"—involves human agency as well. While it is the divine Sovereign who freely gives it ("from the hand of God," "giving to those who are good," etc.), it is up to mortals to make themselves "see." Indeed, there is double, if unequal, agency: enjoyment is a possibility for mortals only by the sovereign power of the deity, but they can only have it when they make themselves "see."

Enjoyment is expressed, in the first instance, in terms of the metaphor of the most basic of life's activities: eating and drinking.[20] That seems obvious enough, and it is borne out by its other appearances in Ecclesiastes, where eating and drinking are associated with explicit terms for enjoyment (3:12—13; 5:17—19; 8:15; 9:7—10). At a most basic level, these activities are intended to sustain the human life force, so much so that "to eat" can mean "to live" (cf. Gen 47:22). People eat and drink in order to live. Beyond this, eating and drinking may also indicate living life to the full. When people eat and drink,

---

18 Seow, *Ecclesiastes*, 141—42.

19 On Qohelet's theology of God's absolute sovereignty, see L. Gorssen, "La Cohérence de la Conception de Dieu dans l'Ecclésiaste," *ETL* 46 (1970): 313.

20 See Rudolf Smend, "Essen und Trinken—Ein Stück Weltlichkeit des Alten Testaments," in *Beiträge zur alttestamentlichen Theologie* (ed. R. Hanhard and R. Smend; Göttingen: Vandenhoeck & Ruprecht, 1977), 446—59; Paul Humbert, "Laetari et exultare' dans le vocabulaire religieux de l'ancien Testament," *RHPR* 22 (1942): 185—214. Humbert identifies eating and drinking as behavioral aspects of the biblical term for joy.

particularly in the context of a shared meal, it is often accompanied by a sense of contentment, well-being, and gladness (cf. Pss 104:15; 128:2—3).[21] By the same token, eating and drinking may also indicate living a miserable life, which is depicted as "eating in darkness" (cf. 5:16). Indeed, in 2:25, eating is juxtaposed with and antonymous to "fretting,"[22] which is clarified as the obsessive preoccupation with amassing and gathering (v. 26).

Besides the metaphor of feasting, enjoyment is also expressed in terms of causing oneself to see good (*her'â 'et-napšô ṭôb*). The verb *r'h* ("to see") connotes more than observation[23] or critical examination.[24] These proposals do not adequately cover the various nuances of the verb present in the book. According to the context, it expresses Qohelet's experience, his examination of it, or the knowledge he derives from it.[25] Indeed, the word is regularly used to mean "to taste" or "experience," as is evident in the idiom "to see/experience life" in Eccl 9:9, which may be contrasted with the idiom "to see/experience death" (Ps 89:49). Elsewhere in the Hebrew Bible, the idioms *rā'â ṭôb* (Ps 34:13; Job 7:7), *rā'â bĕṭôb* (Pss 27:13; 128:5), and *rā'â ṭôbâ* (Job 9:25) may mean "to experience good," or "to live."[26] This use of the verb in Ecclesiastes (2:1; 3:13; 5:17; 6:6) suggests that enjoyment is, in part, a matter of encountering and accepting the good at hand. Likewise, the author uses the related noun sight/seeing (*mar'ēh 'ênayim*, 6:9; *mar'ê 'ênêkā*, 11:9)[27] to refer to the experiencing of what may be present—the situation that one faces and/or the things in one's possession.

---

21   A similar association between eating and enjoyment is found in the Egyptian *Admonitions of Ipuwer*: "Lo, a man is happy when eating his food. Consume your goods in gladness, while there is none to hinder you. It is good for a man to eat his food. God ordains it for him whom he favors" (8.5—6, see Lichtheim, *AEI* I, 157).

22   There is no consensus among scholars on the translation of the Hebrew *yāḥûš*. It probably means "worry" or "fret," a sense clearly attested in Job 20:2. See the exhaustive study by F. Ellermeier, "Das Verbum ḤWŠ in Koh 2,25," *ZAW* 75 (1963): 197—217. Other proposals include "abstain" (Gordis, *Koheleth*, 216—17), "enjoy" (Barton, *Ecclesiastes*, 78, 84), "rejoice" (Murphy, *Ecclesiastes*, 24), and "glean" (Seow, *Ecclesiastes*, 118, 139—40).

23   Loader, *Polar Structures in the Book of Qohelet*, 25.

24   Michel, *Untersuchungen zur Eigenart des Buches Qohelet*, 21—30.

25   See Antoon Schoors, "The Verb *r'h* in the Book of Qoheleth," in *"Jedes Ding hat seine Zeit ...": Studien zur israelitischen und altorientalischen Weisheit* (BZAW 241; ed. A. A. Diesel et al.; Berlin/New York: W. de Gruyer, 1996), 227—241 (241); idem, "Words Typical of Qohelet," 26—33.

26   Conversely, the idioms *r'h r'* and *r'h br'* may mean "to experience evil," or "to suffer" (see Eccl 4:3; Hab 1:13; Num 11:15; 2 Kgs 22:20).

27   Note also the expression "the seeing of the eyes"(*r'yt 'ynyw*) in 5:10. The *Ketib* may suggest *rĕ'iyyat*, which is well attested in Postbiblical Hebrew, meaning "seeing" or "sight" (see Jastrow, *Dictionary*, 1436). *Qere* has *r'wt*, indicating either an abstract

Furthermore, one may note that the verb is one of the author's most frequently used words, occurring forty-seven times in the book. Qohelet repeatedly observes and examines the things that happen in the world—both the good and the bad (see, especially, 7:14). Enjoying life, as Qohelet understands it, does not mean that one is oblivious to and shielded from the pain that is in the world. Neither does it mean that it is anything but ephemeral. Hence, against Whybray, one might note that there is no contradiction between this passage and Qohelet's summary judgment of enjoyment in 2:1−2. It is not that "Solomon's" wrongheaded view in his youth is corrected by Qohelet's more mature retrospection.[28] Rather, from the start, Qohelet's judgment is that enjoyment is but ephemeral, even if it is good and God-given. Indeed, Qohelet raises three questions in 2:1−3, "As for laughter, I thought: '<What> does it boast?'[29] And regarding enjoyment: 'What really does it accomplish?'... Where, really, is (there) good for mortals?" Those questions are given due response in 2:24−26: enjoyment is *hebel*—ungraspable—but is still a divinely willed possibility that those who are "good before God" ought to "see."

The exegesis above corroborates the judgment of Whybray and others, who have noted the theological significance of this text.[30] Beyond the typical treatment of this passage, however, I have argued that enjoyment has nothing to do with the pursuit of joy or pleasure. Rather, it is one's active response as a human agent to God's giving of all that is "good" to those who are "good before God." As such, that gift is not something that mortals can hold on to, since all is *hebel*—"beyond mortal grasp."

---

noun (*rĕʾût*) or infinitive construct of *rʾh* (*rĕʾôt*). In any case, the sense of the word is nearly synonymous to *marʾēh*.

28 On the ironic use of the genre of royal fiction, see Seow, "Qohelet's Autobiography," 257−82.

29 Most translators read *mĕhôlāl* in MT as a Poal participle and take it to be synonymous with *hôlēlôt* "irrationality" or "madness" (so KJV, ASV, NRSV). Here, I follow Seow's emendation, reading *me<h> hôlēl* "what does it boast?" in parallel with *mah-zô ʿōśâ* "what does it really accomplish?" See Seow's discussion, *Ecclesiastes*, 126.

30 See also J. Coppens, "La structure de L'Ecclésiaste," in *La sagesse de L'Ancien Testament* (ed. M. Gilbert; BETL 21; Gembloux: Leuven University Press, 1979), 288−92; Rousseau, "Structure de Qohélet I 4−11 et plan du livre," 200−17; J. S. Reitman, "The Structure and Unity of Ecclesiastes," *BSac* 154 (1997): 308−9.

2.3 The Human Portion (Eccl 3:12−13, 22)

The second commendation of enjoyment in the book (3:12−13) is likewise located in a key theological text. Here, in the prose commentary (3:10−15) to the Catalogue of Times (3:1−8), Qohelet continues and elaborates more fully upon the theological reflections that he began in 2:24−26.[31] Again, he speaks of the preoccupation ('inyān) that God has given to humanity (v. 10; cf. 1:13; 2:26), applying it in this instance to the problem of God's inscrutable determination of all events and the human inability to know or control the times (v. 11). He then goes further to comment on God's purpose behind this mysterious activity: to evoke an attitude of reverence from human beings (v. 14). God is explicitly mentioned six times in these verses, yielding one of the densest concentrations of the word 'ĕlōhîm in the book. Once again, Qohelet's reflections on enjoyment are embedded in this talk of God and God's ways in the world (vv. 12−13), confirming that enjoyment has profound theological significance.

While in 2:24−26, the discussion of God's activity is focused on the divine act of giving to those who are "good before him," Qohelet now comments on God's general and pervasive activity in the world. Up to this point in the book, the verb 'śh has occurred thirteen times. Most of these instances have to do with human activity (2:2, 3, 5, 6, 8, 11 [twice], 12, 17), most notably, the accomplishments of Solomon in the parody of the fictional royal autobiography. In 1:9 and 1:13−14, however, God's activity may be implied. The impersonal and passive construction in the latter ("all the deeds which are done") is in all probability an allusion to God. In 3:10−15, instead of the passive form of the verb 'śh, the author employs active forms, with God unambiguously identified as the subject. God is portrayed as the primary Actor, with the root 'śh repeatedly used in reference to the deity: it is God who has made ('āśâ) everything appropriate in its time (v. 11); mortals cannot grasp the deeds (hamma'ăśeh) that God has done ('āśâ, v. 11); what God does (ya'ăśeh) is in the realm of "eternity" (v. 14); God has acted ('āśâ) so that people may fear him (v. 14).

Yet, as in his previous discussion of enjoyment (2:24−26), Qohelet suggests that a double agency is at work in the human enjoyment of life. Immediately, one notes that the question of human agency is foregrounded by the author's choice of vocabulary in the initial query at 3:9: "What advantage does the doer (hā'ōśeh) have in all the toiling?"

---

31   Note that the infinitives in the Catalogue of Times (3:1−8) continue the infinitives in 2:24−26 (le'ĕsôp, liknôs, and lātēt).

When that rhetorical question is posed elsewhere, "the human" (*hāʾādām*) appears as the subject of the toiling (1:3; 2:22; 6:11). In the formulation of the question here, however, the author suggestively refers to the human being as "the doer," or "actor."[32] Perhaps this is done so with an ironic intent, for the human actor is quickly overshadowed by the all-pervasive activity of the deity. The rhetorical question itself suggests that human actors have no advantage in all their toiling.

Nevertheless, in v. 12, Qohelet emphatically asserts that there is indeed something good for humans "to do." Again employing word-play, he submits that "there is nothing good" (*ʾên ṭôb*) for humanity but "to do good" (*laʿăśôt ṭôb*). The parallelism of the latter expression with "to enjoy" (*lišmôᵃḥ*) suggests that the phrase must mean something like "to see/experience good" (cf. 2:1, 24), which is further confirmed by the occurrence of that very idiom in the subsequent verse along with the metaphors of eating and drinking. Yet, it is noteworthy that elsewhere in the Old Testament, the expression "to do good" typically has moral connotations (cf. Gen 26:29; Deut 6:18; Judg 9:16; 1 Sam 24:18; Pss 14:1, 3; 34:15; 37:3, 22; 53:2, 4; etc.). This more common nuance is present in Ecclesiastes as well in 7:20, where "to do good" is associated with *ṣaddîq* ("a righteous one") and opposite of *ḥtʾ* ("to sin," or "to miss"). Here in 3:12, by juxtaposing the expression "to do good" with the explicit call "to enjoy," Qohelet intimates that the enjoyment of life is indeed a matter of ethical duty.[33] Enjoyment *is* doing good; it is being "good before God" (7:26; 2:26). This "doing" that is enjoyment is further expressed in terms of eating and drinking and "seeing good," and all this human activity is made possible by God alone: "it is the gift of God" (v. 13). Thus, although the human being is supposed to "do good" (// "to enjoy"), the ultimate "doer" is, after all, the deity. The one thing that mortals can and ought to "do," in the end, turns out to be due to God's own doing!

This passage, then, echoes the earlier assertion that the ability to "see good" comes "from the hand of God" (2:24). Qohelet repeatedly underscores this reality. Enjoyment is always contingent upon God's giving, and is an opportunity available only for the moment. Moreover,

---

32 A similar choice of vocabulary occurs at the end of the literary unit, where the author recapitulates his commendation of enjoyment (3:22). There, the author substitutes the word *maʿăśāyw* for *ʿămālô*, the word he employs in every other articulation of the familiar refrain, "to have enjoyment in/from one's toil" (2:10; 3:12; 5:17, 18; cf. 8:15).

33 E. Elster makes a similar observation in *Commentar über den Prediger Salomo* (Göttingen: Dieterich, 1855), 72.

the Hebrew word for gift (*mattat*) inevitably recalls the other instances of the deity's giving (*ntn*) in the book thus far: God "gives" to humanity a terrible preoccupation (1:13; 2:16; 3:10); God "gives" to the human heart "eternity," yet without the incumbent ability to apprehend all that happens "from beginning to end" (v. 11).[34] It is a wholly other God, a transcendent Sovereign, who gives in this utterly perplexing fashion. The God who gives a preoccupation (*'et-hā'inyān 'ăšer nātan 'ĕlōhîm*) to mortals to preoccupy them, perhaps even to afflict and humble them (*la'ănôt bô*),[35] is the same one who places (*ntn*) "eternity" in human hearts, without the possibility for people to grasp it all. Indeed, one may see v. 11 as an explication of the perplexing activity of the deity in v. 10.

It is theologically important to point out, however, that juxtaposed with the assertion of divine dealing of eternity to humanity is the equally important claim that the deity has "made everything appropriate in its time" (v. 11a). The juxtaposition is poignant and emphatically posed in the Hebrew: "[God] has made everything appropriate in its time, *also* eternity he has set in their heart." The God who makes everything fitting in its (His!) time, is the same God who gives that eternity. The God who renders the impossibility of grasping *hā'ōlām* "eternity" is the God who makes everything possible in its/His moment. God the *Giver* is God the *Doer/Maker*. The possibility for humanity resides in the activity of God. Inasmuch as the divine Actor has acted, it is possible for the human actor to act, if only in response to the opportunity availed by God from time to time, season to season (3:1—8). The human doer (*hā'ôśeh*, v. 9) is, in the flash of the moment, a reflection of the divine Doer (v. 11). So, one can act appropriately and "do good," with all that it implies for Qohelet (v. 13), because the Doer

---

34   The word *hā'ōlām* is a well-known crux, lending itself to various interpretations, such as "world" (so LXX *aiōna*; Vulg *mundum*, followed by Gordis); "darkness" or "ignorance," from the Hebrew root meaning "to hide" (so Targ, Rashi, and many recent commentators); "duration" (so Jenni, followed by Murphy); "toil," emending *hā'ōlām* to *he'āmāl* (so Ginsberg, Fox); and "knowledge," (so Hitzig). Given the appearance of the word only three verses later (where the temporal sense of the word is not disputed) and elsewhere in the book (1:4, 10; 2:16; 9:6; 12:5), a temporal understanding of the word seems most probable in this instance as well. The term refers to that which transcends time, and stands in contrast to "its time" (*'ittô*) in the same verse, and the various "times" (*'ēt*) described in vv. 1—8. See E. Jenni, "Das Wort *ōlām* im Alten Testament," *ZAW* 64 (1952): 197—248.

35   The inifinitve *la'ănôt* is typically translated as "to preoccupy," or "to be busy," because of its association with the noun *'inyān*. However, the multivalent root *'nh* also has the meaning "to humble," "to afflict" in the Piel, and indeed, the targumic tradition revocalizes the verb to Piel in 1:13 and 3:10. See P. S. Knobel, *Targum Qoheleth: A Linguistic and Exegetical Inquiry* (Ph.D. diss., Yale University, 1976), 222 n. 1. One cannot rule out the possibility of double-entendre.

has already acted. At the same time, however, God's "giving" — of preoccupation (v. 10), eternity (v. 11), and the possibility of the good life (vv. 12—13) — reminds one of the inevitable transience of human existence. That ephemerality of all human activity is poignantly contrasted with the transcendence of Gods activity: "for everything that God does is *lě'ôlām*" (v. 14). Indeed, the recognition of this immeasurable chasm between ephemeral humanity and eternal divinity is the very *telos* of divine activity: "for God has acted so that [mortals] may fear him" (v. 14c).

The fear of God in Ecclesiastes, as elsewhere in ancient Near Eastern literature, denotes the recognition of humanity's proper place before God—with all its potentialities and limitations.[36] Accordingly, then, the material in 3:15—22 is an explication of that very human place. It is at the climax of this explication that Qohelet reiterates what he has expounded in 2:24—26 and 3:12—13: "there is no good but that humans should have enjoyment (*yiśmaḥ*) in all their activity, for this is their portion" (3:22). The new element here is the reference to the "portion" (cf. 2:10, 21; 5:17, 18; 9:6, 9; 11:2). According to the definition proffered by Kurt Galling, the word *ḥēleq*, in Ecclesiastes, is a technical term for "the space allotted for human existence."[37] Seow has suggested further that the usage of the term in the socioeconomic world of the Persian period, where the term is used of a plot of land or other assets that are acquired as a grant, may be instructive for explicating its meaning in Ecclesiastes.[38] Such lots are inevitably limited in space and time, arbitrarily assigned, and necessarily entail both responsibilities (toil) and benefits (fruits of toil). So it is hardly surprising that Qohelet would speak of toil and the possibility of joy in one breath (cf. 2:10, 24; 3:13; 5:17; 8:15), for such is the nature of granted lots. Moreover, the portion is only temporarily at one's disposal; ultimately, at death, it must be relinquished forever, never to be enjoyed again (cf. 2:21; 9:6, 9). Indeed, Qohelet painfully recognizes that there is a common fate for all living creatures—"all return to the dust" whence they came (v. 20). Thus, in light of this limited lot of humanity, which the fear of God impels one to remember, Qohelet insists that the present moment is what matters. Mortals can only "see/experience" what is present, "for

---

36 See chapter 3.

37 Galling, "Prediger," in *Die fünf Megilloth* (HAT 18, 2d ed., Tübingen: Mohr, 1969), 89.

38 See especially *TAD* II.2.11.2—7; Choon Leong Seow, "Rehabilitating 'the Preacher': Qohelet's Theology in Context," in *Papers of the 1997 Henry Winters Luce III Fellows in Theology* (ATS Series in Theological Scholarship and Research 7; ed. M. Zienowitcz; Pittsburgh: The Association of Theological Schools, 2000), 99—100.

who can bring them to see/experience what will happen afterwards?"
(v. 22).

2.4 The Divine—and Human—"Answer" (Eccl 5:17—19)

With 5:17—19, one comes to what has been considered by some to be
the theological highpoint of the entire book.[39] Such an assessment is not
without warrant. First, the larger literary unit to which these verses
belong (5:7—6:9) constitutes the denouement of the first half of the
book.[40] Furthermore, as others have already observed, this literary unit
exhibits a striking chiastic structure, with 5:17—19 situated at the very
center of the unit.[41] One may contend, therefore, that these verses bring
us to the pivotal section of the climax of the first half of the book. The
theological import of this section is further underscored by the fact that
it, together with its mirror section in the chiasm (6:1—2), contains a
thick cluster of references to God (six references within five verses). It
seems undeniable, then, that these verses constitute one of the most
crucial theological texts in all of Ecclesiastes. Here Qohelet offers his
most extensive reflection on the theme of enjoyment thus far, marking a
further development beyond 2:24—26 and 3:12—13, 22. Even more than
before, the divine gift of enjoyment—and the human response to that
gift—is the central and dominant concern of the passage. Beyond this
claim, however, Qohelet introduces a new theological accent: not only
is enjoyment the appropriate human response, it is the requisite God-
given *responsibility*. The ethical implications of enjoyment, which are
already intimated in 3:12, are here expounded and vividly depicted.

The larger context of the passage has to do with the problems
associated with human greed and discontentment. At the very center of
the unit, the author revisits the familiar theme of enjoyment. The issue
of "what is good" is once again at the heart of the matter, and is now
expressed with an increased decisiveness and verve: "Here is what I
have observed to be good (*hinnēh 'ăšer-rā'îtî'ānî ṭôb*)[42]—it is appropriate

---

39   See, for example, Lohfink, "Revelation by Joy," 631, 636.

40   As noted in chapter 1 above, it seems clear that 6:10 marks the midpoint of the book.

41   There is no consensus among scholars concerning the boundaries of this unit.
Fredericks and Seow (with some modifications) have made a convincing argument
concerning the chiastic structure of this unit. See D. C. Fredericks, "Chiasm and
Parallel Structure in Qoheleth: 5:6—7:9," *JBL* 108 (1989): 17—35; Seow, *Ecclesiastes*,
215—218. Krüger also sees a chiastic structure in the unit, 5:9—6:9, with the center
located at 5:17—19. See Krüger, *Kohelet (Prediger)*, 224—26.

42   The *rebia'* on *'ny* creates an awkward and redundant phrase. It is simply easier to
disregard the Masoretic accents and read *hnh 'šr r'yty 'ny ṭwb*. So, Schoors, *The*

(*yāpeh*) for people to eat and drink, and to experience good in the fruit of all their toil…which God has given to them, for that is their portion" (5:17). The mention of *yāpeh* recalls the earlier assertion that God has made "everything appropriate (*yāpeh*) in its time" (3:11), and the reference to "the gift of God" (*mattat 'ĕlōhîm hî'*) in the following verse is a verbatim reiteration of the earlier judgment in 3:13. But there is a new element introduced here—the notion of God's *authorization* of enjoyment. God "has given" (*nātan*) wealth and riches to human beings and "has authorized them (*hišlîṭô*) to partake of it and to take up their portion (*lāśē't 'et-ḥelqô*)" (5:18). This, says Qohelet, is the gift of God.

God has granted, and God has authorized. The sociohistorical context of the Persian period may, again, give some clues to the relationship between grantor and grantee that is implied in Qohelet's vocabulary. Indeed, the terminology is remarkably close to the language of Persian-period royal grants. Not only are the terms "to give," "to authorize," "portion," and "gift" paralleled in contemporaneous inscriptions from the period, its very phraseology is precisely what one finds in the grant documents. The Aramaic legal formulation of "the authorization to take up the gift" (*dš' šlyṭ lmnš'*) surely lies in the background of Qohelet's exhortation for mortals to "take up the portion" (*lāśē't 'et-ḥelqô*) because God has "authorized them" (*hišlîṭô*) to do so, and that is entirely a grant, a gift (*mattat*).[43]

Within the Hebrew Bible, the root *šlṭ* occurs in late texts, with the meaning "to be master of," or "to give authority to" (Neh 5:5; Esth 9:1; Ps 119:133; also Biblical Aramaic, Dan 2:39; 3:27; 5:7, 16; 6:25). Qohelet's usage of the word, however, may have a more specific connotation. Its appearance in various Aramaic documents from Elephantine and Wadi Daliyeh demonstrates that in the Persian period, the verb was used in legal expressions to refer to the right of disposal of one's assets.[44] Indeed, the use of verb *šlṭ* side by side with *ntn* and the related noun *mattat* ("gift," or "grant") is a particularly suggestive one. Such a clustering is found also in Neo-Babylonian economic and contractual documents, where Akkadian *šalāṭu* ("to have or claim authority to dispose of property") is closely associated with *nadānu* ("to give").[45] In

---

Preachers Sought to Find Pleasing Words, 139 n. 111; Charles Francis Whitley, *Koheleth: His Language and Thought* (BZAW 148; Berlin/New York: de Gruyter, 1979), 55 n. 33; Seow, *Ecclesiastes*, 208; Fox, *A Time to Tear Down*, 239.

43 See H. Z. Szubin and B. Porten, "Royal Grants in Egypt: A New Interpretation of Driver 2," *JNES* 46 (1987): 39—48.

44 Douglas M. Gropp, "The Origin and Development of the Aramaic *šallîṭ* Clause," *JNES* 52 (1993): 31—36.

45 See, for instance, J. N. Strassmaier, *Inschriften von Nabuchodnosor, König von Babylon (605—561 v. Chr.)* (Leipzig: Pfeiffer, 1889), Tablet 283:11; A. Ungnad, *Vorderasiatische*

these contexts, *šālaṭu* invariably refers to the legal authorization to enjoy the benefits of contractual relationships.

In Ecclesiastes, it appears, the legal connotation of the word is still in the background. The verb is used in just this sense in 2:19, where Qohelet speaks of an heir's acquisition of the right of disposal of inherited wealth: "he will have authorization (*yišlaṭ*) over all the fruit of my labor." So, too, the related noun *šallîṭ* (7:19) refers to a person who has authority over a certain piece of property, including the right of acquisition and disposition (cf. Gen 42:6; Ezek 16:20). The economic oppression described in 8:9, in terms of people exercising proprietorship over one another (*šālaṭ*), reflects the language of Aramaic slave contracts from that general period.[46] In a similar vein, when the verb *šlṭ* is attributed to God in 5:18, it may signify a transfer of authority to act and the right of disposal. In other words, the deity, much like a Persian sovereign, authorizes the human grantee to take up (*lāśēʾt*) and enjoy the "portion" that is given to them as a grant.

However, one cannot consider Qohelet's positive reflections on enjoyment without paying heed to its counterpart in the chiastic structure (6:1–2), where the author presents a terrible reversal of the scenario in 5:17–18. The vocabulary in 6:1–2 so closely reflects that of 5:17–18 that one cannot but view them as "mirror passages" in the inner-most core of the larger literary unit, separated only by the pivotal verse 5:19. The similarities, however, only make the existing differences all the more astonishing. In the latter scenario, which, according to Isaksson, portrays the possible exception to the general rule of 5:17–18, we read of a person to whom "God gives wealth, riches, and abundance ... yet God does *not* authorize that one to partake of it."[47] Qohelet speaks of God's gift to humanity—God allows people in

---

Schriftdenkmäler des Berliner Museums, herausgeben von der Generalverwaltung (vol. 6; Leipzig: Pfeiffer, 1908), Tablet 95:21; Albert T. Clay, *Legal Documents from Erech Dated in the Seleucid Era (312–65 B.C.)* (Babylonian Records in the Pierpont Morgan Library, pt. 2; New York: Pierpont Morgan Library, 1913), Tablets 5:6; 6:4; 18:25.

46   *TAD* I, 6.4.4; II, 1.1.11; II.2.11.2–7. See Douglas M. Gropp, *Wadi Daliyeh II: The Samaria Papyri from Wadi Daliyeh* (DJD 28; Oxford: Clarendon, 2001), passim; Choon Leong Seow, "The Socioeconomic Context of 'The Preacher's' Hermeneutic," *PSB*, n.s., 17, no. 2 (1996): 181.

47   The most striking difference between the two texts, of course, is the negation. But there are other notable points of contrast as well. Isaksson observes that 5:18 speaks universally of "all people" (*kol-hāʾādām*), while 6:2 speaks more particularly of "a person" (*ʾîš*). Moreover, the Hebrew verbs attributed to God in 5:18 are perfect forms ("God has given," "has authorized"); the same verbs in 6:2 are in the imperfect ("God gives," "God does not authorize"). See B. Isaksson, *Studies in the Language of Qoheleth: With Special Emphasis on the Verbal System* (Studia Semitica Upsaliensia 10; Stockholm: Almqvist & Wiksell, 1987), 122.

general to enjoy the good things in life. Yet, he also recognizes that there are tragic exceptions—situations where people are, for whatever reasons, simply unable to enjoy. As Qohelet would have it elsewhere, some people are fortunate enough to be *ṭôb lipnê hā᾿ĕlōhîm*, while others are simply *ḥōṭē᾿* (2:26).

These central sections of the literary unit, juxtaposed in sharp relief, raise the question of divine determinism. The sovereign will of an unpredictable God lies behind all that happens or does not happen in life. This theology, which seems to permeate the book, is seen in God's inexplicable decision to allow one (5:17—18)—but not another (6:1—2)—to enjoy the divinely granted riches. Yet, paradoxically, the author of Ecclesiastes makes a significant provision for human agency as well. Indeed, this text proffers one of the fullest expositions of Qohelet's theology of double agency. God is unquestionably the primary Actor in the drama of life, the one who gives and authorizes. Nevertheless, by this very act of giving and authorizing, the deity also bequeaths a "portion" to the human actor as well, and like a beneficiary under the Persian system of royal grants, the human agent is given a responsibility for the proper use of that right of disposal. When the Sovereign grants, the designated grantee is expected "to take up." The "determinism" detected in this text, hence, in no way obviates human agency or "freedom of the will."[48] To be sure, there are innumerable things over which mortals have no control. They do not have power (*᾿ên ᾿ādām šallîṭ*) over the wind, or power (*᾿ên šilṭôn*) over the day of death (8:8). After all, everything is *hebel*, says Qohelet. Yet, over the means of enjoyment, human beings do have the God-given power of disposal, if only for a given moment, and Qohelet urges the vigorous and responsible exercise of that power.

So one reads in 5:19—the pivotal point of the entire unit—that people "should not much call to mind the days of their lives,"[49] for God "gives a preoccupation" (*ma῾ăneh*) through the enjoyment of their heart. According to this translation of *ma῾ăneh* (favored by most interpreters), Qohelet asserts here that God makes it possible to forget the brevity and unpredictability of human existence through the busy enjoyment of life. In other words, God keeps human beings occupied with

---

48 As noted by Murphy, the determinism out of which Qohelet operates is of an unusual kind, at least from the perspective of postbiblical thought. He affirms the sovereign disposition of all things by the deity, but this determinism—sharply distinguished from fatalism—does not exempt human beings from responsibility. Along with the rest of the biblical writers, Israel's sages never engaged in any theoretical discussion concerning the reconciliation of these contraries (cf. Sir 15:11—20). *Ecclesiastes*, lxvi—lxvii.

49 For a defense of the injunctive reading of *yizkōr*, see Seow, *Ecclesiastes*, 209.

pleasure, thereby giving them momentary relief from the painful consciousness of human finitude. This notion is found in Egyptian literature as well, as a number of scholars have noted.[50] In the *Song of Antef*, for example, one finds the similar injunction: "May you be whole, as your heart makes itself forget."[51] Such poems appear in mortuary scenes among Egyptian tombs, which depict people eating and drinking in lavish "entertainment scenes" (Egyptian *shmh-ib*, literally, "diverting the heart"). Despairing of the efficacy of mortuary rites to ensure immortality, the poet urges the audience to divert themselves from thoughts of mortality and enjoy themselves in the present. Likewise, from Jerusalem comes a late Hellenistic tomb inscription exhorting: "You who are living, Enjoy!"[52] Qohelet, too, is fully aware of the transient nature of human existence. Mortals are given but a limited number of days (*mispar yĕmê-ḥayyāw*)[53] under the sun (5:17; cf. 2:3; 3:12, 22); their "portion" is limited in space and time. It appears, then, that the *maʿăneh* in 5:19 is a positive preoccupation that is intended to *distract* people from the transience of their lives and the vexing preoccupation with which God afflicts humanity (cf. 1:13; 3:10). The God who troubles mortals with a terrible *ʿinyān* is the same God who preoccupies them with the possibility of enjoyment in their hearts, if only for a moment.

There is, however, another possible rendering for the multivalent word *maʿăneh*, as Jewish commentators like Rashbam and Ibn Ezra have long recognized.[54] The word *maʿăneh* may, in fact, also be taken to mean "an answer" or "one who gives an answer."[55] Indeed, elsewhere in the Bible, this precise Hebrew form always means "answer" (cf. Prov

---

50 Galling, "Der Prediger," 77, 102—3; Lauha, *Kohelet*, 113—14; Fox, *A Time To Tear Down*, 12—13, 239.

51 Papyrus Harris 500, lines 23—24. See also Michael V. Fox, "Study of Antef," *Or* 46 (1977): 393—423. For other examples of Harpers Songs, see Lichtheim, *AEL* I, 196—97.

52 P. Benoit, "L'Inscription Greque du Tombeau de Jason," *IEJ* 17 (1967): 112—13.

53 The phrase may be read as the adverbial accusative (of time), as in 2:3 and 6:12. Qohelet notes the transitory nature of human life in terms of their numbered days. A similar sentiment is expressed in the *Gilgamesh Epic*: "As for humanity, their days are numbered" (Gilg Y iv 142).

54 For Rashbam's text, see S. Japhet and R. B. Salters, *The Commentary of R. Samuel ben Meir Rashbam on Qoheleth* (Jerusalem: Magnes, 1985). For Ibn Ezra, see Mariano Gómez Aranda, ed., *El Comentario de Abraham Ibn Ezra Al Libro del Eclesiastes: Introducion, Traduccion y Edicion Critica* (Textos y estudios "Cardenal Cisneros" 56; Madrid: Instituto de Filologia del CSIC, 1994).

55 A number of Jewish and Christian interpreters have suggested this rendering for the word *maʿăneh* in this context. See Lohfink's survey in "Revelation by Joy," 625—635. For a lengthy discussion of this meaning of the root *ʿnh*, see Franz Delitzsch, *Hoheslied und Koheleth* (BKAT 4; Leipzig: Dörffling & Franke, 1875), 300—301.

15:1, 23; 16:1; 29:19; Job 32:3, 5). Understood in this way, God is the one who "gives a response" through enjoyment in the human heart.[56] This response is, first, God's answer to the problem of human discontentment. Beyond this, if one reads the participle *ma'ăneh* with the concessive force of the Hiphil, one may posit that the divine answer also permits—indeed, calls for—a response on the part of the human. God not only authorizes human beneficiaries to enjoy the portion assigned to them, God also gives them the *responsibility* to work that lot and enjoy its fruit. In other words, enjoyment is not only a divine gift, but also a human *duty*. Indeed, Qohelet implies that those who fail to enjoy have refused to accept the will of God, and will be called to account, or held *answerable*, as it were (cf. 11:9). So, the *ma'ăneh* in 5:19 is both God's response and humanity's responsibility through the positive preoccupation of joy in the heart (*běśimḥat libbô*).

This latter phrase (*běśimḥat libbô*) further reinforces the notion of human volition and agency. As Yochanan Muffs has demonstrated, the Hebrew expression *běśimḥat libbô* may function as a metaphor for willingness and spontaneity.[57] He notes that the Akkadian expressions *ina ṭūb libbi* ("with goodness/gladness of heart") and *ina ḫud libbi* ("with joy of heart") are common in Akkadian documents spanning the Old Babylonian and Neo-Babylonian periods, where they indicate the idea of freedom and volition in various legal contexts. The Hebrew terms for "goodness" (*ṭôb*) and "joy" (*śimḥâ*), like their Akkadian counterparts, function as terms of volition and spontaneity in Late Biblical Hebrew,[58] arguably the language of Qohelet.[59] Accordingly, then, enjoyment in Qohelet's view is a possibility, even a religious responsibility, that humanity must accept and exercise "with gladness of heart," that is, willingly and without reservation.

The urgency of this responsibility is underscored by the reflections surrounding 5:17—19, which depict the terrible consequences of failing to enjoy. As noted above, the larger unit 5:7—6:9 is primarily concerned with the problem of human greed and insatiability. The prominence of this issue is evident in the recurrence of the verbs *'kl* ("to eat," or "to eat up" 5:10, 11, 16, 17 [twice], 18; 6:2) and *śb'* ("to satisfy," 5:9; 6:3; cf. 4:8),

---

56 Lohfink's proposal (following Levy), that the divine answer indicates "revelation by joy," while provocative, is a strained extension of the root *'nh*.

57 Yochanan Muffs, *Love and Joy: Law, Language Religion in Ancient Israel* (New York: The Jewish Theological Seminary of America, 1992), 121—193.

58 See, for instance, 1 Chr 29:9, 17; 2 Chr 24:10; 15:12—15.

59 Despite the undeniable presence of LBH elements, the language of Ecclesiastes may, more precisely, represent the patois of the Persian-period "market place." See Choon Leong Seow, "Linguistic Evidence and the Dating of Qohelet," *JBL* 115, no. 4 (1996): 643—666.

along with the word *nepeš* (literally, "throat" or "gullet," 6:2, 3, 7, 9; cf. 4:8). The voracious human appetite is vividly portrayed through the imagery of people whose *nepeš* can never be satisfied (cf. 6:7). The use of this language is suggestive, for in Canaanite mythology, Death is portrayed as a monster with a wide-opened maw (*npš*), "one lip to the Earth, one lip to the Heaven" (*špt larṣ / špt lšmm*). Greedy Death is ever a threat to life and world order, for he is never sated (*šbʿ*).[60] Within the Hebrew Bible itself, the language of the insatiable *nepeš* is applied first to Sheol's deadliness (Isa 5:14; Prov 27:20; 30:16).[61] Even more striking is the application of the metaphor to the dangers posed to the social order in the cosmos by the insatiable rich oppressors of the world: "they set their mouth in the heavens, their tongue traverses through the earth" (Ps 73:9). In similar fashion, Habakkuk (2:5) speaks of an oppressor as one who "has widened his maw (*npš*) like Sheol; he is like Death, never being sated (*šbʿ*)." In Ecclesiastes, as Seow has observed, this imagery is shockingly applied not just to oppression or widespread injustice, but more broadly to human discontentment.[62] By recourse to such language, the author suggests that human discontentment may in fact lead to cosmic chaos. Human discontentment is not just an individual inadequacy. It is not viewed psychologically as a personal insecurity. For Qohelet, it is as utterly pernicious as gross injustice in the world: it threatens life itself and endangers the cosmos. So, here at the theological highpoint of his reflections, the author confronts the reader with a choice that is freighted with ethical implications: individuals can preoccupy themselves with the ravenous and deadly pursuit of more and more. Or, they can respond appropriately to the opportunities granted by God, and enjoy. That enjoyment of life is vital for the preservation of life and moral order in the world.

2.5 The Paradox of Joy (7:14)

Having concluded the first half of the book with a compelling call to be glad with one's lot, the author continues in the second half to expound on his theology of enjoyment. With every successive turn in his argument, Qohelet's discourse on joy plays a vital role in moving his thoughts forward and generating a shift in the tone of his teachings. There is a noticeable progression from description to prescription, from

---

60   *KTU* 1.23.61—64; cf. 1.5.2.2—4.
61   P. R. Ackroyd, "Two Hebrew Notes," *ASTI* 5 (1966/67): 82—86.
62   Seow, *Ecclesiastes*, 226—227.

observation to ethical commendation.[63] Throughout the remainder of the book, the persistent appeal to enjoy life appears predominantly in the imperative mood and with greater poetic flourish, infusing the sage's teachings with a heightened urgency and exuberance.[64]

Like the preceding reflections, the opening unit in the second half of the book (6:10—7:14) gives a prominent place to the theme of enjoyment. One notes that its movement broadly mirrors that of 1:12—2:26, discussed above. The introduction (6:10—12) and conclusion (7:13—14) form a theological frame around the unit, being marked by the common themes of divine determinism and human ignorance of the future. Moreover, just as in 1:12—2:26, the theological weight is reserved for the conclusion of the unit; only at the end does the sage speak deliberately about God. In 6:10—12, the references to the deity's governance of events are made only obliquely: "whatever happens has already been named" by "the one who is stronger." In 7:13—14, however, the deity is unambiguously identified as the agent behind all that happens (*maʿăśēh hāʾĕlōhîm*, v. 13a; *ʿāśâ hāʾĕlōhîm*, v. 14b). The assertion that human beings cannot make straight what God has made crooked (v. 13b; cf. 1:15) now makes clear that the deity is "the stronger one" with whom humans cannot dispute (6:10). This explicit talk of God gives the conclusion a distinct theological accent, and it is precisely at this juncture that Qohelet renews his summons to enjoy life. The theological import of enjoyment is thereby underscored yet again.

In this instance, the sage's advice is presented more forcefully, in a series of straightforward directives: "see the work of God" (v. 13), "enjoy" (literally, "be in good," v. 14), and "see" (v. 14). Up to this point, Qohelet has consistently maintained that enjoyment is the gift of a sovereign God who gives freely, according to a mysterious divine logic. At the same time, he has insisted that in order for enjoyment to be complete, the gift must be willingly and actively taken up by the human agent. Divine dispensation is foundational for enjoyment, but human participation is essential for its full realization. So, the sage now *commands* joy.

---

63 See Christianson's graphic depiction of the book's gradual shift from first person narration to second person discourse in *A Time To Tell*, 244.

64 Similarly, Whybray remarks that the joy passages are arranged intentionally throughout the book "to state their theme with steadily increasing emphasis and solemnity." Whybray, "Qoheleth, Preacher of Joy," 87. See also William Brown, "'Whatever Your Hand Finds to do' Qoheleth's Work Ethic," 279; Fox, *A Time to Tear Down*, 318; Ellen Davis, *Proverbs, Ecclesiastes, and the Song of Songs* (Louisville: Westminster John, 2000), 223.

It was noted in the introduction to this chapter that enjoyment, for Qohelet, entails a full acceptance of all the opportunities and experiences that life presents, including the bad along with the good. Nowhere is this more pointedly stated than in the verse at hand: "On a good day, enjoy; on a bad day, see ..." (7:14a). This pithy sentence contains in a nutshell the sage's views on how mortals are to live in a world fraught with contradictory realities. The "good day" and "bad day" alike are of God's doing (ma'ăśēh hā'ĕlōhîm, v. 13a; 'āśâ hā'ĕlōhîm, v. 14b). They exist side by side, even as they do in the parallel lines of the admonition (bĕyôm ṭôbâ ... ûbĕyôm rā'â, v. 14a), and it is impossible for humans to root out the one from the other. The work of God is simply beyond human control and manipulation (v. 13b). The sage insists, instead, that the way of joy is to be open to the work of God in its manifold expressions, accepting each moment for what it is. Rather than straining against the grain and seeking to control what happens, people must reflect on divine activity (rĕ'ēh, vv. 13—14) and respond appropriately. The author employs paronomasia to convey this idea: bĕyôm ṭôbâ hĕyēh bĕṭôb ûbĕyôm rā'â rĕ'ēh. Ṭôb echoes ṭôbâ, and rĕ'ēh echoes rā'â. The alliteration reinforces the point by allowing the mirroring to take place on a linguistic level as well.

The idiom for enjoyment employed by the author in this instance is "being in good" (hĕyēh bĕṭôb). This idiom occurs only here in the Hebrew Bible, but it may be likened to the expression rĕ'ēh bĕṭôb in 2:1. Indeed, the familiar language of "seeing/experiencing" is employed here (twice in vv. 13f) in tandem with this language of "being in good."[65] Up to this point in the book, Qohelet has spoken of enjoyment largely in terms of doing—eating, drinking, seeing good, doing good, and taking up one's portion. Here, however, he describes it in terms of being—being fully present to the goodness of the moment at hand. The use of this particular language suggests that enjoyment is not only a matter of right conduct; it is also a matter of *character* and *disposition*. William Brown has argued that the formation of moral character lies at the heart of wisdom theology.[66] With respect to Ecclesiastes, however, he opines that "only snippets of the contours of right character can be discerned from wisdom so remote and abstract."[67] While it is true that Qohelet's approach to wisdom may be more "philosophical" and convoluted than the conventional wisdom of Proverbs, it offers far more than mere "snippets" of right character. Indeed, one may argue

---

65   See similar expressions in Ps 25:13 and Job 21:13.

66   William Brown, *Character in Crisis: A Fresh Approach to the Wisdom Literature of the Old Testament* (Grand Rapids: Eerdmans, 1997).

67   William Brown, *Character in Crisis*, 129.

that Qohelet's theology of enjoyment offers a comprehensive picture of the moral self.

In speaking of the moral being, ethicists have traditionally identified three dimensions of the self that are constitutive of character: perception, intention, and disposition.[68] One may argue that these very elements are reflected in Qohelet's explication of joy. The sage often speaks of enjoyment in terms of perception ("seeing what is good"). As already noted, this perception is more than mere observation; it involves the experience and meaningful integration of what is at hand. He also alludes to the role of intention in giving moral coherence to human agency, particularly in the notion of "gladness in the heart" (5:19), which brings together the volitional and affective dimensions of joy. Here, he suggests that disposition ("being in good") is also a critical aspect of his ethic. The importance of this "being" is highlighted by the unique syntax of this line; the imperative of the verb *hyh*, followed by an adverbial/temporal predicate (*bĕṭôb // bĕyôm ṭôbâ*), calls attention to the verb itself. The imperative of *hyh* occurs only thirteen other times in the Hebrew Bible, and in each instance, it is followed by a nominal or adjectival predicate to communicate the urgency of establishing a particular identity or attribute.[69] For Qohelet, however, right disposition is not a matter of possessing certain normative virtues, but *being in* a timely relationship with divine activity. One must recognize the work of God as that which transcends human understanding, and then experience it in its immanence, as it unfolds moment by moment.

Qohelet's ethic of joy is essentially an ethic of the moment. It may be likened to Barth's notion of joy as "a moment or a few moments" in which life's movement in time is arrested for the time being, a "temporary abandonment to the changes and circumstances of life ... in the recognition that there is no option." But this "abandonment" is in no way a resignation, because an experience of satisfaction, and even fulfillment, may be gratefully found in the moment.[70] Or, as Qohelet would put it, enjoyment is a matter of embracing the here and the now,

---

68 See the discussion in Bruce Birch and Larry Rasmussen, *Bible and Ethics in the Christian Life* (Minneapolis: Augsburg, 1989), 74—81. Others speak of these dimensions in terms of the affective, cognitive, and volitional. See James M. Gustafson, *Ethics From a Theocentric Perspective* (vol. 1 of *Theology and Ethics*; Chicago: University of Chicago Press, 1981), 117—20. See also, Richard Bondi, "The Elements of Character," *JRE* 12 (1984): 201—218. In biblical studies, see William Brown, *Character in Crisis*, especially 6—12; idem, *Character and Scripture*.

69 See Gen 12:2; 17:1; Exod 18:19; 34:2; Judg 17:10; 18:19; Sam 18:17; Isa 33:2; Ezek 21:15; Pss 30:11; 31:3; 71:3.

70 Karl Barth, *CD*, III.4, 376.

not dwelling nostalgically on former days (v. 10) or seeking to calculate and control what will be in the future (v. 14b; cf. 6:12b). It is a disciplined yet joyous concentration on the present, recognizing that the present moment is endowed with a moral significance all its own and therefore merits the full attention of the moral being. Indeed, the present is the only realm in which human beings may assert and fulfill their moral agency.

But enjoyment is not strictly restricted to the good times. The sage goes on to say "when times are bad, see …." Interpreters commonly render the verb r'h in this case as "consider thoughtfully," "pay attention to," or "bear in mind."[71] Yet, given the fact that this verb figures prominently in Qohelet's vocabulary of joy, one may venture to say that more is intended here. Indeed, when the verb occurs as an imperative elsewhere in the book, it functions as an idiom for enjoyment, directing the reader to *recognize* and *experience* the goodness of life (2:1; 9:9).[72] What is striking about 7:14 is that the command to "see" is associated not with times of good fortune, but with times of misfortune. Moreover, the sage only says "see," without supplying an immediate object; the injunction comes to an abrupt halt, leading only to the emphatic *gam*, the particle that emphasizes the dialectical nature of God's activity: "even the one as well as the other God has made…" With this halting construction, Qohelet suggests that even unfavorable circumstances are to be fully encountered and "enjoyed." Authentic enjoyment does not limit itself to good and pleasurable experiences, but also embraces the unfavorable ones, acknowledging that God is at work in all circumstances. Indeed, Qohelet, with the faithful realism that characterizes his teachings, maintains that the one who fears God must goes forth in life with "both" (7:18).[73]

This inevitable alternation of good and ill is given concrete expression by the proverbial sayings (7:1—12) that lead up to this counsel of enjoyment. In a manner reminiscent of the Catalogue of Times, various occasions are described in conventional antithetical pairs: death and birth (v. 1), mourning and feasting (vv. 2, 4), sorrow and laughter (v. 3), the rebuke of the wise and the praise of fools (v. 5), the end and the beginning (vv. 8, 10), etc. Here, however, they come in the form of "better than" (*tôb*) sayings. Of particular interest is the cluster of sayings on the preferential value of sorrow over joy (7:1—6):

---

71   Schoors, "The Verb r h in the Book of Qoheleth," 240.

72   Compare Deut 33:9, where "see" occurs in parallel with "recognize," "know," and "keep," and Deut 11:2, where, similarly, the expression "see the discipline of YHWH" occurs in parallel with "know."

73   See discussion of this text in chapter 3.

the day of death is better than the day of birth (v. 1b); it is better to go to the house of mourning than to go to the house of feasting (vv. 2a, 4); sorrow is better than laughter (v. 3a). The sage who has been extolling the virtues of joy seems suddenly to reverse himself. Commentators therefore surmise that these sentiments must represent an alternative perspective, which Qohelet cites solely for the sake of argument.[74] Yet, given the absence of formal markers for identifying quotations, this proposal is highly unsatisfactory. Others reckon that the "laughter" and "mirth" mentioned in these verses must denote something quite distinct from the "profound enjoyment (śmḥ)" that he advocates elsewhere. Here, the sage has in mind instead an "empty hilarity" or "thoughtless and irresponsible buffoonery."[75] These proposals, however, fail to note that the same vocabulary of joy is employed here (note especially śimḥâ, v. 4; mišteh, v. 2; yiṭab lēb, v. 3), and there is nothing to suggest that the words denote something qualitatively different in this context.

How, then is Qohelet's "turn-around" to be reckoned with? It is important to note, first, that these ṭôb-sayings are Qohelet's response to the question posed at the introduction of the unit: "who knows what is good (mah-ṭôb) for humanity?" (6:12; cf. 2:3). The rhetorical question already suggests that finite minds cannot in fact determine what is good in an absolute or universal sense. The sage then exploits the rhetoric of proverbs to underscore the fact that no maxim is axiomatic for every place and every moment.[76] Proverbial material is often situational in character and may blatantly juxtapose antithetical sentences.[77] In doing so, biblical wisdom acknowledges the limits of moral principles, and invites moral subjects to engage their environment and exercise discernment in making judgments about what is good. Accordingly, the sage who so persistently commends joy throughout his discourse acknowledges here that joy is not always

---

74   Michel, for example, avers that in light of his other passages concerning joy, Qohelet cannot be proposing the pessimism of 7:1–6 as something "good." It must be that the sage cites these views but summarily rejects them with the verdict of *hebel* in 6b. His genuine views are to be gathered from vv. 7–10, where he purportedly argues against vv. 1–6 (*Eigenart*, 126–37). See also Lohfink, *Qoheleth*, 89–93; Murphy, *Ecclesiastes*, 61–65.

75   Ogden, *Qoheleth*, 103; Whybray, *Ecclesiastes*, 113.

76   A number of interpreters have noted that the aphorisms in 7:1–12 are replete with self-directed irony. The sayings may be a parody of the "many words" of the wise that are derided as *hebel* in 6:11.

77   See the classic example in Prov 26:5–6. Note also Qohelet's antithetical sayings on vexation in 7:3, 9.

better. There are occasions when sorrow and mourning may in fact be preferable.

The internal logic of these sayings also sheds light on how they are to be read in relation to Qohelet's broader teachings. In v. 2b, the preference for the day of death/mourning over against the day of birth/feasting is followed by the rationale: "for this is the end of everyone and the living should lay it to heart." In a statement of ultimate realism, the proverb speaks of death as the universal horizon of every living creature, and insists that everyone ought to contemplate their eventual destiny. Elsewhere in his discourse, when Qohelet reflects on the inevitability of death, he does so in order to motivate people to embrace life all the more (see 3:19—22; 5:14—19; 9:5—10; 11:7—12:8). The "house of mourning" (vv. 2, 4) is particularly effective in this regard. The funereal setting confronts a person with one's own mortality, and gives one pause to consider how best to live the remainder of one's life. Here, also, even as the sage commends mourning and sorrow, his primary concern is the promotion of life. In his own rhetoric, "the heart of the wise is in the house of mourning" (7:4), and "wisdom gives life to those who possess it" (7:12).

Yet, one must not too easily dismiss Qohelet's stated preference for sorrow in these proverbs. Birth and death represent the two extreme poles of human existence (7:1b); joy and sorrow represent the two poles of human experiences. If death is a universal fact, so is the sense of loss and grief that accompanies death. Qohelet faces this reality squarely, readily submitting himself to the full range of experiences and emotions that are a part of being human. He insists that only fools use merrymaking as a means of avoiding the tragic dimensions of life (7:4b). Enjoyment is not intended to be the gift of oblivion, as some have contended.[78] It may function as a redemptive diversion that keeps a person from the trap of brooding over one's mortality *overmuch* (cf. 5:19), from a morbid and debilitating preoccupation with it. But it is not meant to anesthetize the pain, not if it comes at the expense of dulling one's authentic experience of life. So the sage commends sorrow along with joy.

He supplies another rationale in v. 3: "for by sadness of countenance the heart is made glad." According to this statement, sorrow not only coexists with joy; it may in fact be a prerequisite for it. Perhaps he means here what he suggests elsewhere—that the contemplation of human mortality ought to provoke enjoyment. But the spare wording of this proverb refrains from explaining precisely

---

78   Fox, *A Time to Tear Down*, 239; Longman, *The Book of Ecclesiastes*, 168.

how or why sadness leads to gladness. It simply underscores the paradox.[79] A similar sentiment is found in Prov 14:13, where the direction is reversed: "even in merriment the heart suffers, and the outcome of joy is grief." These sentences, taken together, speak of life as alternating mysteriously and unpredictably between times of grief and times of gladness. The authentic life must have its share of both. Indeed, Qohelet suggests here that a person cannot know real joy without experiencing real sorrow.

The thrust of the overall passage (6:10—7:14), then, is that "what is good" is at best a fragile reality. One cannot foresee when it may come or how long it may last. Favorable times may inexplicably give way to unfavorable ones, and vice versa. As in 3:14, Qohelet attributes a divine purpose to this perplexing "pattern": the good and bad are woven mysteriously into the fabric of life "so that humans cannot find out anything after them" (7:14c). The unpredictability of God's dealings, it seems, is meant to be a safeguard against human presumption. The "day of misfortune" (yôm rāʿâ), whenever it is encountered, is a reminder that mortals are profoundly limited in knowledge and power. However, the "day of good fortune" (yôm ṭôb) points to the possibilities that likewise reside in God's hand. The mystery of divine activity thus provokes a profound openness to the future, however uncertain that future may be. Here, what in 3:14 is called the fear of God is more concretely described as the ability to see and be present to this mystery (cf. 7:18).[80]

The saying in 7:14 thus epitomizes the sage's views on how mortals are to live in a world governed by an inscrutable deity. Qohelet's theology of enjoyment acknowledges that human agents are limited in their capacities by the freedom of a sovereign God. Mortals are powerless to control the work of God; their agency is bound to the ethic of the moment. They must therefore reflect on the work of God and live appropriately in response, moment by moment, enjoying the times of favor without recoiling from the times of adversity. There is a refreshing modesty about this counsel, which is in keeping with the sage's realistic piety. God is the author of both weal and woe, and Qohelet would be content to echo the sentiment expressed by the psalmist: "Make us glad as many days as you have afflicted us, and as many years as we have seen evil" (Ps 90:15).

---

79 Note the peculiar logic of the saying: the first line values sorrow over joy ("sorrow is better than laughter"); the second line does the opposite, by making joy the desired end of sorrow ("for by sadness of countenance the heart will be glad").

80 To be discussed in chapter 3.

2.6 By the Sweat of One's Brow (8:15)

In 8:9—17, Qohelet returns yet again to the theme of God's inscrutable activity. This time, he focuses on a particular aspect of this larger theological issue: the apparent failure of retributive justice (cf. 3:16—22; 7:15). As he examines "all that is done under the sun" (vv. 9, 16f), he is deeply troubled by the arbitrary manner in which justice is executed. His vision of a moral society is disrupted by the failure of the system to mete out rewards and punishment in the expected manner. Indeed, the principle of retribution seems to be turned on its head: the wicked are honored in death, while the upright are ignominiously neglected (v. 10); evildoers are not punished but rewarded with long life (vv. 11—12a); the righteous are treated as if they were wicked and the wicked as if they were righteous (v. 14). This state of affairs is utterly incomprehensible to him and he intones three times that this is *hebel* (vv. 10, 14 [twice]), and three more times that no one can grasp the work of God (v. 17). Still, the sage never relinquishes his quest for a meaningful existence; indeed, these perplexing realities impel him to revisit the matter of what, then, is "good" for human beings to do. Again, Qohelet's answer is bound up with his theology of enjoyment. In light of the fact that what happens in this world is largely out of human control, he calls for a channeling of human efforts to that which is most fruitful and life-enhancing. In 8:15, at the climax of the unit, he reaffirms his conviction that enjoyment is the most reasonable—and most ethical—response to injustices in this world. And, as before, he anchors his counsel of joy in the theological datum that life is given by God.

The passage has to do with the absurdity of "what is done" on earth. The root *ʿśh* occurs fourteen times in 8:9—16, with five of those occurrences in the passive Niphal stem. The passage itself is framed by references to Qohelet's examination of "(all) the deeds that are done" under the sun (vv. 9, 16f). The problem, it seems, is that what ought to be done is not done (*ʾên-naʿăśeh*, v. 11), and what ought not to be done is done (*yeš-hebel ʾăšer naʿăśâ*, v. 14; *hāʿinyān ʾăšer naʿăśâ*, 16). Because retribution is delayed or altogether absent, people are only emboldened to perpetuate their evil behavior (v. 11). Indeed, the four-fold repetition of the word "evil" in the surrounding verses (vv. 9—12) performs the proliferation of evil on a literary level. Over against this deleterious reflex, Qohelet suggests a better way. The text moves from observation of the injustice (vv. 10—12a) to Qohelet's response to that observation, in which he considers how a person ought to live in such an arbitrary world (vv. 12b—13), and again from observation (v. 14) to response (v.

15). In the midst of all the talk of "evil," he speaks of two things that are "good": the fear of God (vv. 12b—13) and the enjoyment of life (v. 15). This "good" is described in an altogether unpretentious and modest fashion, in terms of a piety of eating, drinking, and being glad in the midst of toil. Yet, in the logic of the text, it is this "good" that counters the proliferation of evil.

As he has often done before (2:24; 3:12, 22), Qohelet presents this commendation of enjoyment in the form of an 'ên-ṭôb saying. All of its stock components are recapitulated here: "there is nothing better for humanity under the sun but to eat and drink and be glad" (v. 15). In this final occurrence of the formula, however, there is a notable variation on the theme. The familiar refrain is now prefaced and accentuated by the enthusiastic declaration: "So I extol (šbḥ) enjoyment." The Piel form of šbḥ occurs only a handful of times in the Old Testament, mostly in the Psalms where it is typically rendered as "praise," with God or the works of God as its object (see Pss 63:4; 117:1; 145:4; 147:12; cf. its Aramaic equivalent in Dan 2:23; 4:31, 34; 5:4, 23). Apart from these several instances, it appears only in Ecclesiastes, here and in 4:2. And the usage may reflect something larger about the progression of Qohelet's thoughts. Notably, the two occurrences of the verb share a similar context: in each place, Qohelet is pondering the abuse of power and the perpetration of injustices in human society. Yet the word šbḥ is used for drastically different ends in the two texts. In the first, the sage's observation of human misery precipitates the bitter declaration: "I extol (šbḥ) the dead who have already died more than the living who are still alive." Ironically, he employs the language of praise in order to lament the plight of the afflicted. In doing so, Qohelet seems to turn his back on life. As he moves forward in his discourse, however, his persistent concentration on the redeeming value of enjoyment engenders a pronounced change in tone. The fervor with which he commends enjoyment escalates, and in 8:15, it reaches a more spirited pitch in which he breaks out into his praise of life-centered joy. The very language previously used to express despair over life is now used for the purpose of embracing life. The language of praise is thereby reclaimed to affirm what is "good."

Still, as always, Qohelet's praise of joy is tempered by his realism concerning life's contradictions. He goes on to say that enjoyment will accompany people "in their toil." Toil ('ml) is an important word in Ecclesiastes. Not only is it featured prominently in the book's leading rhetorical question in 1:3 ("What profit do people have in all the toil at which they toil under the sun?" cf. 3:9; 5:15; 6:11), it also occurs frequently throughout the book, which claims nearly seventy per cent of all occurrences of this root in the Hebrew Bible. It is the author's preferred word to speak of human work, and often has a somber connotation, signifying arduous and wearisome work, or *overwork*.[81] By extension, the word may also denote difficulties and misery apart from labor. Indeed, in Qohelet's rhetoric, the word broadly signifies the burden of living in a troubled world, and on occasion, appears to be functionally equivalent to life (see 3:12f; 2:17f; 9:9). For Qohelet, toil is what characterizes life.

In this regard, Qohelet's perspective is not altogether different from the biblical view of work, which begins with work in the garden. In Gen 1—3, work is given by God and intended to sustain life and give it meaning, but becomes inextricably linked to strenuous labor. Humanity is forever destined to eat of the ground in toil, by the sweat of their brow (see Gen 3:17—19). In Ecclesiastes, the problem of toil is further exacerbated by its association with the futile quest for "profit" (*yitrôn*, see 1:3; 3:9; 5:16). Qohelet affirms the value of work—he declares that only fools idly fold their hands to their detriment (4:5; cf. 10:18). But he also knows the human propensity to *overwork* in the misguided attempt to secure some kind of profit or advantage. Qohelet resists this association of labor with profit and joins it instead with enjoyment.

Qohelet has established the relationship between toil and enjoyment before. Indeed, in all but one of the enjoyment texts where the explicit vocabulary of *śmḥ* is found, it is collocated with the language of toil (2:24; 3:13; 3:22a; 5:17f; 9:9c; cf. 2:10). Now in 8:15, the connection is cemented inextricably through the use of the verb *lwh* "to accompany." The Qal of *lwh* occurs only here in the Hebrew Bible (cf. Sir 41:12). Typically, the verb occurs in the Niphal stem, with the meaning "to join" or "ally oneself with." It denotes an intimate and binding union, often of members that do not normally belong together, or have somehow become alienated from one another. Hence, the unloved Leah, after bearing a third son for Jacob, hopes that "now this time my husband will be joined to me" (Gen 29:34). Moreover, the union signified by *lwh* may fundamentally change the status or identity of the members involved. Israel's prophets envision a time when foreigners will join themselves to YHWH and become his people (Isa 56:3, 6; Zech 2:15).

Although joy and toil are not easy companions, Qohelet insists on an organic bond between the two. This bond reveals two things about his theology of enjoyment. First, it reinforces the point made above that

---

81   See Fox's helpful study of this word in *A Time to Tear Down*, 97—102.

Qohelet's conception of enjoyment must be clearly distinguished from any notion of hedonism. Enjoyment is not about avoiding or minimizing unpleasant experiences. It takes place in the midst of back-breaking toil, which Qohelet accepts as an inescapable feature of life. But even as humans live by the sweat of their brow, they can savor the moments of sweet respite and be refreshed by the fruit of their toil. This point leads to the second: when labor is allied with joy, it gives birth to work that is meaningful and fulfilling. It is joy that sustains and redeems the labor. The enjoyment of life—described in terms of eating and drinking—is what sustains a person in the toilsome work of living. Qohelet has in mind more than just the physical nourishment provided by food and drink. The pleasurable aspect of these activities is just as important for bolstering the desire and strength to carry on. It is what enables a person to fully engage life despite its difficulties. As these pleasures accompany a person in work, work is thereby relieved from its onerous sting, and can become vocation.

For Qohelet, enjoyment is not to be equated with the pursuit of gain or profit. The enjoyment of life's simple gifts—sustaining meals and sleep that rejuvenates in the night—displaces the vain prospect for gain. Hence, as Brown notes, joy is "both trivialized and elevated." Qohelet has, in effect, "integrated the solemn Sabbath command into the mundane rhythms of daily living, and in so doing consecrated them."[82] Qohelet refuses to let toil take over and have the decisive word. Indeed, the word itself tapers off toward the end of his discourse,[83] and human work is described in increasingly positive terms (see especially 9:10; 11:6).

Finally, as in each of the previous instances, the sage's call to enjoy is grounded theologically in the conviction that life is a gift of God. As Qohelet rounds off his counsel, the deity again appears as the subject of giving. It is not entirely clear what the object of this giving is. The relative particle *'ăšer* in v. 15c has a number of possible antecedents: life, days, toil, or enjoyment. Indeed, in Qohelet's theology, all of these things are given by God. In this case, the most immediate referent is *yĕmê ḥayyāyw* "the days of one's life." This phrase is an abbreviated version of the fuller expression *mispar yĕmê ḥayyîm* "number of days of one's life" (2:3; 5:17), or *mispar yĕmê ḥayyê heblô* (6:12; cf. *yĕmê ḥayyê heblekā* in 9:9; *yĕmê heblî* in 7:15), all of which signify the ephemerality of human existence. Qohelet repeatedly notes that human beings are

---

82   William Brown, "'Whatever Your Hand Finds to Do' Qoheleth's Work Ethic," 280–81.

83   The frequency of the word in both verbal and nominal forms is heavily concentrated in the first half of the book (31 out of 35 occurrences).

allotted a limited number of days. However, he emphasizes that this allotted time is time *given by God*. The ability to enjoy reflects, at base, a contentment with the human lot as a divine gift. One may even say that it betrays a kind of resignation. Yet, for Qohelet, it is not a bitter resignation. No, this hard-earned acquiescence to the place of humanity is a liberating one, and is accompanied by an enlivening appreciation of the limited but real possibilities that come with that place. The time that humans have under the sun will quickly come to an end. And that limited time will be marked by toil. It will, moreover, be accompanied by perplexing injustices. Yet, the fact that life is given by God should engender gratitude and contentment, not dejected resignation. To borrow the words of Barth, one can then see life as "an unfathomable and inexhaustible reality,"[84] worth living to the full and even celebrating.

2.7 To Life! (9:7—10)

I have argued that Qohelet's theology of enjoyment calls us back to *life*, the chief concern of the wisdom enterprise. The primary focus of the sage's teachings is the cultivation of habits and attitudes that are vital for the flourishing of human life. This includes the regular exercise of those activities that nourish the body and gladden the heart. It also entails a disposition marked by a realistic appreciation of and contentment with the human lot. In 9:7—10, Qohelet returns to this vital notion, but again, with a noticeable modulation. This commendation of enjoyment comes at the climactic conclusion of a passage in which he broods over the inevitability of death—the "one fate" (vv. 2, 3) that comes indiscriminately to all who are alive.[85] And it is his most exuberant and most expansive endorsement of enjoyment thus far. It is as if the awful contemplation of death stirs him to embrace life all the more and to urge his audience to do the same. He shifts abruptly from his reflective first-person discourse to address the reader directly and forcefully. The movement from the indicative to the imperative mood is all the more pronounced because of the heaping up of imperatives and jussives: go, eat, drink, let them be white, let it not

---

84   Barth, *CD* III/2:555.

85   Whenever Qohelet speaks of "fate" (*miqreh*), it is always in reference to death (2:14, 15; 3:19 [three times]; 9:2, 3). See Peter Machinist, "Fate, *miqreh*, and Reason: Some Reflections on Qohelet and Biblical Thought," in *Solving Riddles and Untying Knots* (ed. Z. Zevit et al.; Winona Lake, Ind.: Eisenbrauns, 1995), 159—75.

be lacking, enjoy life, act! Never has Qohelet been so profuse in his enthusiasm for life.

What he presents here is an anatomy of enjoyment, an elaborate description of the concrete activities that together make up a comprehensive picture of joy. He begins with verbs that typified his previous calls to enjoyment and lavishes upon them additional verbiage that speaks of joy: "eat your bread with enjoyment and drink your wine with a merry heart" (v. 7a). If there was any question that these verbs constituted a call to enjoy, the addition of "with enjoyment" and "with a merry heart" effectively dispels it. In addition, the imperatives are now accompanied by the specific objects of bread and wine. Elsewhere in the Old Testament, these elements, often occurring in tandem, are symbolic of the good life—one that is marked by sufficiency and gladness.[86] As Qohelet says elsewhere, "bread is made for laughter and wine gladdens (yĕśammaḥ) life" (10:19a; cf. Ps 104:15). Moreover, in the rhetoric of sapiential discourse, they may represent not only physical sustenance but also nourishment of the mind that cultivates understanding and fortitude of character. In Prov 9:5—6, Wisdom calls to the simple, "Come, eat of my bread and drink of the wine I have mixed. Lay aside immaturity, and live, and walk in the way of insight." Bread and wine thus promote life in the fullest sense. By incorporating these elements now into his call to enjoy, the author firmly anchors his ethic of joy in its potential to enhance life.

Then in vv. 8—9, Qohelet further augments his portrayal of enjoyment:

> At all times, let your garments be white;
> And let oil not be lacking upon your head;
> Enjoy life with your beloved wife[87] all the days of your fleeting life...

Enjoyment is characterized, first, by the donning of special garments. Particular types of clothing apparently could symbolize either sorrow and mourning or joy, as suggested by the psalmist's declaration that "you have turned my lamenting into dancing, you have taken off my sackcloth and clothed me with joy" (Ps 30:12). Although the symbolic usage of *white* garments is found only here in the Old Testament, it is

---

86 See, for example, Gen 14:18; Deut 29:5; Judg 19:19; Ruth 2:14; 1 Sam 10:3; 16:20; 25:18; 2 Kgs 18:32; Isa 36:17; Sir 31:27f; 39:26; cf. Lam 2:12. Bread and wine, of course, may also appear individually to represent the good life. Bread represents the basic component of a meal; wine typically adds an extra dimension of joy.

87 The word 'iššâ without the definite article may refer to one's wife when the context calls for it (e.g., Gen 30:4, 9; 1 Sam 25:43; Deut 22:22). Moreover, as noted by Seow, the Akkadian word in the parallel text in the *Gilgamesh Epic* is marḫitu "wife," rather than sinništu "woman." Seow, *Ecclesiastes*, 301.

more widely attested in rabbinic literature, where Israelites who celebrate the Passover are said to "rejoice with clean clothes and old wine" (*b. Pesahim 71a*).[88] Anointing with oil is a more common sign of joy and well-being in the Old Testament. Ps 104:15 includes "oil to make the face shine"—along with "wine to gladden the human heart" and "bread to strengthen the human heart"—among YHWH's good provisions.[89] The same could be said of conjugal relations (cf. Prov 5:18—19).[90] Indeed, all the activities that are catalogued here are concrete enactments of joy and well-being. With these embellishments, Qohelet moves a step beyond his former endorsement of simple everyday pleasures. He now infuses it with an air of festivity, and it swells into a veritable celebration of life.

As numerous scholars have pointed out, a similar counsel is also found in the *Gilgamesh Epic*. The similarity between the two texts is remarkable not only for the various elements that appear in both, but for the identical sequence in which they are enumerated. When Siduri the tavern keeper encounters a Gilgamesh who is despondent over his futile search for immortality, she gives him the following admonishment:

> As for you, Gilgamesh, let your belly be full,
> Enjoy yourself day and night.
> Find enjoyment every day,
> Dance and play day and night.
> Let your garments be clean,
> Let your head be washed; bathe in water.

---

88 For further discussion and citation of other literature, see Gary Anderson, *A Time to Mourn, a Time to Dance* (University Park: Pennsylvania State University Press, 1991), 48. This literary convention is found also in Egyptian didactic literature. *The Tale of Sinuhe* includes "bright clothing" among the things that characterize the good life (Text B 153; see Lichtheim, *AEL* I, 228). Conversely, the absence of "white garments" signifies impoverishment and sorrow in *The Admonitions of Ipuwer* (Text 2, 8; see Lichtheim, *AEL* I, 151).

89 See Pss 23:5; 133:2; 92:11; and the expression "oil of gladness" in Ps 45:7; Isa 61:3; Matt 6:16—17, where Jesus instructs those who are fasting to avoid looking dismal by anointing their heads with oil. This convention is also evident in Egyptian reliefs of banquet scenes that depict the guests with oil upon their heads (J. A. Thompson, "Ointment," *IDB* 3:594).

90 Rejoicing with one's wife may refer to the physical pleasures of lovemaking (Prov 5:18—19; Song 1:4; Deut 24:5; cf. Deut 20:5—7; 28:30). Anderson notes many instances in rabbinic literature, where the expression *śimḥat 'ištô* "the pleasure of his wife" denotes the necessity of providing one's wife with pleasure during lovemaking. See Gary Anderson, *A Time to Mourn, a Time to Dance*, 27—37, 55—56, and literature cited therein.

Look upon the little one who holds your hand,
Let your spouse enjoy herself in your embrace!
(Gilg M iii 6—14)

These parallel passages are often identified as *carpe diem* texts, and appropriately so. They make the point that since mortals cannot hold on to life forever, they must make the most of the present. Siduri tells Gilgamesh that his quest for immortality will come to naught, since the gods have ordained death for all humanity, retaining life "in their own hands" (Gilg M iii 4—5; cf. Eccl 9:1). With this *carpe diem*, she in effect says to him, the life you are offered is not eternal life—but life in this world, lived to the utmost.

However, to see these texts merely as a *carpe diem* would be to miss an important dimension. A more specific nuance may also be present in these passages. Gary Anderson has demonstrated that in ancient Israel and its cognate cultures, there is a behavioral dimension of joy that is specialized and ritualized. The behavioral dimension includes eating and drinking, anointing with oil, donning festal garments, and conjugal relations—precisely the activities enumerated in both Ecclesiastes and *Gilgamesh*.[91] Anderson argues that these activities are regular features in the ritual of terminating a mourning cycle. They are the signs of the living in contrast with the dead, and as such, signal the transition from grieving over death to reincorporating oneself into the normalcy of life.[92] Anderson contends that in the case of *Gilgamesh*, the passage likely has a highly specific function in its literary context. When the ruler of Uruk arrives at Siduri's abode, he is in a state of mourning over the death of his friend Enkidu. Having become a denizen of the steppe and having adopted a state of ritual dishevelment, Gilgamesh has identified himself with the realm of the dead.[93] He laments that since Enkidu's passing, he has not "found life" (Gilg M ii.10). According to Anderson, the alewife's exhortation to rejoice is in effect an exhortation to conclude his period of mourning, leave the world of the dead, and reincorporate himself within the world of the living.

Anderson, who largely limits his study to legal and ritual texts, does not include Eccl 9:7—10 in his discussion of the ritual significance

---

91 Gary Anderson, *A Time to Mourn, a Time to Dance*. In addition to these activities, Anderson discusses a fifth category: singing and dancing in praise of God.

92 In the *Gilgamesh Epic*, before Enkidu descends to the underworld, Gilgamesh admonishes him to abstain from just such activities, because, as Tigay puts it, "they are the marks of human life which will provoke the jealous anger of the dead who no longer enjoy them." Jeffrey H. Tigay, *The Evolution of the Gilgamesh Epic* (Philadelphia: University of Pennsylvania Press, 1982), 211.

93 G. Anderson, *A Time to Mourn, a Time to Dance*, 74—77.

of these activities. This text does not have the specialized function that the *Gilgamesh* counterpart may have; there is nothing in the context to suggest that the prescribed activities are meant to be ritualistic in the strict sense of the word. Nevertheless, it would be remiss not to consider the implications of Anderson's findings for Qohelet's call to enjoy life, particularly given the striking similarities with the *Gilgamesh* text. The author of Ecclesiastes does not trace Qohelet's quest through the vehicle of a biographical narrative, at least not in the same way as in the Mesopotamian tale.[94] Yet, as others have noted, his attempt to find a meaningful existence in light of human finitude has close affinities with Gilgamesh's odyssey.[95] Ruminations on the inevitability of death permeate Qohelet's teachings, so much so that some see death to be the prevailing theme of the book.[96] The preoccupation with mortality, however, is balanced by another "preoccupation" (5:19)—a commitment to enjoyment and life while the possibility remains. Qohelet's discourse moves back and forth between the two. The unit 9:1—10, in particular, displays a dramatic movement from contemplation of death to reaffirmation of life. As noted above, the first segment (vv. 1—6) is occupied with the certainty of death, which befalls every living being, regardless of character or conduct.[97] It is the one thing that humans can know with any confidence (v. 5).[98] Qohelet

---

94   Most interpreters agree that the autobiographical element in Ecclesiastes is confined to the opening chapters. Christianson, however, explores the narratival and biographical dimensions of the book as a whole in *A Time to Tell: Narrative Strategies in the Book of Ecclesiastes.*

95   A comparison between Gilgamesh and Qohelet figures prominently in Brown's recent commentary on Ecclesiastes. See also Brian W. Jones, "From Gilgamesh to Qoheleth," in *The Bible in the Light of Cuneiform Literature: Scripture in Context III* (ed. W.W. Hallo et al.; Lewiston, N.Y.: Edwin Mellen, 1990), 349—79.

96   Shannon Burkes, *Death in Qoheleth and Egyptian Biographies of the Late Period* (SBLDS 170; Atlanta: Society of Biblical Literature, 1999).

97   A similar reflection on the leveling effects of death is found in the Babylonian "Dialogue of Pessimism." This farcical conversation between a master and his slave explores "what is good" to do, and leads to the comment that ultimately it matters not what one does:
    Do not perform, sir, do not perform.
    Go up on to the ancient ruin heaps and walk about;
    See the skulls of high and low.
    Which is the malefactor and which is the benefactor?
    (ll. 75—78, see Lambert, *BWL*, 149)
    The dialogue concludes on a despairing note, with the answer that "what is good" is death.

98   *biṭṭaḥôn* in v. 4 does not indicate a feeling of "hope," as some English translations would have it (thus, KJV, NRSV, NIV), but something that one can count on as

descends into thoughts of the numb subhuman existence in the underworld, devoid of any knowledge or passion or recompense (vv. 5f, 10). Then, much as Siduri does with Gilgamesh, he calls a halt to his own mournful reflections by calling his audience to enact joy through these symbolic activities. He ardently urges a full-blooded engagement with the community of the living. His impassioned summons to enjoy is, in short, a summons to go on with the business of living. In the exercise of life itself—through these "performances" of enjoyment—one can experience the vitality of joy.[99]

Qohelet then caps his call to enjoy with a summary admonition: "Whatever your hand finds to do, do with your strength" (v. 10)![100] Throughout his discourse, Qohelet has indicated that joy and labor belong hand in hand. He reiterates that point here: vigorous work is entirely consonant with the festive enjoyment of life. The use of the verb "to find" is noteworthy in light of Qohelet's repeated assertion that mortals "cannot find" the things they seek (3:11; 7:14, 24—28; 8:17 [three times]). The word recalls the bankruptcy of human efforts to grasp the totality of God's work. Up to this point, whenever the sage has bemoaned this inability, he has balanced it with the advice to focus instead on enjoyment (3:12—13; 7:13; 8:15). Here, he goes one step

---

certain. Compare 9:1b, where the sage remarks that "no one knows anything before them," *'ên yōdēaʿ hāʾādām*.

99　According to Fox, the notion of *śimḥâ* in Ecclesiastes is reduced to (1) the sensation of pleasure, and (2) the means of pleasure (i.e., something that induces the sensation of pleasure, such as wine or music). In his insistence that the word never means happiness or joy, he creates a sharp dichotomy between a sensation/means of pleasure and the "inner experience" of joy. He writes: "There is no need to urge people to be happy; everyone wants happiness.... It is in any case pointless to *advise* happiness ... because happiness is not something people can impose upon themselves.... On the other hand, the advice to undertake pleasurable activities *can* be carried out. One can indulge in such things even when the heart is heavy" (Fox, *A Time to Tear Down*, 113—15). Fox is both right and wrong in this explication of *śimḥâ*. He is right that Qohelet recommends the undertaking of pleasurable activities. But his sharp distinction between pleasure and the inner experience of joy may be a false one. As argued by Anderson, ritual activity is not only expressive of human experience and emotions, but may also *produce* them (G. Anderson, *A Time to Mourn, a Time to Dance*, 51—55). This insight is an important one. Anderson's insistence that modern readers must attend to the *performative* dimension of joy reminds us that Fox's dichotomy may not be appropriate to this ancient text. Qohelet advises—indeed, commands—these pleasurable activities. But the joy that he espouses is not a hollow experience of pleasure that is somehow divorced from a person's inner life. The inner emotion may follow these enactments of joy. Indeed, these enactments may be intended to produce just such an internal transformation.

100　Reading against the Masoretic punctuation, which indicates that *bĕkōhăkā* ought to be read with the preceding infinitive *laʿăśôt* ("Whatever your had finds to do with strength, do!").

further and overturns the frustration of "not finding." In fact, from this point on, there is no longer any talk of "not finding"—only the possibility of finding the modest yet redeeming means of enjoyment (11:1). Finite beings cannot grasp the infinite. But there are some things that human beings can indeed find and grasp with their hands: those things that are immediately before them. And this they are called to do vigorously, "with strength." Concerning this, Brown observes that the rhetorical force with which Qohelet casts his prescription for work approximates that of the Shema (cf. Deut 6:5).[101] The work under the sun is to be taken up seriously and yet joyously. Or, as Miskotte puts it: "altogether earnestly, but not nervously, but rather with a light hand, without much pressure, and not without the light of the Sabbath running through it all."[102]

As always, the value of enjoyment is given theological grounding. The text includes three motivational clauses with this series of imperatives, each one introduced by the particle *kî*. The first is the most striking: "for God has already approved your deeds" (*ma'ăśêkā*).[103] The verb *ṛsh* expresses favor and pleasure (divine or human), and is often used to denote God's delight in right sacrifice or faithful service (among numerous examples, see 1 Chr 29:17; Ps 147:11). Here in 9:7, the object of divine pleasure is "your deeds"—the various joyous activities catalogued in this text. The celebration of life is not only sanctioned, but elevated to the status of religious duty, the fulfillment of which brings God pleasure. When human beings take pleasure in the gifts of God, God responds in kind, with pleasure. In this instance, the divine agent reflects the human agent! Human agency in the practice of enjoyment is thereby given a remarkable validation.

This validation is reinforced in the second rationale as well. Enjoy life "all the days of your fleeting life that are given you under the sun," says Qohelet, "for that is your portion (*ḥelqĕkā*) in life and in your toil" (v. 9). The sage returns to his earlier theological claim that the days of one's life is allotted and given by God.[104] Yet, the expression "your portion" in this instance refers to something more concrete and more specific. For the first time in the book, the word *ḥeleq* appears with the second person possessive pronoun. In fact, in addition to the copious usage of imperatives in vv. 7—10, there is a preponderance of the

---

101 Brown, *Ecclesiastes*, 95.

102 Kornelis H. Miskotte, *When the Gods Are Silent* (New York: Harper & Row, 1967), 454.

103 Some commentators posit that the divine approval precedes human enjoyment, i.e., enjoyment is a *post facto* sign of the divine approval (Crenshaw, *Ecclesiastes*, 162; Fox, *A Time to Tear Down*). But such a reading makes for a strange motivational clause.

104 In v. 9b, God is not explicitly named but understood to be the subject of the verb *ntn*.

second person pronoun. The sage speaks of *your* bread, *your* wine, *your* deeds, etc., utilizing the pronoun no less than twelve times to designate what belongs to the human agent. He addresses his audience directly, in effect proclaiming: "All of these things are *your* portion. It has been given to *you*, and it is *yours* for the taking and enjoying." In affirming the human portion so profusely, Qohelet underscores the importance of human agency in his ethic of joy. The giftedness of life is revealed not only in the concrete means of enjoyment enumerated in these verses, but also in the empowerment of the human agent to exercise good stewardship over those means.

Some may demur that the notion of stewardship cannot properly be attributed to a depiction of enjoyment that appears to be largely self-oriented and self-serving. This text exhibits minimal concern for a larger community outside the narrow confines of the self and the immediate circle of the family. Yet, it is significant that the next time the word *ḥeleq* appears in the book, the sage commands that it be shared broadly and liberally: "give a portion to seven, and even to eight, even though you do not know what trouble may occur upon the earth" (11:2). That counsel is coupled with the admonition to "release your bread upon the waters; after many days, you may find it" (11:1). These sayings are often interpreted as a counsel concerning the wisdom of diversifying one's investment portfolio. But, as noted by Seow, the expression "give a portion to" does not mean "divide your portion among" as indicated by the NRSV; it suggests, instead, the distribution of property to one or more recipients (cf. Josh 14:4; 15:13; Eccl 2:21).[105] Neither is "releasing bread upon the water" a metaphor for foreign investment,[106] but a call to perform charitable deeds with abandon, without calculating the potential returns (11:1b).[107] The earliest interpreters understood the text in this way,[108] and similar proverbs

---

105 Seow, *Ecclesiastes*, 335. The word *ḥeleq* may refer to a share in anything, including wealth (Gen 14:24; 1 Sam 30:24) and food (Hab 1:16; Deut 18:8), and the preposition *lĕ* identifies the recipient(s) of the distributed portion.

106 The Hebrew word *leḥem* may be taken to mean "grain," as in Isa 28:28 and Prov 30:23, but not merchandise.

107 The imperfect verb *timṣā'ennû* should probably be taken in the modal sense. The reference to finding one's bread "after many days" is often read as the motivation for the command to "release your bread." However, in the context of Qohelet's repeated assertion that people cannot "find" or "grasp" anything, any "finding" of bread here would be serendipitous. It is possible to take the particle *kî* as a weakened asseverative and leave it untranslated (see Joüon-Muraoka §164.b). For various alternative interpretations of this expression, see Michel, *Eigenart*, 207–8; Ellermeier, *Qohelet* I/1, 255; Fox, *A Time to Tear Down*, 311–14.

108 Luther explains the meaning of the sayings as follows: "Share your food, which the Lord has given you … [t]he fact that you have been generous with others will not

from other cultures support this reading. In the Egyptian *Instruction of Onchsheshonqy*, for example, we find "Do a good deed and throw it in the water; when it dries you will find it" (19, 1).[109] Similarly, an Arabic tale instructs one to "Do good, cast bread upon the waters; if the fish does not know it, God will."[110] In Qohelet's particular rendition, the expression "your bread" recalls the command to "eat your bread with enjoyment" in 9:7. The commands to "release your bread" and "give a portion," therefore, constitute an important expansion of Qohelet's ethic of enjoyment. One must enjoy the bread/portion that is in one's possession with relish; one must also gladly release it for the benefit of others. This text speaks not of economic investment, but an investment in joy. It commends the value of community over commerce.

Other Old Testament texts speak of the communal dimension of joy, with vocabulary that closely echoes Qohelet's. In Nehemiah, the returned exiles are commanded to celebrate (*laʿăśôt śimḥâ gĕdôlâ*) the public reading of the Law by *eating, drinking,* and *sending* (*šlḥ*) portions to those who have none (Neh 8:10, 12). Similarly, in the book of Esther, the description of the festival of Purim, rich with terms of joy and feasting (*śimḥâ, mišteh, yôm ṭôb*), includes the clause that it be "a day of *sending* (*mišlôᵃḥ*) gifts of food to one another and presents to the poor" (9:22; cf. 9:19; 2:18). The sequence of joy overflowing in a generous concern for the neighbor is made explicit in extra-biblical sources as well. In his study of the ritual of hosting the messenger in Akkadian epistolary literature, Meier notes that the display of joy was always interpersonal—the king had to be present with the messenger when he ate and drank. He observes, moreover, that numerous texts display the movement from joy to generosity. He remarks, "In the ancient Semitic world, communal joy without food, oil, wine, song, or *the giving of gifts* was not joy at all" (italics added).[111] All of these texts speak of the impossibility of being "merry in isolation."[112] Similarly, in the Egyptian *Instruction of Anii*, one finds the admonition: "Eat no bread, while another stands nearby and you neglect to stretch out your hand to him"

---

perish, even though it seems to perish." *Luther's Works* (ed. J. Pelikan; St. Louis: Concordia, 1972), 15:171. Or, as Goethe puts it: "Why do you want to find out where generosity flows! Throw your bread into the water! Who knows who will enjoy it?" Westöstlicher Divan (ed. H. A. Maier; Tübingen: Niemeyer, 1965), 111, cited by Seow, *Ecclesiastes*, 343.

109 Lichtheim, *AEL* III, 174.

110 Cited by H. F. von Diez, *Denkwürdigkeiten von Asien* (vol. 1; Berlin: Nicolaischen Buchhandlung, 1811), 115.

111 Samuel A. Meier, *The Messenger in the Ancient Semitic World* (HSM 45; Atlanta: Scholars Press, 1988), 219.

112 Barth's expression, *CD* III.4, 379—80.

(Text B 21.4).[113] Ben Sirah speaks of this correlation between one's own enjoyment and generosity to others in this way: "If you are mean to yourself, to whom will you be generous? You will not enjoy your own riches" (Sir 14:5). And he goes on to say:

> My child, treat yourself well, according to what you have ...
> Remember that death does not tarry, and the decree of Hades has
> not been shown to you. Before you die, do good to friends and
> reach out and give to them as much as you are able. Do not
> deprive yourself of a day's enjoyment; do not let your portion of
> desired good pass you by. (Sir 14:11——14)

Ben Sirah approaches the matter from a different angle. He suggests that enjoyment is important because it prepares and enables a person to practice generosity. According to his logic, a person who does not know how to enjoy will not know how to do good to others. Qohelet may not spell out the connection as overtly, but he does observe the case of a miserly individual who toils away without end, depriving himself of all enjoyment (4:7f). And this man, says Qohelet, tragically lives in complete isolation (*yēš 'eḥad*), without son or brother, without any companion at all (*'ên šēnî*). Through the carefully crafted rhetoric of his discourse on joy, Qohelet too suggests that there must be a salutary balance between an individual's experience of enjoyment and generosity toward others. One must gladly take up every opportunity of enjoyment; one must also liberally share the means of enjoyment with those who may be in need.

Finally, Qohelet urges all these things because none of it will be possible when this life is over. He puts it in no uncertain terms: "for there is no activity, or thought, or knowledge, or wisdom in Sheol, where you are going" (v. 10b). The realm of the living is the only theater of human activity. The dead never again have any portion (v. 6); they have nothing to enjoy for themselves, and nothing to give to others. Given the inevitability of death, one can either languish in despair over the eventual "going" to Sheol (v. 10b), or one can "go" and live life (v. 7a). For this sage who loves life, the awareness of mortality does not drive to despair but arouses an invigorated zest for life. He is adamant that those who still have a portion ought to enjoy while they can, in the full sense of the word. So, he counsels: keep life simple yet festive, every moment (*kol-'ēt*, v. 8a) and every day (*kol-yĕmê ḥayyê heblekā*, v. 9a) that is at their disposal. One day — and all too soon — there

---

113 See Lichtheim, *AEL* II. Cf. Isa 58:6—7. See also the *Eloquent Peasant*, which asks: "what are you doing to satisfy the hunger of your dependents ... He who has bread should be merciful" (101b).

will be a complete cessation of all human activity (*lĕʿôlām*, v. 6b). Before the dawning of that final day, Qohelet urges living life to the utmost.

2.8 Farewell to Joy (11:7—12:7)

With 11:7—12:7, the author comes to the dramatic culmination of his work. These are Qohelet's very last thoughts, his final impartation, before the *hebel* epigram in 12:8 draws it all to a close. And with his final breath, Qohelet makes his most stirring appeal for enjoyment. As numerous scholars have noted, the passage is a masterful composition in which various images and ideas are skillfully interwoven.[114] Most prominently, the dual themes of rejoicing and remembering bind the reflections together into a cohesive and distinct unit, with the verbs *śmḥ* and *zkr* appearing first as jussives in 11:7—8,[115] and then as imperatives in 11:9—12:1. Then, to conclude his impassioned address, the sage speaks through a poem, a haunting evocation of death's finality. Structurally, the poem in 12:1—7 completes the *inclusio* with the introductory poem in 1:3—11. Thematically, it rounds out many of the key issues addressed throughout his discourse. These reflections are, then, Qohelet's grand finale. They represent his final and decisive counsel, appropriately summing up the whole of his teachings.

To heighten the power of his final plea, the sage marshals all the resources at his disposal. In the discourse style of Proverbs, he identifies the figure of the youth as his principle audience, thereby appealing to his authority as an elder and seasoned instructor of the young. As a skilled poet, the aesthetics of his language allows him to effectively arrest the imagination and move the heart. Moreover, with poetic license, he casts an eschatological overtone to his depiction of death to make the astounding suggestion that his ethic of enjoyment has significance of eschatological proportions. The theological foundation to his ethic is thus expanded: enjoyment is not only a divine gift but also a divine imperative with ultimate implications.

---

114 See, for example, Graham Ogden, *Qoheleth*, 193—198; idem, "Qoheleth XI 7—XII 8: Qoheleth's Summons to Enjoyment and Reflection," *VT* 34, no. 1 (1984): 27—38; Étienne Glasser, *Le Procès du bonheur par Qoheleth* (LD 61; Paris: les Éditions du Cerf, 1970), 167; Maurice Gilbert, "La Description de la vieillesse en Qoheleth 12:1—7, est-elle allégorique?" in *Congress Volume, Vienna, 1980* (ed., J. A. Emerton; VTSup 32; Leiden: Brill, 1981), 98; Witzenrath, *Süss ist das Licht*, 20—28.

115 Contra Ellermeier (*Qohelet*, I/1, 303—06), Lauha (*Kohelet*, 208), and others who take these to be indicative.

The unit begins with a simple affirmation of the goodness of life: "Sweet is the light; it is good for the eyes to see the sun" (11:7). Light and sun are familiar metaphors for life in the Old Testament (see Job 3:16; 33:28, 30; Pss 36:10; 56:14). By extension, "to see the sun" is an idiom meaning "to be alive" (see 6:5; 7:11; cf. Pss 49:20; 58:9; Job 3:16).[116] The worldly-wise teacher, who has confronted all that transpires under the sun, speaks here with a disarming simplicity and charm, employing the word "sweet" to describe the sheer experience of being alive. Yet, he knows that it is all too possible to be alive without truly living, without experiencing the delight of the sun's rays. In the introductory poem, the sun's trek across the skies is described as a wearying series of rounds; those who live under it are subject to its circuitous routine, fixed in the cycle of rising and sleeping, toiling and resting. Yet, if one has "eyes to see" (11:7), to appreciate this natural rhythm of life and be nourished by it, then even an activity as mundane as sleep may become "sweet" (5:11). Qohelet therefore urges that "even those who live many years should be glad (yiśmaḥ) in all of them." Every moment and every season has its potential for joy, and it should be exercised to the full, regularly and intentionally.

The summons to relish the sweetness of life is then balanced by the second admonition: "Let them remember (yizkōr) that the days of darkness will be many." If light signifies life, then darkness signifies death. Yet darkness may denote more than death. It may, in fact, impinge upon those who are still alive, as in 5:16, where Qohelet speaks of miserable people who "eat in darkness, in much vexation, sickness, and resentment."[117] Although Qohelet affirms the goodness of life, he is aware that life may be clouded by times of wretchedness and gloom (cf. 7:14). Moreover, as the subsequent reflections indicate so poignantly, "days of unpleasantness" are likely to increase as a person's vitality and ability to experience pleasure diminish with age (12:1). Finally, there will be an eclipse of the sun—indeed of all the celestial luminaries—which will make the darkness permanent (12:2).

With this sober realism about the dark side of life, Qohelet then pronounces that "all that comes (kol-šebbā᾿) is hebel." As noted by Seow,

---

116 This literary convention is also evident in other ancient Near Eastern literature. In the Gilgamesh Epic, one finds the statement, "May my eyes see the sun so that I may have my fill of light" (Gilg M 13; cf. Gilg X I 13). For Gilgamesh, the alternative to life (seeing light) is the darkness of the netherworld. Similarly, in The Descent of Ishtar, the inhabitants of the netherworld see no light and must dwell in perpetual darkness. See "Descent of Ishtar to the Netherworld" (Benjamin Foster, Before the Muses: An Anthology of Akkadian Literature [Bethesda, Md.: CDL Press, 1996], 2:402—409). Compare also Job 10:21f.

117 See also Job 3:4—5; 15:23; Amos 5:18.

the precise expression *šebbāʾ* occurs two other times in Ecclesiastes, each time in reference to a life that comes into being only to go (*hlk*) back whence it came (5:14f; cf. 6:4). Every human life that comes into existence is destined to pass away. Every generation that comes must likewise go (cf. 1:4). So, the sage calls his audience to remember the mortal boundary of human existence. But this *memento mori* is inextricably bound to his *carpe diem*. In the syntax of the verse, the verbs *śmḥ* and *zkr* stand in tandem, separated only by the conjunction. The author has married these keywords before, at the theological conclusion of the first half of the book (5:17—19).[118] At that pivotal juncture, Qohelet remarks that "one should not much call to mind (*zkr*) the days of one's life because God gives an answer though the gladness (*śmḥ*) in one's heart" (v. 19). That earlier statement may seem to directly contradict the advice presented here in 11:7—12:7. There, however, Qohelet speaks against a different kind of remembering—an excessive (*harbēh*) brooding—that threatens the potential of enjoyment. In this text, at the very end of his discourse, he urges the kind of contemplation that will inspire enjoyment. In both of these texts, then, memory is intended to serve the ethic of the moment.

The relationship between remembrance of death and enjoyment of life is reinforced in the remainder of the passage, where the verbs are reiterated as imperatives. Qohelet has spoken in imperatives before (9:7—10). Now, however, he addresses an imaginary youth for the first time. The figure of a youth fulfills several rhetorical functions. First, it enables the sage to appeal to his status as elder and veteran of life and endows his instructions with greater authority and credibility. A community of learning is thereby evoked, in which the wisdom of one generation is passed down to the next. Second, the figure of the youth allows Qohelet to address his audience as one who is eminently receptive to his instructions. Throughout his discourse, Qohelet has led his reader through the tortuous terrain of his thoughts. The reader has accompanied him on his quest to search out all that happens upon the earth, witnessing the frustrated attempts and coming in danger, together with the sage, of becoming jaded and world-weary. Now, by addressing the reader as "youth," Qohelet calls forth a rhetorical persona that reflects, as it were, Ricoeur's "second naiveté."

Furthermore, the various references to youth (*bāḥûr*, *bĕḥûrôt*, *yaldût*, *haššaḥărût*), which occur no less than six times in 11:9—12:1, suggest that there is something about this particular stage of life that makes the

---

118 Ogden notes the vocabulary shared by 5:17—19 and 11:7—12:1 and suggests that the two texts were intended to be read together closely. Ogden, "Qoheleth XI 7—XII 8," 35.

sage's counsel especially pertinent. As the parallel terms demonstrate, youth represents the prime of life (*bāḥûr*, *běḥûrōt*), the height of vitality and vigor.[119] In Proverbs, this youthful liveliness is often associated with impulsive conduct, and viewed with a wary eye. The parental voice in Proverbs therefore champions discipline and restraint as the cardinal virtues of youth.[120] By contrast, Qohelet identifies these peak years as the time designated for enjoyment. For him, youth incarnates the ideal of unrestrained exuberance, a radical openness to life. He insists that while one is young and strong, one ought to capitalize on the opportunities of enjoyment, reiterating his positive charge three times: "rejoice ... let your heart cheer you ... follow the ways of your heart and the sight of your eyes."

The last of these instructions, in particular, is unparalleled in its validation of youthful spontaneity. Indeed, it seems to fly in the face of the injunction in Num 15:39: "Do not search after your own heart and your own eyes." The contradictory perspective in Ecclesiastes apparently troubled interpreters of antiquity, who took measures to correct or at least temper its liberalism.[121] There are, however, some important differences between the two texts that bear mentioning. The verb used to describe the inclinations of the human heart in Numbers is *twr* "to seek out" or "to spy out"—the very word used by Qohelet to speak of his futile attempts to discover matters beyond his ken (1:13; 2:3; 7:25). Moreover, in the Numbers text, the verb *twr* occurs in conjunction with the verb *znh* "to commit fornication, be a prostitute."[122] The heart and eyes thus function as a figure for idolatry and are pitted against the divine commandments, which the people are

---

119 As noted by Fox, *běḥûrōt* represents youth extending into adulthood. A *baḥûr* is a young man of the optimal age for military service (e.g., 1 Kgs 12:21 and 2 Chr 25:5). Fox, *A Time To Tear Down*, 318.

120 As noted by Brown, Qohelet's perspective may function as a necessary counterbalance to the austere admonitions in Proverbs. Brown suggests that the combined effect of the two constitutes the formative education of youth (*Ecclesiastes*, 106).

121 LXX adds *amōmos* "blamelessly" after the first phrase in Eccl 11:9b, and some Greek witnesses include a negative particle in the next line: *kai mē en horasei opthalmōn sou* "and not in the sight of your eyes." Likewise, one finds in the Targum a tendency to moralize: "walk in humility with the ways of your heart and be careful with what your eyes see that you do not see evil...." Ben Sirah displays a similar wariness, reversing Qohelet's advice altogether: "Do not follow your heart and your eyes, to go in evil delights" (Sir 5:2). The early rabbis who debated whether the book was "safe" for the general public were likewise unsettled by this particular advice in 11:9, because they feared that the ostensibly hedonistic sentiment might provoke licentious behavior.

122 The Hebrew reads *lō' tātūrû 'aḥărê lěbabkem wě'aḥărê 'ênêkem 'ăšer-'attem zōnîm 'aḥărêhem*.

charged to remember instead (Num 15:40). According to this anthropology, the moral self must choose between its natural proclivities and the will of God.

By contrast, Qohelet's expression, "follow the ways of your heart," is an idiom for enjoyment. This is borne out, first, by the context: in the preceding line, the heart is identified as the agent of joy; it is what cheers the person (wîṭîbkā libbĕkā). It is also corroborated by an analogous idiom in Egyptian, šms-ib "follow the heart," which likewise means "enjoy."[123] The phrase marʾê ʿênêkā "the sight of your eyes" in the subsequent line confirms this reading as well. In 6:9, marʾēh ʿênayim "the sight of the eyes" denotes the experience of what is immediately present to the person, as opposed to the overreaching cravings of the nepeš. Related to the expression rāʾâ ṭôb (already established as an idiom for enjoyment in Ecclesiastes), both of these nominal forms must likewise signify enjoyment. Contrasting this idiom with the Numbers text, Seow concludes that the saying in Ecclesiastes "has nothing to do with how one makes ethical decisions (i.e., whether one follows one's heart or obeys divine orders)."[124] Nevertheless, by employing language that so closely resembles the Torah prohibition, Qohelet elicits an intertextual conversation. His affirmative counsel deliberately counters the move to set the human heart and its desires in opposition to the divine will. Qohelet's text, too, makes a statement about how ethical decisions are made. According to his theology, gladness in the human heart redeems that inner space (cf. 5:19), making it and its desires an appropriate vehicle of moral agency. Indeed, joy in the heart becomes the divine answer to the problem of wayward desire and the destructive side of the human appetite (cf. 6:7).

So, Qohelet goes on to invoke divine accountability for enjoyment: "know that for all these things, God will bring you into judgment" (11:9b). Because of the reference to divine judgment, many interpreters disregard this statement as a moralistic gloss. They opine that a pious scribe must have inserted this annotation as a caveat to Qohelet's call to enjoy, in order to set proper boundaries to his hedonism. The effect is: "enjoy, but[125] know that God will judge you for your deeds." However, as already noted above, the notion of human accountability before the

---

123 Similarly, the expression swt nt šms-ib (literally, "places of following the heart") denotes "places of enjoyment." See WbÄS IV, 483–4. Compare also The Instruction of Ptahhotep, where the counsel to "follow your heart" caps off a series of geriatric complaints (Lichtheim, AEL I, 66), and The Song of Antef, which includes the injunction to "follow the heart" while one is yet alive (II.v.26; see Fox, "A Study of Antef," 407).

124 Seow, Ecclesiastes, 350.

125 Reading the waw as an adversative.

deity is not alien to Qohelet (see 3:17; 5:4−7; 8:6a) and need not be written off as a later intrusion. Rather, by appealing to God's judgment, the sage lends his counsel of joy all the weight of a divine commandment. He insists more strongly than ever that enjoyment is the will of God, for which human beings will be held answerable. Or, as a text in the Talmud has it: "Everyone must give an account before God of all good things one saw in life and did not enjoy" (y.Qidd. 4:12).

While Qohelet affirms the ideal of youthful exuberance, he is not unaware of the potential pitfalls of youth. People in the prime of life are particularly susceptible to the drive to go out into the world and make a place for themselves. They are more often fixated on achievement and accumulation, less able to curb their ambitions and rest content with what they have. So, the veteran of life charges his apprentice: "remove vexation (ka'as) from your heart" (11:10a). Elsewhere in the book, ka'as is antithetical to enjoyment. It is the possession of those who strive at things inordinately (see 1:18; 2:23; 5:16). Its companions are "darkness," "pain," "sickness," and "resentment." When it resides in the "heart," usurping the place of joy, it prevents sleep in the night (2:23) and fills the days with pain so that even "eating" becomes a joyless task (5:16). To those who are prone to such frenetic activity and straining beyond their means, Qohelet insists that they must not let vexation rob them of the opportunities for enjoyment.

To this he adds: "banish unpleasantness (rā'â) from your flesh." The choice of the term "flesh" suggests that Qohelet is speaking here of physical discomforts, such as may be caused by over-working or depriving oneself of sleep (cf. 12:12). More broadly, the term "flesh" often points to the frailty of human existence.[126] The "flesh" is entirely dependent on God's giving and preservation of life. Early in the history of humankind, God sets a limit to the human lifespan, determining that "my spirit will not dwell in mortals forever, for they are flesh" (Gen 6:3). And when God withdraws the breath from the creature, "all flesh would perish together, and all mortals return to dust" (Job 34:14f; cf. Eccl 3:20; 12:7). Yet people in their prime are least likely to think of death and dying. That day seems far off in the distant future, and their optimism about life's possibilities may slip into a false sense of invincibility. To such a one, Qohelet issues a sobering wake-up call: You are but flesh, destined for mental and physical decline, and eventually, the extinction of all vitality. Enjoy life while you are able,

---

126 Among the various terms for humanity in the Old Testament, this term is often used to contrast humanity from God (e.g., Ps 78:39; Job 10:4; 2 Chr 32:8; Isa 40:6.). See Hans Walter Wolff, *Anthropology of the Old Testament* (Philadelphia: Fortress, 1974), 30−31.

because "youth and the dawn of life[127] are *hebel*" (11:10b), as ephemeral as the morning mist that evaporates in a moment. "The days of unpleasantness" will come, surely and inexorably, until one can no longer remove the unpleasantness (12:1).

These thoughts on human frailty naturally lead into the charge to "remember your Creator" (12:1). There has been much scholarly discussion about the proper rendering of the object of remembrance, *bôrĕ'ēkā*.[128] The unusual spelling of the word may be explained either as the plural of majesty,[129] or as an instance of the common confusion between III-*'Alep* and III-Weak roots in Late Hebrew.[130] But some interpreters contend that the reference to God as "Creator" is suspect, since nowhere else in the book does the author use an epithet for the deity. Hence, various emendations and alternative readings have been proffered: *bĕrû'ēkā* "your well-being,"[131] *boryāk* "your vigor,"[132] *bĕ'ērêkā* or *bôrĕkā* "your well," as a metaphor for wife (cf. Prov 5:15, 18),[133] and *bôrĕkā* "your pit," an allusion to the grave.[134] Given the author's penchant for wordplay, it is possible that the unique orthography was meant to engender multiple meanings and connections. The multivalence is already suggested by Rabbi Akabya ben Mahallalel, an early interpreter from the first century who is reported to have said: "Know whence you came [*b'rk*, 'your source'], whither you are going [*bwrk*, 'your grave'], and before whom you are destined to give an accounting [*bwr'yk*, 'your creator']" (m. *'Abot* 3:1; Qoh. Rabb. on 12:1; *Lev. Rabb.* section 18). Indeed, these various levels of meaning are all appropriate to the poem in 12:1−7. Remembrance of the creator calls attention to the end in which the life-breath, given in the beginning, will return to the One who gave it (12:7).[135] The charge to "remember your Creator," then, is a reminder of one's creaturely status, and the eventual destiny of all created beings. The object of reflection is God, the giver and sustainer of life, who also determines its end.

---

127 The unique noun *haššaḥărût* is a metaphor for juvenescence. Most commentators read "blackness of hair" (as *śêbâ* "gray hair" is a metaphor for old age). The word may also be related to *šaḥar* "dawn," which is also associated with youth (see Ps 110:3).

128 Although some MSS read the singular form *br'k/bwr'k*, they probably represent an attempt to correct the more difficult plural form in *BHS*.

129 So Delitzsch, *Commentary on the Song of Songs and Ecclesiastes*, 389.

130 So Gordis, *Koheleth — The Man and His World*, 330; Seow, *Ecclesiastes*, 351.

131 Ehrlich, *Randglossen zur hebräischen Bibel*, 103.

132 Zimmerman, *The Inner World of Qohelet*, 160.

133 Graetz, *Kohelet*, 133−34; followed by Crenshaw, *Ecclesiastes*, 184−85.

134 Galling, "Prediger," 120−22.

135 Gilbert, "La Description de la vieillesse en Qoheleth 12:1−7," 100.

Then follows a vivid depiction of that end. Here, at the climactic conclusion of Qohelet's discourse, the author appeals to the aesthetics of poetic language to captivate the imagination, to stir the emotions, to evoke a sense of terror and desolation at the prospect of death. The enigmatic poem has been variously interpreted as a portrayal of an aging body,[136] an approaching thunderstorm,[137] an estate in disrepair,[138] the onset of winter,[139] a funerary procession,[140] the eschatological demise of the cosmos,[141] or some combination thereof. Most commentators agree that the poem must function on multiple levels, and that it is impossible to fix some univocal setting or meaning. Indeed, it is likely that the poet intended it to be so. However, although the precise meaning of the individual images remains obscure, the poem does not fail to communicate. Indeed, the ambiguities and uncertainties only serve to draw the reader deeper into the world of the poem—a world of decay, fear, and silence. Qohelet's final poem is a powerful and hauntingly beautiful evocation of death. The horror and melancholy with which he depicts the final eclipse of life reveals all the more his profound love of life. This ode to death is, in effect, Qohelet's swan song to life, his farewell to joy. And with the final *hebel* in 12:8, only a breathtaking, hushed silence lingers.

The poet creates this effect in stages, building his thoughts through a series of subordinate clauses, each one introduced by the phrase *'ad 'ăšer lō'* "before" (vv. 1b, 2a, 6a): he urges remembrance *before* the arrival of unpleasant days (12:1), *before* the darkness and the cessation of all activity (12:2—5), *before* the total disintegration of life (12:6—7). The cadenced repetition of this "before" calls attention to itself. It conveys at once the certainty of the deterioration that is to come and the urgency of the *now*. In short, the sage urges the youth to remember, and enjoy life, *now*, before it is too late, before the possibility of joy is irretrievably lost.

---

136 Various images in the poem are interpreted (allegorically/symbolically) as parts of the body: the women gazing out the window are the dimming eyes, the grinders are the teeth, etc. It is possible that the author may have reworked an existing composition on old age and impending death to create this evocative poem. See Seow's argument in "Qohelet's Eschatological Poem," 209—212.

137 Ginsburg, *Coheleth, Commonly Called the Book of Ecclesiastes*, 457—58; M. Leahy, "The Meaning of Ecclesiastes 12, 1—5," *ITQ* 19 (1952): 297—300.

138 J. F. A. Sawyer, "The Ruined House in Ecclesiastes 12: A Reconstruction of the Original Parable," *JBL* 94 (1976): 519—31; Witzenrath, *Süss ist das Licht*, 44—55.

139 Loretz, *Qohelet und der alte Orient*, 190—93.

140 C. Taylor, *The Dirge of Coheleth in Ecclesiastes XII* (London: Williams & Norgate, 1874).

141 Seow, "Qohelet's Eschatological Poem," 209—34.

Upon initial reading, the poem seems to be about the debilitating effects of old age that eventuate in death.[142] Yet, the poem is not just about the demise of an individual, as devastating as that is in its unmitigated loss. The imagery in these verses—the ominous darkening of the luminaries (v. 2), the abrupt cessation of all life-sustaining activities (v. 3f), the languishing of nature (v. 5)—carries cosmic and eschatological overtones.[143]   Until this point in Qohelet's discourse, although the specter of death has been an ever-present threat, there has always been the possibility of enjoyment. Here, as the argument of the book is brought to its staggering denouement, the sage suggests that there will come a day when all possibilities will come to an end, not only for the individual but for the whole of creation. Indeed, creation itself will be decisively and irreversibly overturned. In the movement of the poem, then, the death of the individual presages nothing less than the end of the world. The individual's life is a microcosm, and the individual's death the undoing of the cosmos. With this hyperbolic imagery, the poet raises the magnitude of his ethic of enjoyment to eschatological proportions. Earlier in the passage, God appeared as judge (11:9); now, God is the Creator (12:1) who will one day recall the life-breath and bring about the permanent end of all things. In juxtaposing these theological claims, the poet—however subtly and tongue-in-cheek—hints at the possibility of an eschatological judgment. With poetic license, he conveys the urgency of his call to enjoy in startling terms. To remember one's "Creator" is to do the will of God and enjoy life now—before it is too late, and with the knowledge that there will one day be a final reckoning.

2.9 Conclusion

A close analysis of Qohelet's discourse on enjoyment demonstrates that the "joy passages" in Ecclesiastes are not, as other scholars have argued, merely the author's random philosophical reflections, or narcotic doses to counter the larger reality of life's travails, or even lapses into wishful thinking. Second only to the *hebel* refrain in its purposeful redundancy, these commendations of enjoyment are essential to the author's rhetorical strategy and theological argumentation. They appear at critical junctures in Qohelet's discourse,

---

142 Indeed, it is possible that the author may have reworked an existing composition on old age and impending death to create this evocative poem. See "Qohelet's Eschatological Poem," 211.

143 Seow, "Qohelet's Eschatological Poem," 214, 233–34.

moving it forward, shaping its general contours, and creating its complex yet distinct timbre. Despite his stark realism concerning life's limitations, Qohelet's love of life pulsates throughout his discourse, at the start in a muted beat but growing steadily until it swells into a veritable celebration of life. When his reflections finally come to a close, it is with a mournful farewell to all possibilities of joy. Qohelet's persistent call to enjoy life simply cannot and must not be written off as a contradictory strain or a peripheral digression. It is *vital* to his teachings.

For Qohelet, enjoyment is all about *life*. From beginning to end, his theology of enjoyment is resolutely life-centered. This means, first, that the practice of enjoyment commended by this theology must be true to the realities of human life. The sage who undertakes the ambitious task of examining "all that is done under the sun" confronts contradictions and inconsistencies everywhere he turns. This he attributes to the inscrutable work of God, which alternates unpredictably between good and ill, blessing and bane, leaving humanity only to marvel at the incomprehensible logic of it all. Indeed, the purpose of divine activity is to engender the fear of God in humanity (3:14; cf. 7:14). The enjoyment that Qohelet espouses, because it is borne of his profound realism, is one that confronts and experiences life more completely and more authentically. It takes place in the midst of the grueling labor of living. It takes place with the full awareness that the joy may at any time be interrupted by an occasion for sorrow. Finally, it takes place with the specter of death ever looming in the near horizon. The window of opportunity for enjoyment is small because, as Qohelet frequently reminds his reader, life is bounded by death. That window is even smaller because the ability to fully experience life is diminished by age. And finally, all possibilities of joy will sadly come to an end, for God will one day recall the life-breath from all of creation. Enjoyment, like all things under the sun, is ultimately *hebel*.

Yet, for Qohelet, the clear boundaries of life emphasize not the grim limits, but the importance of making the most of this life where meaning is to be found. Hence, his theology of enjoyment is life-centered in another sense: it promotes life in the fullest sense. Its primary concern is human flourishing in the context of daily life.[144] True to the practice of the sages, Qohelet does not speak about the

---

144 Indeed, the semantic horizon of the root *śmḥ* in Northwest Semitic suggests that there is a close relationship between "rejoicing" and "flourishing." J. C. Greenfield argues that the Hebrew root *śmḥ* is cognate to the Akkadian *šamāḫu*, which means "to grow, flourish." See his analysis in "Lexicographical Notes II," *HUCA* 30 (1959): 141—51.

mighty works of God in history, but about how a person may cope with the challenges provoked by one's immediate experience of the world. Daily life is what matters most to him. So, what Qohelet says most often about enjoyment is that there is nothing better, nothing better than the basic activities that sustain human life and make it meaningful. Eating and drinking, working and resting, being with one's beloved—these simple and mundane pleasures reveal the giftedness of life and make life worth living.

Finally, Qohelet's theology of enjoyment has important ethical implications for the life of the human community. It has been argued that Ecclesiastes reflects a social world marked by an acquisitive spirit. Qohelet's validation of enjoyment bears an important ethical dimension that addresses just such a society. Enjoyment is commanded because it is good and right to be glad with one's portion in life. In the sage's own diction, enjoyment *is* "doing good" (3:12). It is good not only because of the experience of pleasure and its potential to promote the health and vitality of the individuals who practice it. But, just as important, it is good because of its potential to safeguard and improve the vitality of social relationships. This kind of enjoyment does not condone self-aggrandizement at the expense of neighbor. Indeed, it speaks directly against it (5:7—6:9; 10:16—19). It insists that moral beings must exercise responsible stewardship over the means of enjoyment, not only for their own benefit but the benefit of the larger human community as well (11:1—6).[145]

The ethical dimension of joy is also evident in its close relationship to the fear of God in Qohelet's discourse. The following chapter will be devoted to the explication of that important theme and its relationship with Qohelet's theology of enjoyment.

---

145 Further discussion of Qohelet's ethic of joy is reserved for the final chapter of this study.

Chapter Three

The Fear of God: The Dialogics of Piety

3.1 Introduction

In a bold rejoinder to an observation of Heinrich Heine regarding the book of Job, Franz Delitzsch described Ecclesiastes as "the supreme song of the fear of God," proclaiming the book to be the quintessence of biblical piety.[5] This enthusiastic endorsement of Ecclesiastes' place in the canon has by no means found a receptive audience. Quite the contrary, most commentators regard the author of the book to be a consummate pessimist, possibly the most strident among the voices of skepticism preserved in the Bible. There is, nevertheless, some basis for Delitzsch's positive assessment. Fear of God may not be *the* dominant theme of the book, as Delitzsch would have it, but it certainly is *one* of its dominant themes. Indeed, the book concludes with the command to fear God (12:13b), which arguably serves as an important hermeneutical key for reading the whole.[6] To be sure, most scholars contend that this "postscript" is likely the work of a redactor and not properly a part of Qohelet's reflections. Yet the author expounds on this theme elsewhere in the body of the book, at critical junctures where the most pressing theological matters are considered (3:14; 5:6; 7:18; 8:12–13). So, in some ways, the exhortation to fear God is an entirely appropriate way to bring the book to a close.

It is hardly surprising that this ancient Near Eastern idiom for religion would figure so prominently in Ecclesiastes. Fear of God is a central concern in Israel's sapiential literature. Not only does it occur numerous times in this corpus, it occupies a critical place in each book. In Proverbs, the theme frames the first collection of sayings (Prov 1:7; 9:10) as well as the book in its entirety (1:7; 31:30), suggesting that its teachings are to be read in light of the cardinal principle that "the fear of the Lord is the beginning of wisdom." In the opening verses of Job,

---

5   Delitzsch, *Commentary on the Song of Songs and Ecclesiastes*, 183.
6   See Sheppard, "The Epilogue to Qoheleth as a Theological Commentary," 182–89; Childs, *Introduction to the Old Testament as Scpriture*, 585–588.

fear of God is the virtue that characterizes its main protagonist (Job 1:1, 8; 2:3); it is what sets up the book's central dilemma as posed by the Adversary: "has Job feared God for nothing?" (1:9). Indeed, as Michael Barré has argued, the fear of God lies at the heart of the worldview of wisdom.[7] Wisdom has to do with recognizing and living constructively within the network of relationships that is built into the order of creation, and fearing God is the basic stance necessary for such a meaningful existence. In other words, fearing God means understanding humanity's place before God, within this order of creation.

Ecclesiastes, too, seeks to determine how humanity may achieve a meaningful existence, and naturally reflects at crucial moments on what it means to fear God. However, because the "pious" theme seems at odds with the pessimistic outlook of the book, the references to the fear of God have often been dismissed as the work of an orthodox glossator, or the perspective of traditional wisdom cited by the author solely for the sake of dismantling it. Given the evidence for the book's integrity presented in chapter 1, however, this approach is no longer viable or fruitful. To excise this critical motif in an *ad hoc* fashion would be to undercut seriously the theological and ethical claims of the book. Any interpretation of the book must consider carefully the meaning and function of fearing God in Ecclesiastes.

Yet, when statements concerning the fear of God are taken to be an integral part of the author's thought, scholars more often than not bring them in line with the pessimistic interpretation of the book. Accordingly, the fear of God in Ecclesiastes is said to depart radically from its general meaning in the rest of the wisdom corpus (and much of the Old Testament). The notion of fearing God in this book, they argue, reflects the intense skepticism of Qohelet's thoughts and regresses to its primitive notion of enervating terror before an unpredictable God. There is nothing positive about this fear: Qohelet can establish no relationship with the distant deity he encounters, and he cannot base any form of piety or morality on the basis of his experience of this God. Instead, he warns that human beings must be vigilant, or "on guard *against* Elohim," [8] lest they provoke the deity's displeasure. Such interpretations, however, seem unduly skewed by the pessimistic interpretation of the book. They fail to account for Qohelet's positive—sometimes even exuberant—counsel concerning the good gifts of God, which often occurs in those very places where he

---

7   Michael Barré, "'Fear of God' and the World View of Wisdom," *BTB* 11 (1981): 41 – 43.

8   Bickerman, *Four Strange Books of the Bible,* 149.

expounds on the meaning of fearing God. The close association between fear and joy in Qohelet's rhetoric suggests that enjoyment is a vital aspect of Qohelet's vision of piety.

Yet the alternative "optimistic" approach is no more satisfactory in its explication of the fear of God. Whybray, for example, maintains that Qohelet's notion of fearing God is no different from the view found in the rest of the Old Testament: it signifies obedience, service, conformity to God's moral command, avoidance of sin, honest conduct, etc. — "in short, the reverence for, and worship of God, characteristic of sincere Yahwists...."[9] While such assessments are a welcome counterpoint to the prevailing view, comments such as these are too sweeping and generic to be helpful. They say little about what is distinctive and unique in Qohelet's conception of piety.

Unlike the other wisdom books, Qohelet never uses the nominal expression "the fear of God." Fear occurs only in its verbal forms, and this exclusive preference is perhaps not insignificant.[10] For Qohelet, fear of God is not a fixed principle. It is not a quality that one can possess, and there are no guarantees associated with it. Instead, he speaks of fearing God in terms of what one can and cannot do in light of God's mysterious activity. Qohelet's discourse on fearing God is firmly rooted in a theology of divine transcendence. God is in the realm of the eternal; humanity is confined to individual times and moments (3:11—14). God dwells in heaven; humanity is earthbound (5:1). God's activity is pervasive, but humanity cannot comprehend it (8:17; 11:5). It is this essential Otherness of the deity that elicits humanity's response of "fear." To fear God, in short, means to recognize and respect the distance between the divine and the human.

This worldview implies that the human place is marked by profound limitations. Humanity cannot know, grasp, or hold on to anything. Their existence is bounded by the uncertainties of this life, by death, by the freedom of a sovereign God who governs the world in an utterly confounding manner. However, Qohelet's conception of fearing God emphasizes not only these impossibilities but also the possibilities that come with the human place. And these possibilities are summed up in his call to enjoyment. Human potentialities lie in the "portion" that is granted them under the sun: in the daily exercise of life, in the mundane pleasures of eating and drinking, in the work that is right now in one's hands. *These things* people are free to desire, hope for, and work diligently for. Indeed, they are enjoined to do so. Moreover,

---

9   Whybray, "Qohelet as a Theologian," 264—65.
10   The same is true for Deuteronomy, which employs a very similar grammar and
     syntax in its treatment of this theme.

Qohelet's recognition of the distance between deity and humanity does not indicate a complete alienation from God. Qohelet rarely speaks of cultivating a relationship with God, and then, only cautiously (4:17—5:6).[11] Divine presence is experienced not so much through prayer, worship, or other forms of religious observances (although he does address this aspect of piety as well), but through God's giving and humanity's taking up of the gift of enjoyment. Qohelet's form of piety is practiced in the moral stewardship of these gifts, because to enjoy the gifts of God is to be mindful of one's Creator (11:7—12:7).

The following analysis of the pertinent passages in Ecclesiastes (3:14; 5:6; 7:18; 8:12f; 12:13b) demonstrates that (1) Qohelet's comments on the fear of God are indeed part and parcel of the author's thought; (2) Qohelet's notion of fearing God entails a recognition of humanity's proper place in the order of creation, a place that is marked by both its limitations and possibilities; (3) the enjoyment of life constitutes a vital component in Qohelet's conception of religious duty. It is this essential connection between joy and fear that is most distinctive about the explication of the fear of God in Ecclesiastes.[12] The bulk of this chapter will focus on the first two claims stated above. Some attention will be given to the relationship between joy and fear; however, a full synthesis will be reserved for chapter 4.

3.2 The Inscrutable Work of God (3:14)

D. Michel has posited that the first three chapters of Ecclesiastes may be seen as an extended introduction to the book.[13] Whether or not one agrees with this particular nomenclature, one may at least argue that these initial chapters introduce many of the themes that the author will develop in the rest of his work. In 3:9—22, at the denouement of this extended introduction, the author reaches a significant theological crescendo in his argumentation. The dominant theme in the passage is the work of God. Here, the author packs together a host of active verbs with God as its subject, yielding a thick description of divine activity. In

---

11   To be discussed below.

12   Although a number of scholars have alluded to the relationship between these two themes, there has not yet been an extended investigation of this interplay in the theological rhetoric of the book. See Polk, "The Wisdom of Irony: A Study of *Hebel* and Its Relation to Joy and the Fear of God in Ecclesiastes," 3—17. Ricky William Byargeon, "The Significance of the Enjoy Life Concept in Qoheleth's Challenge of the Wisdom Tradition" (Ph.D. diss., Southwestern Baptist Theological Seminary, 1991), 202, 241.

13   Michel, *Untersuchungen zur Eigenart des Buches Qohelet*, 1—2, 83.

addition to the fourfold occurrence of the verb "to do/act/make" (ʿśh, twice each in vv. 11, 14), nearly all the verbs attributed to God in Ecclesiastes make an appearance in this chapter: God "gives" (ntn) a preoccupation (v. 10); "puts" (ntn) eternity in the human heart (v. 11); "seeks" (bqš) what is pursued (v. 15); "judges" (špṭ) the righteous and the wicked (v. 17); "sets apart" (brr) humanity (v. 18). Qohelet's God is indeed an active God.[14] It is at the climactic moment of this key theological text that the author first introduces the theme of fearing God. In the midst of an expansive description of divine activity, Qohelet identifies the fear of God as the purpose and end of that activity: "God has acted so that they [humanity] will fear him" (v. 14).[15]

This statement concerning the fear of God is an inextricable element of Qohelet's discourse, and to excise, ignore, or otherwise downplay it would be to dismiss an important theological conclusion. Thematically, it flows with the rest of the text and its primary concern with the work of God; indeed, it makes a crucial claim about the very *telos* of divine activity. Formally, v. 14 is tied to the surrounding verses by a number of grammatical and syntactical features. Like the verses immediately preceding it (v. 12), this verse is introduced forcefully by the verb *yādaʿtî*. The emphatic position of the subject (*wĕhāʾĕlōhîm ʿāśâ*, v. 14c) links this verse with the subsequent one, where the same syntax is employed (*wĕhāʾĕlōhîm yĕbaqqēš*, v. 15b). Beyond this immediate context, the use of the infinitives *lĕhôsîp* and *ligrōaʿ* in v. 14b recalls the string of infinitives in the Catalogue of Times (vv. 2−8).[16] Given this remarkable coherence, most exegetes—including those who posit orthodox glosses in other places—accept v. 14b as integral to the passage.[17]

The primary question concerning this first reference to the fear of God, then, is not *whether* it belongs in the text but *how* it ought to be interpreted in this particular context. Regarding this matter there is no consensus. For those who see the author as a thoroughgoing skeptic,

---

14   See Roland E. Murphy, "Qoheleth and Theology?" *BTB* 21 (1991): 30−33.

15   The *š* particle, like *ʾăšer*, can introduce a purpose/result clause (see Gen 11:7; 13:16; 22:14; Deut 4:10). See also GKC 165.b According to Murphy, this statement represents the one place in Ecclesiastes where a purpose is attributed to divine activity (*Ecclesiastes*, lxv.). But see also 7:14, where Qohelet says that "God acts … so that mortals may not grasp anything after them."

16   The infinitives in 3:2−8, in turn, hark back to the string of infinitives that conclude preceding unit (*leʾĕsôp, liknôs, lātēt*, 2:26).

17   Crenshaw, "The Eternal Gospel (Eccl. 3:11)," 25. See also Galling, "Der Prediger," 59; Louis Derousseaux, *La crainte de Dieu dans l'Ancien Testament: royauté, alliance, sagesse dans les royaumes d'Israël et de Juda; recherches d'exégèse et d'histoire sur la racine yārēʾ* (Paris: Éditions du Cerf, 1970), 341.

Ecclesiastes is the *one book* in the Old Testament where the fear of God deviates from the notion of religious duty and lapses into a literal terror.[18] The "primitive attitude" reasserts itself only for Qohelet, "who has been drained of faith in life's possibilities."[19] This text is said to have none of the consoling elements that are usually associated with the fear of God among the sages. Instead, it portrays God as an indifferent, even cruel deity whose only concern is to guard divine prerogatives. Zimmerli puts it in this way:

> Gottesfurcht ist hier das Gehen unter einem geheimnisvoll verschlossenen Himmel, nie gesichert vor der Möglichkeit, daß aus ihm jäh ein Blitz hervorzuckt und den Wanderer trifft, auf Schritt und Tritt allein angewiesen auf die freie Beschenkung Gottes, auf Schritt und Tritt aber auch gerufen, bereitwillig das Rätsel und die Bedrängnis zu tragen, die Gott verhängen kann.[20]

By placing *hāʿōlām* in the human heart but deliberately withholding the ability to grasp the work of God in its totality (v. 11), "the divinity has played a desperate trick upon humanity."[21] This act of "divine sabotage" is intended to keep people off balance and elicit the appropriate response of trepidation before the unknown. Crenshaw is even more audacious in his interpretation, saying that the description of God's activity here borders on "demonic."[22]

But it seems amiss to single out this one book as being somehow deviant in its treatment of the fear of God, particularly when numerous biblical texts uphold divine inscrutability as a basic theological affirmation. Perhaps Ecclesiastes is distinct in its unrelenting accent on this aspect of divine activity, but it is hardly "primitive" or "demonic" in its perspective. Qohelet makes the divine mystery his preeminent claim about God, and thereby becomes a difficult but crucial witness to the *deus absconditus*. He repeatedly emphasizes what mortals cannot know, cannot have, cannot do. However, that is not the only claim that Qohelet makes about divine activity. Even here in 3:14, the inscrutable work of God does in fact include a consoling element. The fear of God

---

18   Derousseaux contends that the grammatical construction (the object of the verb *yr'* marked by *millipānāyw*) connotes a literal terror before the deity. Derousseaux, *La crainte de Dieu*, 341 n. 128; 344–45. He makes too much of this syntax, however; it occurs elsewhere in the Old Testament in contexts where terror is not signified (2 Sam 3:28; cf. 1 Chr 16: 30, 33; 1 Kgs 21:29).

19   So, Gordis, *Koheleth — the Man and His World*, 223.

20   Zimmerli, "Das Buch des Predigers Salomo," 169. Similarly, Hertzberg, *Der Prediger* (KAT 17/4; Gütersloh: Mohn, 1963), ad loc.; Longman, *The Book of Ecclesiastes*, 123–24.

21   Murphy, *Ecclesiastes*, 39.

22   Crenshaw, "The Eternal Gospel," 43.

also has a positive dimension that affirms what humans can know, can have, and can do—and that positive dimension is found in the possibilities of enjoyment.

As noted above, the passage identifies fear of God as the purpose of divine activity. In the logic of the text, this fear is engendered, in the first place, by the recognition that "whatever God does is for eternity; one cannot add to it and one cannot take away from it" (v. 14). This formulaic expression is used elsewhere in the Old Testament to emphasize the invariable and decisive authority of the word of God (see Deut 4:2; 13:1; Jer 26:2; Prov 30:6; cf. Rev 22:18−19). In Deuteronomy, the application of the "canonical formula" underscores the binding force of the commandments, which are to be diligently observed at all times and all places, without exception. There, too, the formula appears in conjunction with the command to fear God; the authoritative character of the commandments demands a response of "fear" on the part of the people (4:10; 13:5).[23] What is peculiar about Qohelet's usage is that the formula is applied not to the word of God but the *work* of God (cf. Sir 18:6; 42:21). Qohelet's God does not speak with authority, but *acts* with authority. Divine activity is always and everywhere in force, imposing itself upon human subjects who are incapable of escaping or controlling it in any way. Qohelet repeatedly examines "what is done" upon the earth (*na'ăśâ*, 1:9, 13; 2:17; 4:3; 8:9, 16; 9:3, 6) and concludes that, ultimately, all of it is the work of God (8:17; cf.11:5). As he says here, "God has made/done everything ..." (3:11) and "whatever happens has already happened, and what will happen has already happened" (3:15). The latter statement picks up the language of 1:9a, where Qohelet makes the point that despite all the frenetic activity in the cosmos, nothing can decisively interrupt the grand course of events ordained by the deity. Only God successfully seeks out and apprehends whatever is sought by human beings (3:15b).

---

23 This connection between the immutable Law and the people's fear of God is maintained throughout the book, where the call to observe the commandments is frequently juxtaposed with the injunction to fear YHWH (4:10; 5:29; 6:2, 13, 24; 8:6; 10:12−13; 13:4; 17:19; 28:58; 31:12−13). Indeed, the two are virtually synonymous. In other words, fearing God means demonstrating absolute loyalty to the covenant God through the diligent observance of the commandments. Hence, the call to fear God in Deuteronomy often appears with other terms that denote loyalty: to serve/worship (6:13; 10:12; 13:4; 10:20), to love (6:2−5; 10:12; 10:20−11:1; 13:4−5), to hold fast to (10:20; 13:4−5) to follow (13:4), to listen to YHWH's voice (13:5), to swear by his name (6:13; 10:20). For a discussion of the covenantal dimension of fear, see Bernard J. Bamberger, "Fear and Love of God in the Old Testament," *HUCA* 6 (1929): 39−53. See also C. J. de Catanzaro, "Fear, Knowledge, and Love: A Study in Old Testament Piety," *CTJ* 9 (1963): 166−73; William L. Moran, "The Ancient Near Eastern Background of the Love of God in Deuteronomy," *CBQ* 25 (1963): 78.

This activity of God may be experienced as an oppressive reality, particularly when it violates the principles of justice and condones human suffering (3:16; 4:1—3). Indeed, in the majority of its occurrences, "what is done" is evaluated negatively by Qohelet (2:17; 4:3; 8:9, 14, 16; 9:3). Here, too, Qohelet alludes to the perplexing dimension of divine activity, in the remark that "whatever God does is for eternity" (3:14a). The expression "for eternity" (*lĕʿōlām*) reinforces the notion of God's immutable activity. But it also harks back to the earlier statement that "God has put *hāʿōlām* in the human heart (3:11b).[24] Humans are given a sense of "eternity"—that which transcends the "time" availed to the mortal (*ʿēt*, v. 11a, cf. vv. 1—8), but this sense comes without the concomitant ability to grasp "what God has done from beginning to end" (v. 11c). Humanity is caught between the moment at hand and an awareness of the eternal, a bind created by none other than the deity. This tension, on the one hand, provokes a restless impulse to transcend the moment and grasp the totality of God's work. This, too, is directly attributed to the deity. According to Qohelet, it is God who "has given" humanity this "preoccupation" (*ʿinyān*) in order to "preoccupy"—or perhaps "oppress"—them with it (v. 10; cf. 1:13).[25] On the other hand, the impossibility of that task occasions a profound appreciation of the deity's essential otherness. Fearing God thus means recognizing and accepting humanity's creaturely status, and with it, its impossibilities, its tragic dimensions.

However, Qohelet affirms that fearing God has a positive dimension as well. In v. 12, he states that there is something else that he "knows" (*yādaʿtî*), and he declares it as emphatically as he does his other claim concerning the immutability of divine activity. The "I know" of v. 14 cannot be read apart from the "I know" of vv. 12—13; the structure of the text binds these verses together closely. What Qohelet knows is this: "there is nothing better for [humanity] than to be glad and enjoy life as long as they live." The God who gives (*ntn*) humanity a terrible preoccupation by placing (*ntn*) eternity in the human heart also grants the redeeming possibilities of enjoyment. This, too, is the activity of God. Qohelet acknowledges that enjoyment itself has its limits: it is circumscribed by the limited days of one's life (*bĕḥayyāyw*, v. 12), and hampered by the toil that is endemic to human life (*bĕkol-ʿămālô*, v. 13). Nevertheless, as long as they are alive, even in the midst of their toiling, people may engage in activities that make life

---

24 See my discussion of the interpretive crux concerning *hāʿōlām* in chapter 2, footnote 34.

25 The root *ʿnh* is multivalent, and may mean "preoccupy" as well as "oppress" (usually in the Piel).

enjoyable and meaningful. This possibility is described in terms of gift, not profit (*yitrôn*, v. 9). It is something that is received in the moment (*bĕʿittô*, v. 11), not achieved by straining for what is beyond. For Qohelet, the appropriation of these modest but redeeming activities as the gift of God for humanity is an expression of fearing God.

When Qohelet revisits the theme of God's work for the final time in the book, he concludes that "you cannot know the work of God, who does everything" (11:5; cf. 8:17). In the end, what Qohelet knows for certain is that mortals are *unable to know* or grasp the mysterious ways of God. As he remarks in 8:5—7, "the wise heart knows ... that no one knows what will be." So, fearing God means acknowledging what one can and cannot know. Mortals cannot know what tomorrow holds (3:22; cf. 7:14b), let alone apprehend the whole of God's activity. Yet, for this sage who grapples valiantly with the inscrutable work of God, not knowing is not always debilitating. The uncertainty may point to a disaster in the making (*rāʿâ*, 11:2), but it may also point to a future that will present good possibilities (*ṭôb*, 11:6): "*you do not know* which will prosper, this or that, or *whether both alike will be good.*" So, fearing God means recognizing that the human lot includes both its oppressive limitations and its liberating possibilities. The one who fears God lives at every moment with this tension, and goes forth in life with both (cf. 7:18).

3.3 In the Presence of the Wholly Other (5:6)

In 4:17—5:6, the author introduces a new theme: appropriate attitude and conduct in the presence of the divine. More specifically, the passage offers concrete instructions about liturgical practices and proper behavior in the temple. The introduction of this subject matter is accompanied by a shift in the mode of discourse. The language of reflection gives way to the language of admonition, and for the first time in the book, the sage addresses the reader directly.[26] The pronounced change in tone has led some commentators to identify this text as a critical turning point in the movement of the book. Taking his cue from this shift, Castellino identifies the primary division in the book precisely at this point (4:17).[27] For Seow, the shift in tone from the indicative to the imperative signals the beginning of an explicit and

---

26 The imperatives that occur previously function either as an interjection (1:10; 2:1), or as self-directed discourse in the Solomonic fictional autobiography (2:1).

27 Castellino, "Qohelet and His Wisdom," 16—17.

sustained engagement with *ethics*.[28] Lohfink, too, recognizes the ethical significance of this text. He in fact places these religious instructions at the very pivot of his palindrome design. As he sees it, the fear of God is at the "center of Qohelet's thought," and this text is the very "centerpiece" of the book.[29] One need not agree with every aspect of these structural proposals to recognize that this text is indeed self-consciously theological in its concern. The subject matter, by its very nature, is a theological one. This is underscored by the dense clustering of the word *'ĕlōhîm* (six times) within these seven verses. The text's concern with right behavior is evident in the predominance of the imperative mood: nine times the sage issues commands about what a person ought to do and ought not to do in the presence of God. At the culmination of these instructions, Qohelet issues the command to "fear God" (5:6). This decisive command sums up the contents of the unit and is its capstone.

The disjunction in theme and style, however, has led some scholars to cast doubt on the integrity of the unit. It has been argued that the concern with cultic matters is alien to sapiential literature and must represent the views of an editor.[30] That assessment, however, is not an entirely accurate one, as demonstrated by Leo Purdue's comprehensive study on wisdom and cult.[31] While it is true that the wisdom tradition was not primarily occupied with matters of the cult, neither was it antithetical or hostile to it. The sages addressed people who had cultic obligations, and allusions to cultic rituals naturally found their way into sapiential discourse. Indeed, given the comprehensive scope of the wisdom enterprise, it was bound to touch upon this important aspect of Israelite religious life. Hence, every wisdom book of the Old Testament includes some reflections on ritual worship (e.g., Prov 15:8; 21:27; 17:1; 20:25; 28:9; Job 1:4—5; 42:8—10; 8:5—6; 11:13—15; 22:27), and Ecclesiastes is no exception (see also 9:2). Indeed, Michael Barré has argued that the fear of God has a behavioral component, which in some

---

28 Seow, *Ecclesiastes*, 46—47. Compare Franz J. Backhaus, *"Denn Zeit und Zufall trifft sie alle": Studien zur Komposition und zum Gottesbild im Buch Qohelet* (BBB 83; Frankfurt am Main: Anton Hain, 1993), 1—332.

29 Norbert Lohfink, *Kohelet* (NEBib; Würzburg: Echter Verlag, 1980), 40. See also his; "Warum is der Tor unfähig, böse zu handeln? (Koh 4:17)" in *Augewählte Vorträge* (ZDMG Supplement 5; ed. F. Steppat; Wiesbaden: Steiner, 1983), 113—20.

30 McNeile, *An Introduction to Ecclesiastes*, 25.

31 Leo G. Perdue, *Wisdom and Cult: A Critical Analysis of the Views of Cult in the Wisdom Literature of Israel and the Ancient Near East* (SBLDS 30; Missoula: Scholars Press, 1977). See also Paul Humbert, *Recherché sur les sources égyptiennes de la literature sapientiale d'Israël* (Neuchâtel: Paul Attinger, 1929).

contexts is "translated concretely into *cult*."[32] In other words, the cult
was a primary locus in which the fear of God could be concretely
practiced and taught (see 2 Kgs 17:24—28). There is, therefore, no
warrant for dismissing this passage as a secondary accretion on the
basis of its subject matter.

If not jettisoned *in toto* on the basis of its cultic orientation, various
portions of the text are dismissed as secondary material. The final
injunction to fear God, in particular, is written off as a pious gloss.
Michel opines that the command to fear God must be the work of the
epilogist, who issues the same command—in identical formulation (*'et-
hā'ĕlōhîm yĕrā'*)—at the end of the book (12:13b).[33] However, one may
just as well argue that the epilogist modeled his words on an important
injunction that was already present in the book. Along with the
reference to the fear of God in 5:6b, the proverbial sayings in 5:2 and
5:6a are often deemed to be the work of a glossator with a wisdom
orientation.[34] To be sure, the sayings are reminiscent of conventional
wisdom, but there is no reason for concluding that the author himself
could not have composed them. Indeed, Qohelet excoriates wordiness
elsewhere in his discourse (Eccl 6:11; 10:13—14). Even more to the
point, the vocabulary of these maxims uniquely reflects Qohelet's
diction. The noun *'inyān* (v. 2) is an important one for Qohelet (1:3; 2:23,
26; 3:10; 4:8; 5:2, 13; 8:16), and is attested in no other biblical book. The
reference to *ḥăbālîm* (v. 6), of course, is also vintage Qohelet.

Beyond these lexical clues, there are a number of formal
connections that tie the unit with the surrounding material. The "better-

---

32 Barré, "Fear of God and the World View of Wisdom," 42. Barré's brief article is in no
    way comprehensive in its treatment of the cultic dimensions of fear. But it is odd
    that he does not consider the cultic dimensions of the fear of God in wisdom
    literature, given that his study identifies itself as a study of the fear of God and the
    worldview of wisdom. Nevertheless, his discussion of ancient Near Eastern texts
    that reflect this understanding of the fear of God confirms that fearing God did in
    fact have a visible behavioral dimension.
33 Michel attributes 5:6b to the second epilogist. Michel, *Untersuchungen zur Eigenart des
    Buches Qohelet*, 257. Similarly, Morris Jastrow, *A Gentle Cynic: Being a Translation of
    the Book of Koheleth, Commonly Known as Ecclesiastes, Its origin, Growth, and
    Interpretation* (Philadelphia: J. B. Lippincott, 1919), 217.
34 Barton, *A Critical and Exegetical Commentary on the Book of Ecclesiastes* 123—24;
    Podechard, *L'Ecclésiaste*, 338; similarly, V. Zapletal, *Das Buch Kohelet* (Freiburg:
    Gschwend, 1905), 14—35; Galling, "Der Prediger," 76. Another popular strategy—
    not entirely different in approach—is to argue that these verses are quotations of
    existing proverbs. So, Gordis, *Koheleth*, 101, 248; Lauha, *Kohelet*, 97. For Michel, 5:2 is
    a quotation, and 5:6b an addition by the second epilogist (*Eigenart*, 257).

than" saying in 5:4 (cf. 4:17b[35]) continues the style of the preceding unit, which consists of a string of such maxims. The comment concerning fools who sacrifice without knowing that they are doing wrong (4:17) comes at the heels of 4:13, where Qohelet speaks of a foolish old king who does not know how to take advice. These various stylistic features further link the whole of this passage to Qohelet's own thought, and one may therefore reasonably accept 4:17–5:6 in its entirety as integral to the book.

The outstanding question, then, is what the command to fear God means in this passage. As in the case of 3:14, many scholars interpret the reference to fear in this context as a literal terror.[36] According to this view, the admonitions in 4:17–5:6 depict a deity who is distant, even dangerous. An "aroma of paranoia" lingers over it all.[37] The call to "guard your feet" (4:17a) has a tone of "fearful foreboding."[38] The reference to the chasm between God and humanity (5:1c) indicates the deity's cold indifference toward the devout and their prayers. The admonition in 5:5 warns against a wrathful and destructive God who must be appeased by the punctual fulfillment of vows. Throughout the text, the argument goes, Qohelet's counsel regarding the cult emphasizes solely its terrifying side, with no attention to its beneficent, life-giving dimensions.[39] The sage's command to fear God thus reflects a cynical resignation to the fact that people must dutifully fulfill their religious obligations in order to escape the deity's menacing attention.

To be sure, this passage issues a strong cautionary word against relating to God in a casual manner, leaving no room for glib complacency in the presence of the divine. One must note, however, that this emphasis is not markedly different from the respect for God that is commanded elsewhere in the Old Testament. In fact, the admonitions in this text have biblical parallels that are readily accepted as normative. The echoes are numerous, and sometime nearly verbatim. Qohelet's admonitions in this passage deal with common

---

35   The word *qārôb* should be read as the adjective meaning "acceptable," rather than an infinitive absolute functioning as an imperative. As such, the saying closely approximates a "better-than" saying.

36   Perdue, *Wisdom and Cult*, 179–82; R. H. Pfeiffer, "The Peculiar Skepticism of Ecclesiastes," *JBL* 53 (1934): 103; Longman, *Ecclesiastes*, 36, 150–56; W. H. U. Anderson, *Qoheleth and Its Pessimistic Theology*, 113–14, 20; Lauha, *Kohelet*, 99, 115–118; Macdonald, *The Hebrew Philosphical Genius*, 70.

37   Zimmermann, *Inner World of Qohelet*, 37–41; see also Christianson, *A Time to Tell*, 116.

38   Perdue, *Wisdom and Cult*, 179.

39   Perdue, *Wisdom and Cult*, 182; W. H. U. Anderson, *Qoheleth and Its Pessimistic Theology*, 120.

wisdom topoi: (1) thoughtful and restrained speech (5:1—2; cf. Prov 10:14, 19; 21:23; Eccl 6:11; 10:13—14), and (2) accountability for vows (5:3—5; cf. Prov 20:25; Sir 18:22; Ps 66:13—14). Moreover, Qohelet's admonition concerning vows (5:3—4) has a precise parallel in Deut 23:22—24. It is identical in substance, with only minor variations that represent characteristic wisdom adaptation.[40] There is nothing out of the ordinary about these admonitions. As elsewhere in the Old Testament, the sage insists that religious commitments are a serious matter, and protestations of inadvertence (šĕgāgâ; cf. Num 15:22—31; Lev 4:2, 22, 27—30) will not safeguard a person from the consequences of breaking a vow. There is no warrant for arguing that Qohelet's conception of fear in this text represents a perverse re-imagination of this biblical principle.

The passage opens with the charge to "guard your feet when you go to the house of God" (4:17). The feet often functions as a figure for human conduct in biblical poetry (see Prov 1:15—16; 4:27; 5:5; 6:18; 19:2; Job 23:11; 31:5; Pss 26:12; 119:59, 101; Isa 59:7). Hence, to guard one's "feet" means to watch one's *conduct*.[41] Qohelet urges those who enter the presence of the God to tread carefully. As noted above, the fear of God could be practiced concretely in the cult. So, in explicating the meaning of the fear of God, Qohelet transports his audience to the sacred precincts. Yet, the emphasis here is not on the ritual acts themselves, but on *how* they are to be performed. Qohelet implies that the acts of going to the temple and engaging in religious activities, in and of themselves, do not constitute piety. The fear of God is properly demonstrated, not by the offering of sacrifice, prayers, and vows, but by the exercise of appropriate restraint and reverence when doing so. The rationale he offers first is a familiar one: it is more acceptable to listen/obey than to offer sacrifices (4:17b).[42] Similar sayings are found elsewhere in the Old Testament (1 Sam 15:22; Prov 15:8; 21:3, 27), and Qohelet's remarks are not essentially different from the common

---

40 Where the Deuteronomic injunction states as its motive "for the LORD your God will surely require it of you, and you would incur guilt," Qohelet says that it is foolishness not to fulfill vows.

41 One may note a similar emphasis on appropriate attitude in the Egyptian wisdom text *The Instruction Addressed to King Merikare*: "The character of the upright is preferred to the ox of the evildoer" (see Lichtheim, *AEL* 1:105—107).

42 The word qārôb should be read as the adjective meaning "near to God's favor" or "acceptable," rather than an infinitive absolute with imperative force (contra Aq, Syr, and Vulg). In 1 Kgs 8:59, Solomon's words of prayer are said to be "near to the Lord," meaning acceptable to him. The word denotes an intimate relationship, whether divine (Pss 34:19; 85:10; 119:151) or human (Ps 148:14; Ezek 43:19; Lev 10:3). See Fox, *A Time to Tear Down*, 230 and Seow, *Ecclesiastes*, 194.

critique of cultic abuses in the Old Testament (see also Isa 1:12—17; Hos
6:6; Amos 5:22—24). Its formulation, however, displays a unique
syntax. First, in a text that underscores the distance between God and
humanity (5:1c), Qohelet ironically employs the adjective that typically
connotes proximity (*qārôb*) to speak of that which is more acceptable to
the deity. He says, in effect, that God's favor (or "nearness") is better
experienced through listening rather than the mindless and
perfunctory giving of sacrifice. Secondly, the phraseology in this text
highlights the verbal aspect over against the nominal (*lišmōᵃᶜ mittēt
hakkĕsîlîm zābaḥ*; cf. especially *šĕmōᵃᶜ mizzebaḥ*, 1 Sam 15:22; *mizzābaḥ*,
Prov 21:3). Qohelet is comparing the acceptability, not so much of
obedience versus sacrifice, but of the acts of *listening* versus *giving*. For
Qohelet, who repeatedly identifies God as the subject of the verb *ntn*,[43]
giving is the prerogative of the deity. Worshippers must therefore
acknowledge that mortals have little to give to God but reverential
attentiveness and mindfulness (cf. Hab 2:20). So, the sage continues his
thought with the admonition to thoughtful in speech: "do not be rash
in your speech, or hasty with your heart to bring a matter before God."

Qohelet then supplies another rationale, this one explicitly
theological in orientation: "for God is in heaven, while you are on
earth" (5:1). In the Old Testament, God's heavenly abode may signify a
number of things: sovereignty over all creation, omnipresence, ability
to see and judge everything under heaven (Job 28:24; Pss 33:12; 102:20;
113:6; 115:3—7, 12—13). Most comprehensively, it speaks of divine
supremacy, which commands the fear, worship, and loyalty of all who
dwell on earth. In the Deuteronomistic history, YHWH is described as
"God in heaven above and on the earth below" (e.g. Deut 4:39; Josh
2:11). When this confession is made, it is in the context of recounting
the deity's awe-provoking acts on behalf of Israel, which are seen to be
an attestation of God's supremacy over all the earth. Qohelet's
statement here, while affirming divine supremacy, underscores the
distance between God and humanity: God is in heaven; humanity is on
earth. Earlier in 3:11, he spoke of divine transcendence in temporal
terms; here, he does so in spatial terms. The distance between God and
humanity is insuperable in every regard. But this emphasis on the
distance need not reflect a view of God who is far-removed from
human concerns and indifferent to prayer.[44] Nowhere does God's
heavenly abode signify an aloofness from earthly affairs. It signifies,
instead, the inscrutability of God who is Wholly Other. The sentiment

---

43   Eccl 1:13; 2:26; 3:10, 11; 5:18; 6:2; 8:15; 9:9; 12:7.
44   Contra Michel, *Eigenart*, 289; Gordis, *Koheleth*, 248; Hertzberg, *Der Prediger*, 226.

is perhaps most closely echoed in Isaiah: "For my thoughts are not your thoughts, nor are your ways my ways, says YHWH. For as the heavens are higher than the earth, so are my ways higher than your ways and my thoughts than your thoughts" (Isa 55:8—9). The heavenly vantage point means that God is aware of all that takes place on earth. It speaks of the utter freedom with which the deity governs the affairs on earth. As the psalmist puts it, "Our God is in the heavens, he does whatever he pleases" (Ps 115:3).

The subsequent proverb provides yet another rationale for his counsel: "For a dream comes with much preoccupation, likewise the voice of a fool with much talk" (5:2). The second portion of the aphorism is clear enough; Qohelet echoes the conventional wisdom that teaches brevity of speech as the indelible mark of the wise person (Prov 10:14, 19; 21:23; cf. Eccl 6:11; 10:13—14). The first line, however, is more obscure. It is generally understood as a warning that too many preoccupations during the day may cause disturbing dreams at night. But this reading does not seem appropriate for this context, as scholars often concede. Instead, the point of the aphorism is that just as excessive preoccupation amounts to nothing more than an illusory dream,[45] so does excessive verbiage produce only vapid noise. As noted above, the word ʿinyān is fraught with meaning for Qohelet. In his discourse, it generally refers to obsessive yet futile activity, such as the quest to understand all that happens on earth (1:13; 3:10), or the compulsion to amass goods without being able to enjoy them (2:24; 5:12f). The comparison between the prattle of a fool and the preoccupation with illusory things in this context cautions that worship in the temple—ostensibly the most natural setting for the practice of piety—is just as susceptible to the folly of obsessive behavior. The ostentatious display of religiosity may be nothing more than a compulsive preoccupation. If religious observance is characterized by such glib verbosity or mindless fanaticism, then even the practice of piety may be precarious.

Qohelet gives one final rationale for his admonitions. With respect to the wisdom of fulfilling one's vows promptly without making any

---

45 In ancient Near Eastern literature, a dream is often a figure for anything that is illusory or "unreal." See A. Leo Oppenheim, *The Interpretation of Dreams in the Ancient Near East, with a Translation of an Assyrian Dream-book* (Philadelphia: American Philosophical Society, 1956), 228, 234; Hermann Grapow, *Die bildlichen Ausdrückes des Ägyptischen* (Leipzig: Hinrich's, 1924), 140. Hence, Seow posits that the "significance of 'dream' here approximates *hebel*—it is something ephemeral and unreliable." See his discussion in *Ecclesiastes*, 199—200, where he cites relevant biblical and Egyptian literature. See also Sir 34:5, which says that divinations, omens, and dreams are but *hebel* (μάταιά).

excuses, he asks, "why should God be angry at your voice and destroy
the work of your hands?" The root *qṣp*, typically rendered as "to be
angry" or "to be wrathful," expresses the displeasure of an authority
figure. Most often, it is used of God to signify divine anger over sin,
disobedience, or rebellion, and may be accompanied by the threat of
destruction, as here in Ecclesiastes (cf. Num 16:22; Deut 1:34; 9:19; Josh
22:18; Isa 47:6; 57:16f; Zech 1:2, 15; Lam 5:22). Its frequency in other Old
Testament texts flies in the face of the contention that Qohelet's
commendation of the fear of God somehow represents a perverse
aberration from a biblical norm.[46] The sage simply restates what
others—and he himself—have claimed before: God's sovereign
judgment is to be taken seriously. God does not govern capriciously or
erratically, even though it may often appear that way.[47] The way a
person lives does make a difference. So, Qohelet urges those who
would be wise to be accountable for their actions, especially in
commitments made before the deity.

Finally, the imperative "fear God" (v. 6b) sums up the contents of
the entire passage. The passage closes as it began, with the
admonishment to conduct oneself with proper trepidation before the
deity (cf. 4:17). Several conclusions may be drawn. First, the fear of God
is expressed through the concrete behaviors that are recommended in
this text. Just as joy has a behavioral dimension, so, too, does fear. But
as noted above, the sage's principle concern is not with the specific
rituals of the cult, but with appropriate attitude and conduct as one is
engaging in these activities. Von Rad observed that sapiential literature
in general takes up matters pertaining to the cult but does so in order to
address "human presuppositions which are indispensable for cultic
participation."[48] One may then posit that the fear of God is not limited
to these particular ritual activities, but transcends them. Although the
immediate purview of the passage is the specific setting of the cult, the
instructions hold general principles that may be applied to affairs
outside the sacral realm as well. The scope of its ethics extends beyond
the cult and into daily life. Hence, Lohfink is not amiss to liken the
subject matter of this text to the ethical instructions of 9:7—12:7: "Both
offer advice, not to draw us away from the world, but rather to root us
more deeply in what is normal, albeit in the light of a wholly new

---

46 In fact, the numerous references to and echoes of other Old Testament texts in this
    passage indicate that the views espoused here constitute no radical departure.

47 Qohelet will address this precise problem in his subsequent exposition of the fear of
    God.

48 Gerhard von Rad, *Wisdom in Israel* (trans. James D. Marton; London: SCM Press,
    1972), 186—87; trans. of *Weisheit in Israel* (Neukirchen-Vluyn: Neukirchener, 1970).

knowledge."[49] This is especially true for Qohelet, who sees all of life—
for better or for worse—as the realm of divine presence.

To summarize, Qohelet's notion of godly fear is rooted in a
theology of divine transcendence that underscores the insuperable
distance between the divine and human. To fear God means to be fully
aware of God as Wholly Other, who reigns over every aspect of life in
justice (Qohelet affirms this), yet resides utterly beyond the bounds of
human comprehension. It also means to know that humanity's place is
"on earth," under heaven, or, as the sage more commonly puts its,
under the sun. [50] This place comes with the most severe limitations.
Throughout his reflections, Qohelet describes life under the sun against
the backdrop of inevitable death—the days under the sun are *hebel*. But
it also comes with its invigorating possibilities. Eternity belongs to God;
but humanity has the gift of individual moments. God's abode is in
heaven; but earth is humanity's domain. As the Psalmist puts it: "The
heavens are YHWH's heavens, but the earth he has given to human
beings" (Ps 115:16). And mortals are given the charge to exercise good
stewardship over their ephemeral days on earth with humility and
grateful acceptance.

3.4 A Morality of "Both" (7:18)

In 4:17—5:6 Qohelet discussed the meaning of the fear of God in the
specific arena of cultic life. Now, he speaks more generally of the
characteristic behavior of "one who fears God." As in 3:14, his
comments here are situated in a text that deals with the inscrutability of
divine activity (see especially 7:13—14, 23—24). In this context, what is
incomprehensible to him is the blatant violation of retributive justice:
"there are righteous people who perish in their righteousness, and
there are wicked people who prolong their lives in their evildoing"
(7:15). When he bemoans a similar breach of justice in 3:16, he simply
consoles himself by recalling that "God will judge the righteous and the
wicked." Here, however, he considers its implications for piety. If
retribution is unreliable and righteous behavior makes no difference in
the quality of one's life, how then should a person live? He evaluates
two alternatives: strive all the more for righteousness in the hopes that
more may secure a good life (v. 16); or forego such impossible attempts

---

49 Lohfink, *Qoheleth*, 75—76.

50 The expressions *taḥat haššemeš* (29 times) and "under heaven" (3 times) are virtually
synonymous. In a number of instances, the phrase "on earth" (cf. 5:1) has a similar
nuance (8:14, 16; 12:17; cf. 7:20 [with the preposition *bĕ*]).

altogether and indulge in wickedness (v. 17). Qohelet refuses to settle
for either of these extreme options. Instead, he proposes another way:
"it is good that you should take hold of the one without letting go of
the other, for the one who fears God goes forth with *both* of them" (v.
18). Genuine piety, for Qohelet, entails negotiating and living with the
contradictions of human existence.

Commentators generally reckon that the verse has a traditional cast
to it, despite the ambiguity concerning the expression "go forth with
both of them." Whether one interprets the verb *yṣ'* as "succeed,"[51]
"fulfill one's duty,"[52] "escape,"[53] or "go forth,"[54] it is difficult to make
the case that the fear of God in this context signifies a disabling terror.[55]
Hence, because of its "pious" tone, some scholars have questioned the
text's integrity, suggesting that v. 18b is an interpolation by an
orthodox glossator.[56] But such dismissals are all too convenient and fail
to attend to the tensions in the text, the very thing that conveys
Qohelet's message in this instance.

There is another significant flaw in the theory of interpolation. The
putative annotation (7:18b) is intertwined syntactically and structurally
with the surrounding material, which is agreed to be original. The
statement "the one who fears God goes forth with both of them
(*kullām*)" is the logical conclusion of first half of the verse which states,
"it is good that you should take hold of the one (*bāzeh*) without letting
of the other (*wĕgam-mizzeh*, v. 18a)." The phrase "both of them" (*kullām*)
in v. 18b refers to the couplet expressed by demonstrative pronouns
(*zeh … zeh*) and completes the thought. The antecedents of "the one …
the other" (*zeh … zeh*), then, are found in the pair of admonitions that
are cited in vv. 16—17. These three verses (vv. 16—18) are thus closely
bound together. But the connections do not stop there. The phrase
"both of them" (*kullām*) harks back also to the statement "both have I
seen" (*'et-hakkōl rā'îtî*) at the beginning of the unit (v. 15), which in turn

---

51   NAB, REV, NRSV.
52   On the basis of the Mishnaic idiom. Gordis, 277—78; Delitzsch, *Commentary on the
     Song of Songs and Ecclesiastes*, 323; Whybray, *Ecclesiastes*, 121; Fox, *A Time to Tear
     Down*, 262; cf. Jerome, *nihil negligit*.
53   So Hertzberg, *Der Prediger*, 237; Michel *Eigenart*, 151.
54   Thus LXX, Sym, Syr [read *npq* "go forth" for *nqp* "adhere"]. So also Ginsburg,
     Coheleth, 233; Seow, *Ecclesiastes*, 255. This plain sense of the verb recommends itself
     above the others.
55   Longman comes the closest to doing so. Longman, *Ecclesiastes*, 197.
56   Graetz, *Kohelet*, 96; Barton, *A Critical and Exegetical Commentary on the Book of
     Ecclesiastes*, 144. Among recent commentators, Crenshaw supposes that the
     "optimism" of this statement is irreconcilable with the depressing observation in v.
     15 and casts doubt on its authenticity (*Ecclesiastes*, 142).

is further linked to the preceding unit by the language of "seeing" ("see the work of God," vv. 13—14) and another dialectical construction with *zeh...zeh* ("the one as well as the other God has made," v. 14).[57] These extensive connections demonstrate that v. 18b is integral—indeed indispensable—to the unit. The teacher's closing statement concerning "both of them" (*kullām*) is his final word on how mortals are to make their way in a world rife with ambiguities and tensions. The statement in v. 18b is "the point and climax of the preceding, without which it would be meaningless."[58]

What, then, does this text say about "the one who fears God"? And what does it mean to "go forth with both of them"? As the above structural analysis demonstrates, a recurring theme in vv. 13—18 is the dialectic of "both." The ambiguity concerning the referent of "both of them" (*kullām*) in v. 18b opens up the possibility of multiple connections and layers of meaning. First, as already noted, the expression refers most immediately to the pair of injunctions that Qohelet considers in vv. 16—17. In the first, he warns, "Do not be overly righteous,[59] and do not be too wise." In the second, he cautions against the opposite extreme: "Do not be overly wicked, and do not be a fool."[60] Qohelet's own conclusion is that *both* must be embraced: "It is good that you should take hold of the one and not let go of the other" (v. 18a). But what do these peculiar admonitions mean? Surely, the diligent pursuit of virtue should be commended rather than denigrated, as Qohelet seems to do in v. 16. Moreover, v. 17 seems to condone a certain measure of vice.[61] Are these statements a reflection of Qohelet's belief in God as a "morally neutral being, beyond good and evil"?[62] Are they a mockery of the traditional belief in divine retribution?[63]

---

57   The strategic position of the word *hakkōl* strengthens this linkage all the more. The object *'et-hakkōl* in 7:15 is in the emphatic position, as is *gam 'et-zeh lĕ'ummat-zeh* in 7:14b, causing the two ideas to be read together. The expression *hakkōl* in 7:15 is both prospective and retrospective and functions effectively as the link between the two units.

58   Gordis, *Kohelet*, 268.

59   Whybray is probably right to stress that the adverb *harbēh* modifies not the adjective *ṣaddîq* "righteous," but the verb *tĕhî* "be." The sage has in mind the manner in which righteousness is pursued.

60   The virtual synonymity of righteousness/wisdom and wickedness/folly, typical of traditional wisdom, is implied here by the parallel constructions in vv. 16—17.

61   Barton, *A Critical and Exegetical Commentary on the Book of Ecclesiastes*, 144.

62   Bickerman, *Four Strange Books of the Bible*, 149. See also MacDonald, who characterizes Qohelet's God as "a completely amoral being" in *The Hebrew Philosophical Genius*, 86—87.

63   Murphy, *Ecclesiastes*, 72—73. See also Lauha, *Kohelet*, 82.

Scholars offer varying interpretations for these puzzling admonitions. Regarding the first saying in v. 16, Whybray's proposal—that Qohelet is issuing a warning against *self*-righteousness and *pretensions* to wisdom—may be appealing.[64] His argument, however, has some logical difficulties that make it ultimately untenable. He suggests, on the basis of the estimative usage of the Hithpael,[65] that the form *tithakkam* denotes hypocritical wisdom. However, while *tithakkam* may theoretically mean "pretend to be wise," the phrase *těhî ṣaddîq* cannot mean "claim to be righteous," nor can the parallel injunctions in v. 17 be taken to indicate pretense. What is at issue for Qohelet is not pretense but *presumption*—the misguided *over*confidence that a person may somehow attain a level of righteousness that will guarantee the rewards of a good life. Qohelet disabuses his audience of any such naiveté, first by noting that "there are righteous people (*yēš ṣaddîq*) who perish in their righteousness" (v. 15b), then by stating unequivocally that "there is no one righteous (*'ên ṣaddîq*) on earth, who does good without ever erring" (v. 20). To err is human, and no human being can be perfectly righteous. It is important to note that this insistence on human fallibility is meant not as a condemnatory word but a *therapeutic* one. The rationale that Qohelet supplies for his counsel is that straining to achieve the unattainable will only leave a person devastated (*tiššômēm*). This verb (*šmm*) may refer not only to physical ruin but psychological ruin as well (e.g., Ps 143:4; Isa 59:16; 63:5; Dan 8:27; Sir 43:24), and Qohelet may have in mind a state of stupor or acute despair precipitated by frustrated efforts.[66] In other words, one must avoid being over-scrupulous and over-ambitious in the pursuit of righteousness because it can have debilitating effects on a person's physical and emotional health. Wickedness and folly are known to destroy life (v. 17). But so, too, can zealous religiosity damage a person's vitality and well-being. Qohelet therefore urges those who are prone to such over-righteousness to cease striving, and allow mistakes in themselves and others as well (cf. vv. 21—22). Fear of God must be accompanied by an appropriate and realistic knowledge of the self if it is to be life-giving.

---

64 R. N. Whybray, "Qoheleth the Immoralist? (Qoh 7:16—17)" in *Israelite Wisdom* (ed. J. G. Gammie et al.; Missoula, Mont.: Scholars Press, 1978), 191—204. So also Castellino, "Qohelet and His Wisdom," 15—28; Delitzsch, *Commentary on the Song of Songs and Ecclesiastes*, 326.

65 See, for example, 2 Sam 13:5 ("pretend to be ill") and Ezek 13:17 ("play the prophet").

66 Similarly, Seow, *Ecclesiastes*, 254; Fox, *A Time to Tear Down*, 261.

Qohelet then addresses the other extreme: since no one can be entirely righteous and the principle of retribution is unreliable in any case, should people be free to act wickedly/foolishly? Elsewhere in his discourse, he observes that the failure of retribution does indeed embolden some people to brazenly perpetrate evil (8:11). He cautions here that such an approach to life remains under the threat of judgment, affirming with traditional wisdom that wickedness will indeed hasten one's demise. The fact that he cautions against being *overly* (*harbēh*) wicked is not a recommendation of wickedness in moderation.[67] As Fox rightly notes, "to condemn much is not to approve of a little."[68] Rather, the qualification is a concession to the fact that no life remains untouched by folly.

The one who fears God, then, goes forth with both righteousness and wickedness, wisdom and folly. This is not to say that piety and ungodliness in Ecclesiastes are "identical for all practical purposes," as Pfeiffer contends.[69] Neither is it an endorsement of an Aristotelian *via media*, a "golden mean" between two extremes, as many have argued in the past.[70] Rather, it is a warning against being too much of either. Straining inordinately in either direction is a sign of presumptuous confidence in one's own abilities, and a form of hubris.[71] And such presumptions can destroy a person. The fear of God, by contrast, embraces both the possibilities and the impossibilities of being human. It acknowledges that people are invariably *simul iustus et peccator*.[72] Humanity's best efforts at righteousness and wisdom will be found wanting. But that shortcoming is not necessarily a failure of piety. So, Qohelet makes the surprising claim that genuine piety inevitably includes a measure of wickedness and folly, for such is the reality of the human condition. His faithful realism leads to a form of piety that is more modest (and less demanding), and therefore more able to instill life in those who would pursue it.

---

67 Contra Barton, *Ecclesiastes*, 144.

68 Fox, *A Time to Tear Down*, 262. Similarly, the curse on slaying a neighbor in secret (Deut 27:24) is not a license to do so in public, as noted by Crenshaw, *Ecclesiastes*, 141.

69 R. H. Pfeiffer, "The Peculiar Skepticism of Ecclesiastes," 106.

70 For example, Delitzsch, *Commentary on the Song of Songs and Ecclesiastes*, 324; Gordis, *Kohelet*, 265–68.

71 Hertzberg, *Der Prediger*, 154; Fox, *A Time to Tear Down*, 260–61.

72 Delitzsch, *Commentary on the Song of Songs and Ecclesiastes*, 325; similarly, Rüdiger Lux, "Der 'Lebenskompromiss'–ein Wesenszug im Denken Kohelets? Zur Auslegung von Koh 7,15–18," in *Alttestamentlicher Glaube und Biblische Theologie* (ed. J. Hausmann and H.-J. Zobel; Stuttgart: Kohlhammer, 1992), 276–78; Seow, *Ecclesiasates*, 268.

The insistence that piety must be grounded in the reality of the human condition is echoed in the larger context as well. As noted above, the expression *kullām* "both of them" in v. 18b recalls the reference to *hakkōl* "both" in v. 15. There the sage makes a twofold observation: "there are righteous people who perish in their righteousness and there are wicked people who prolong their lives in their evil-doing." The structure of the text suggests that this twofold observation may be another referent of *kullām* in v. 18b. In other words, the one who fears God must "go forth" with the knowledge that the principle of retribution may be overturned in the affairs of the world. Contrary to the teachings of conventional wisdom (cf. Prov 3:1—18; 4:10—27), the experiences of life reveal that upright behavior does not always lead to rewards, and villainy is not always promptly punished. The one who fears God must confront these contradictory realities, however painful that may be. Piety is not a doctrinaire adherence to a rigid system of beliefs. Theological principles must be evaluated rigorously in light of their truthfulness to and relevance for the human condition. Probing questions must be asked. One must recognize that even the most cherished truth claim may be qualified, perhaps even overturned, by its encounter with real life. Indeed, one must "consider the work of God" (7:13)—the crooked and inscrutable work of God—which impinges upon human constructs and disrupts the tidiness that people instinctively desire. For Qohelet, any form of religiosity that presumes the ways of God is not genuine fear of God. Indeed, this point is so important to Qohelet that he will return to it again in his subsequent exposition of the fear of God (8:9—15).

Finally, following the structural analysis above, the word *kullām* in v. 18b harks back also to the "good day" and "bad day" noted in v. 14. The perplexing contradictions in life do not keep Qohelet from affirming the good along with the bad. The one who fears God, he maintains, must experience fully both the times of good fortune and times of misfortune in the course of one's life. Prosperity and adversity are not explained in terms of reward and punishment. Although Qohelet maintains vigorously that there is *some* relationship between personal morality and the quality of one's life, he is forced to admit that the relationship is neither self-evident nor always reliable. Instead, Qohelet portrays the turns and tides in fortune as integral to the natural rhythms of life. Just as humans must accept a mix of virtue and vice in themselves (and others), so too must they accept a mix of sorrow and joy, prosperity and adversity, in the circumstances of life. For a second time in the book, Qohelet attributes a purpose to this mysterious design of the deity: "God has made the one as well as the other so that humans cannot grasp what lies ahead of them" (v. 14b; cf. 3:14). To fear God means to encounter and accept the reality that "humans cannot grasp what lies ahead." In the same breath, however, he affirms what humans can and must do: they must consider the work of God and respond appropriately at every given moment (7:14a). As Lohfink observes, what is called the fear of God in 3:14 is now defined concretely as the ability "to allow oneself to fall into the happiness offered us, but also to know that God is at work in misfortune, and therefore to accept it."[73] As in 3:9—15, the notion of godly fear and life-centered joy are closely bound together in Qohelet's discourse. The one who fears God must take hold of every given moment as an opportunity to experience life in all its variegated fullness, neither shrinking back from the hardships nor bypassing the pleasures. The fear of God is a disposition toward life—and toward the self—that enables one to endure difficulties with a tough-minded realism, and to be "surprised by joy" whenever a good thing is encountered. Good and ill, justice and injustice, pleasure and pain—*both* are inevitable features of human life, and the one who fears God goes forth with both. That this basic insight has perennial value is evidenced in the poetry of William Blake, which closely echoes the sentiment: "It is right it should be so; man was made for joy and woe; and when this we rightly know, through the world we safely go."[74]

3.5 To Believe or Not to Believe (8:12b—13)

In 8:1—17, Qohelet returns yet again to the theme of God's inscrutable activity. And as before, at the heart of the matter is the problematic of retributive theology and its implications for the one who fears God (vv. 10—14). In 7:15—18, Qohelet notes the violations of retribution and suggests that genuine piety must be attentive to these troublesome realities and live constructively with these ambiguities. Here, he continues along the same vein but underscores the contradictions much more explicitly and deliberately. The passage registers a series of disturbing observations concerning the failure of moral governance in the world: the wicked are given ceremonial burials at death while those who have lived uprightly are publicly castigated (v. 10); evil deeds are not summarily punished (v. 11); sinners prolong their lives (v. 12a); the righteous are treated as miscreants and vice-versa (v. 14). Embedded in

---

73   Lohfink, *Qoheleth*, 97. He asserts—inaccurately—that this is the first time that the fear of God is defined in this way. The relationship between fear and joy has already been established in 3:9—15, 22.

74   From *Auguries of Innocence*.

this litany of grievances is a curious statement concerning the fear of God: "it will go well for those who fear God because they fear him, but it will not go well with the wicked … because they do not fear God" (8:12b—13). The statement is peculiar not because of what it says—it is, in fact, a forthright affirmation of the traditional precept concerning the fear of God (cf. Prov 14:27; 10:27)—but because of its seemingly naïve placement in this particular context. On either side of these remarks, Qohelet records examples that patently contravene the principle. The resultant tension in the text raises some crucial questions. How are these conflicting claims to be interpreted? Does Qohelet doggedly uphold the principle of retribution in spite of the troubling exceptions, or does he refer to it merely to disabuse his readers of the traditional belief? Or is something else at stake in the passage?

The glaring contradictions make this text particularly amenable to a source-critical analysis. Because the claim in 8:12b—13 has the stamp of conventional wisdom, which associates the fear of God with well-being and long life, scholars have commonly assigned it to an orthodox revisionist who allegedly was intent on toning down Qohelet's unsettling views.[75] There are some difficulties with this approach, however. If an editor had indeed been at work to offset Qohelet's subversive observations, one would expect the text to conclude on the corrective note. It is highly unlikely that the putative glossator would have reserved the final word for the very voice that was to be suppressed (v. 14).[76] As it stands, the effect is not to mollify Qohelet's skepticism, but to call attention to it all the more by the jarring juxtaposition. One notes, moreover, that the statements in 8:12b—13 are composed in Qohelet's own language and style.[77] The expression $k\hat{\imath}$ gam (cf. 4:14, 16; 7:22; 8:16; 9:12), the comparison of human life with a shadow (cf. 6:12), and not least of all, the theme of fearing God—all belong to his repertoire. There is, then, no warrant for assigning these verses to an orthodox hand. Indeed, doing so only flattens out a crucial

---

75 Barton, *A Critical and Exegetical Commentary on the Book of Ecclesiastes*, 153; Braun, *Kohelet und die frühhellenistische Popularphilosophie*, 97; Ellermeier, *Qohelet I/1*, 125—29; Lauha, *Kohelet*, 157; Siegfried Plath, *Furcht Gottes: der Begriff yr' im Alten Testament* (ArbT 2/2; Stuttgart: Calwer, 1963), 82 n. 228. Among contemporary commentators, Crenshaw subscribes to such an approach, albeit more cautiously. He believes that the sayings are most likely the work of the epilogist, who similarly portrays the fear of God as religious devotion. Crenshaw, *Ecclesiastes*, 155. Similarly, Brown, *Character in Crisis*, 147 n. 78.

76 Fox makes a similar argument. See his astute comments in *A Time to Tear Down*, 18—19.

77 Cf. Gordis, *Koheleth*, 282—83. Even Crenshaw, who subscribes to the theory of an orthodox glossator, agrees that the style is distinctively Qohelet (*Ecclesiastes*, 89).

dimension of the text and undercuts both the message and the method of theological inquiry modeled therein.

Another popular way of dissipating the tension in this text is to posit the presence of quotations. According to this strategy, Qohelet cites a traditional saying only to debunk it, or at least seriously qualify it. Gordis, a major proponent of this method, embellishes his translation of v. 12b as follows: "though I know the answer that 'it will be well in the end with those who revere God'...."[78] However, in the absence of quotation marks or some other objective criterion for identifying a citation, there is no control over such *ad hoc* methods. As Fox aptly points out, one may just as well attribute 8:11—12a, 14 (the "skeptical" remarks) to another hand, and conclude that Qohelet rejects the ideas cited there.[79] The epilogue portrays Qohelet as a sage who taught the people, and it is hardly surprising that his teachings would include sayings of a traditional cast alongside his more subversive observations. Indeed, if other conventional statements are acknowledged to be from the author's pen (e.g., 3:17; 4:17—5:6; 7:1—12; 10:8—20, and other scattered maxims), there is no reason to deny him this affirmation of retributive justice.

How, then, is this piece of conventional wisdom to be interpreted in its context? The arguments turn, in part, around the expression *kî gam yōdēaʿ ʾānî*, which introduces vv. 12b—13. Many translators and commentators reckon that the concessive nuance is operative in *kî gam*, and that the participle in the phrase *yōdēaʿ ʾānî* signals common knowledge over against some truth that Qohelet himself has come to know from his own investigations, in which case the perfect form *yādaʿtî* (1:17; 2:14; 3:12, 14) is employed.[80] The combination yields a sense not unlike Gordis's amplified translation. Qohelet acknowledges conventional wisdom, but only reluctantly as a concession to popular wisdom. The point he wants to dwell on, ultimately, is the unreliability of retribution. As Seow remarks, "this concession is merely parenthetical, it seems, and without much conviction, for he quickly

---

78 Gordis, *Koheleth*, 105, 287; and widely followed. Loretz, *Qoheleth und der alte Orient*, 123; Loader, *Polar Structures*, 100—1; Lohfink, *Qoheleth*, 108. In a variation of this approach, others designate the remark as an example of a *zwar-aber* saying (Hertzberg, *Der Prediger*, 30).

79 He notes that traditional commentators did, in fact, make such an interpretive move. Fox, *A Time to Tear Down*, 23. See also Whybray, "The Identification and Use of Quotations in Ecclesiastes," 435—51.

80 Isaksson, *Studies in the Language of Qoheleth*, 67. Hertzberg makes a similar argument, but emphasizes that the participle introduces someone else's ideas (*Der Prediger*, ad loc.).

returns to note the injustice … in v. 14."[81] However, as noted by Fox, the phrase *kî gam*, much like *wĕgam*, typically introduces a concomitant fact.[82] Here, the conventional truth is upheld on an equal plane with the contradicting cases cited around it. Qohelet knows the principle of retributive justice and nowhere denies it (cf. 3:17; 5:5b; 7:17; 8:5; 11:9b). He also knows that there are cases that breach the rule.[83] Furthermore, even if the participial expression "I know" signifies general knowledge, there is nothing inherent in its usage that indicates the sage's own position toward that knowledge. One must look to the context to determine that.

The rhetorical design of the text accomplishes two things: the first is felt immediately, the second only after closer analysis. The immediate impact of the text is dissonance and disorientation. Fox is right to insist that Qohelet makes the contradiction linger in its unrelieved tension. In one breath, he upholds the traditional belief concerning retribution and declares that he knows it to be true. In the next, without hesitation or apology, he cites empirical evidence that directly invalidates the principle. The deliberate repetition of certain vocabulary heightens the incongruity all the more. In v. 12a, Qohelet claims that sinners who do evil nevertheless prolong their lives (*ma'ărîk*). Only one verse later, in clear opposition, he submits that evildoers will not in fact prolong their days (*lō'-ya'ărîk*). The structure and language of the discourse creates a clash between conflicting claims: the claim of traditional theology on the one hand, and the claim of human experience on the other. As in 7:15—18, Qohelet insists that questions about the moral life must take place in the encounter between theology and life. That encounter is not always a hospitable one; indeed, Qohelet suggests an agonistic relationship between the two in this case. The principle of retribution is on trial, as it were. Although Qohelet cherishes the principle, he allows it to be scrutinized by the hard facts of life. The positive affirmation is flanked on both sides by contravening examples, forcing the reader to wrestle with the question of its credibility. Indeed, the rhetoric of the text underscores the ambiguity and presses the dilemma upon the reader.

However, the contradictions do not leave the reader forever in the impasse. Beyond its initial impact, Qohelet's rhetoric suggests a way of pressing past the contradictions to a new vision of piety. It has been argued that Qohelet, by juxtaposing these contradictory claims,

---

81   Seow, *Ecclesiastes*, 288, 294—95.

82   Fox, *A Time to Tear Down*, 286.

83   Fox writes, "it is because Qohelet holds to the axioms of Wisdom that he is shocked by their violation and finds the aberrations absurd." *A Time to Tear Down*, 286.

relativizes traditional wisdom. But rarely is that argument accompanied by an explication of *how* that is accomplished. The text forces the reader to reevaluate the affirmation of retribution in very specific ways. Through the details and subtleties of his language, Qohelet redefines the "good life" associated with piety. First, the two corresponding statements in vv. 12b−13 are not precise parallels. "Those who do not fear God" are equated with the wicked in v. 13, but "those who fear God" are given no further explication; they are not explicitly identified with the righteous. Granted, that is the probable implication, given the conventions of sapiential rhetoric and the contrast (the righteous opposite the wicked) plainly established in v. 14. But in v. 12c, the text purposively refrains from making this overt identification. In addition, less verbiage is dedicated to describe the fate of those who fear God. Regarding the wicked, the sage submits that "it will not go well" with them, and then offers the elaboration: "they will not prolong their days...." When the author describes the fate of the devout, however, the expected promise of long life is conspicuously omitted. In somewhat of a tautology, Qohelet simply says that "it will go well for those who fear God, because they fear [God]."[84] Noting the redundant construction, Ellen Davis observes that for Qohelet, "Fearing God *already* constitutes the well-being of the righteous. The reward for fearing God is fearing God."[85] That observation has merit.[86] Beyond that insight, however, the gap created by the sparing and indistinct description forces the reader to look beyond its immediate context to determine *how* "it will go well" (*yihyeh-ṭôb*) for those who fear God.

It is not until v. 15 that Qohelet gives the particulars of the good life: "there is nothing better (*ṭôb*)" than to eat, drink, and be glad. When he expounds on the good things that are availed to the devout, his commendation of enjoyment reasserts itself, confirming yet again the intimate relationship between fear and joy in Qohelet's theology. Qohelet deliberately abstains from defining well-being in terms of longevity. He cannot be so optimistic. He knows that no one has power over the day of death (v. 8), and that every human life is limited in

---

84 By virtue of the parallel, many commentators infer that the "good" is long life. Ogden, for example, argues that this text teaches that "Fear of God is the only way to success ... and the nature of the success or 'good' we infer from the context: long life.... Qoheleth here throws his full support behind the tradition." *Ecclesiastes*, 137.

85 Davis, *Proverbs, Ecclesiastes, and the Song of Songs*, 209.

86 This reading also accords with Bamberger's observation that throughout the Old Testament, "fear and love of the Deity are not urged as motives for the good life, but are themselves the good life. They are not means, but ends." Bamberger, "Fear and Love of God in the Old Testament," 40.

number (implied by the expression *yĕmê ḥayyāyw* in v. 15b).[87] Yet the transient days under the sun are accompanied by God-given opportunities to eat and drink and be glad, however tenuous these opportunities of enjoyment may be. The good life that Qohelet envisions for those who fear God is far more modest and ordinary than that claimed by traditional wisdom. But it is good nevertheless.

In his attempt to acknowledge both the principle of retribution and its failure, Qohelet exposes the limits of human knowledge. Indeed, he is almost forced to give up sure knowledge altogether. The one theological truth he returns to again and again is the inscrutability of God who acts in utter freedom, whose mysterious ways are inaccessible even to those who dedicate themselves religiously to such pursuits (8:16). This aspect of divine activity conditions everything that humans know. The unit thus ends fittingly with a three-fold repetition of the admission that mortals "cannot grasp" the work of God (8:17). If the fear of God is demonstrated by acknowledging what one cannot know, then the enjoyment of life—its vital counterpart in Qohelet's theology— is "being free not to know."[88] Embracing the mundane yet vital pleasures of eating and drinking frees the sage to let God be God, and humans truly human.

3.6 The End of the Matter (12:13b)

Qohelet's own thoughts come to a close with the *hebel* epigram in 12:8. Beginning with 12:9, the epilogue retrospectively evaluates the sage's work and, more broadly, the work of the wisdom enterprise in general. The book proper is then sealed with the notice: "the end of the matter; all has been heard" (12:13a). But the book does not end there. One last time, it recommends religious duty: "Fear God and keep his commandments, for thus should everyone be" (12:13b). This final injunction to fear God, identified as "the kernel and star of the whole book" by Franz Delitzsch,[89] is the decisive note on which the whole project is brought to conclusion. Its privileged position at the very culmination of the book suggests its critical significance for the interpretation of the whole. Indeed, as noted by Fox, the Masoretes

---

87 Compare 2:3; 5:17; 6:12, where the fuller expression (with *mispar*) is employed to communicate the idea of transience more explicitly. A number of Hebrew manuscripts include *mispar* at this point as well.

88 Davis, *Proverbs, Ecclesiastes, and the Song of Songs*, 210.

89 Delitzsch, *Commentary on the Song of Songs and Ecclesiastes*, 438.

apparently wanted to mark the special status of this "postscript" when they made the *samekh* of *sôp dābār* a *samekh rabbati*, "a large *samekh*."[90]

Delitzsch's glowing assessment of these closing words derives largely from the function he assigns to them in relation to the larger teachings of Qohelet: the orthodox theme, he argues, counterbalances the book's radical pessimism and "hallows" its potentially dangerous eudaemonism. Many commentators have followed a similar line of interpretation. The book's conclusion undoubtedly functioned this way in the early history of its interpretation.[91] Jerome, for example, defended the book from its fourth-century detractors by invoking the pious ending:

> [Some] say that, among other writings of Solomon which are obsolete and forgotten, this book ought to be obliterated, because it asserts that all the creatures of God are vain, and regards the whole as nothing, and prefers eating and drinking and transient pleasures before all things. [But] *from this one paragraph* [12:13f] it deserves the dignity that it should be placed among the number of the divine volumes, in which it condenses the whole of its discussion, summing up the whole enumeration, as it were, and says that the end of its discourse is very easily heard, having nothing difficult in it, namely, that we should fear God and keep his commandments (italics added).[92]

Indeed, at its very inception, the book's orthodox conclusion was a crucial factor in the early rabbis' decision to declare it safe for public reading despite its troublesome contradictions: it "ends with words of Torah" (*b. Shab.* 30b).

It is clear that long before the age of critical interpretation, readers of Ecclesiastes felt some measure of dissonance between the body of the book and its conclusion and exploited the interpretive possibilities of that dissonance. In the modern era, this tension led, of course, to the expedient of historical criticism. The postscript (typically, along with the whole epilogue) was attributed to a conservative redactor who allegedly attempted to tone down the sage's radical skepticism by appending the parallel injunctions to "fear God and keep his commandments." Indeed, both thematic and formal considerations seem to support the conclusion that at least the final two verses most likely originate from a different hand. This general consensus,

---

90   The *samekh rabbati* does not appear in the Leningrad codex proper, but is listed in its Masorah Finalis and is noted in *Dikduke Ha-Těamim* (ed. Baer-Strack, §61), cited by Fox, *A Time to Tear Down*, 358−9.

91   See K. J. Dell, "Ecclesiastes as Wisdom: Consulting Early Interpreters," *VT* 44 (1994): 301−29.

92   Cited by Ginsburg, *Coheleth*, 15.

however, does not obviate the question of how the postscript is to be read in relation to the teachings of Qohelet. Is the explication of the fear of God in terms of observance of divine commandments compatible with the views found in the body of the book, or is it completely antithetical to it? Is the postscript a legitimate and salutary extension of Qohelet's teachings, or is it a regrettable retreat into orthodoxy that obscures the book's true message? The discussion of the postscript's relationship to the body turns on the kind of piety espoused in each.

Some interpreters, following the reading strategy of Jerome (and Delitzsch), continue to herald the postscript (and more broadly, the epilogue) as the normative voice that overrides Qohelet's difficult teachings. Tremper Longman's views are representative. He argues that Qohelet's skeptical thoughts are recounted by the epilogist (the implied author of the book, following Fox) as a parade example of the kind of theology that must be avoided. Qohelet's theological orientation thus functions as a foil for genuine piety, and the book essentially warns against the deleterious effects of speculative wisdom. With the blunt expression "the end of the matter," the orthodox epilogist in effect says, "Enough of Qohelet, let's get on with what is really important."[93]

But Longman represents a relatively small minority of scholars. The majority see the assertion of orthodoxy at the end of the book not as its crowning attribute but as an unfortunate failure of nerve on the part of a later redactor that distorts the book's true message.[94] According to Crenshaw, the summation of the postscript is "totally alien to Qohelet's thinking," and only witnesses to the fact that "[f]ew people can endure … the conclusion that life is utterly futile!"[95] Newsom seconds that conclusion when she characterizes the postscript as the first (and not altogether innocent) "*mis*-reading" of Qohelet.[96]

Others, while acknowledging that a different perspective is showcased in the postscript, are less insistent about the tension. The perspective of the final verses, they argue, is not "entirely alien" to Qohelet's teachings, but a reasonable conclusion to them. Gerald Sheppard has demonstrated that there are a number of thematic and linguistic correspondences between the postscript and the body of the

---

93 Longman, *Ecclesiastes*, 32–39, 282. See also Perry, *Dialogues with Kohelet*, ad loc.
94 Michel, *Untersuchungen zur Eigenart des Buches Qohelet*, 286; Newsom, "Job and Ecclesiastes," 189; Christianson, *A Time to Tell*, 114–17.
95 Crenshaw, *Ecclesiastes*, 192.
96 Newsom, "Job and Ecclesiastes," 189–90.

book that provide some clues to the nature of their relationship.[97] He suggests that the epilogist has extracted a particular aspect of Qohelet's teaching and presents a schematizing interpretation of it, one that is discriminating but nevertheless legitimate. More specifically, he posits that the postscript responds to the dilemma of delayed justice raised by Qohelet and speaks to it with an assurance likewise contained in the book itself. He maintains, "It effectively conditions the hearing of the book precisely because of these points of literary continuity."[98] This interpretation of the book, however, is made to coexist with another "thematizing" rubric, seen in the summary *hebel* verdict that frames the book (1:2; 12:8).[99] Sheppard makes the critical observation that the preservation of these disparate orientations warns against reducing the book to a single meaning. The postscript provides the reader with some "emphatic guides" to the book's interpretation without flattening or trivializing of contents.[100] Christianson, who, contrary to Shepphard, sees a tensive relationship between the epilogue and the body, makes the same observation about the function of the orthodox frame.[101] Although these two scholars essentially disagree about the compatibility of Qohelet's thoughts with the perspective of the "epilogist," they both recognize that the frame and the body of the book must be read in relationship to one another.

While the emphasis on the divine commandments in the postscript may suggest a different orientation, the final command to fear God cannot be read in isolation from Qohelet's teachings on the theme throughout the book. Indeed, the postscript deliberately makes literary and theological connections with the body of the book that indicate that they ought to be read closely together. The correspondences are, in fact, more numerous than those identified by Sheppard. The most obvious connection is with 4:17—5:6. The syntax of the command in 12:13b is identical to that in 5:6b, with the object preposed emphatically (*'et-*

---

97 Sheppard, "The Epilogue to Qoheleth as Theological Commentary," 182−89. Wilson, makes the even bolder (and less compelling) claim that there is a correspondence between the prologue of Proverbs and the ending of Ecclesiastes (the reference "words of the wise") that implies a hermeneutical principle for wisdom: the fear of God and obedience is "the proper context within which to understand and evaluate the wisdom endeavor." G. H. Wilson, "'The Words of the Wise': The Intent and Significance of Qoheleth 12:9−14," *JBL* 103, no. 2 (1984): 175−92.

98 Sheppard, "The Epilogue to Qoheleth," 186.

99 First noted by Kurt Galling, "Der Prediger," 124−25; cf. his "Koheleth-Studien," *ZAW* 50 (1932), 279−82.

100 Sheppard, "The Epilogue to Qoheleth," 186.

101 Christianson, *A Time to Tell*, 114−120.

hā'ĕlōhîm yĕrā'). Furthermore, the structural and thematic counterpart to the imperative in 5:6b is the command to "guard one's conduct" (*šmr*) in the presence of the divine (4:17). As noted in the discussion of 4:17—5:6 above, the two imperatives frame the passage and the former is an important explication of the latter. The postscript establishes the same parallel, but instead of human conduct in general, it makes the commandments the specific object that must be observed. Yet even in Qohelet's explication of religious duty in 4:17—5:6, there are already references—both implicit and explicit—to the commandments (Deut 23:22—24; Num 15:22—31; Lev 4:2, 22, 27—30). Elsewhere in his reflections, too, he alludes to the wisdom of obeying the commandments. In 8:5, he remarks that "whoever keeps a command (*šōmēr miṣwâ*) will experience no harm." Admittedly, the "command" in this text refers most immediately to the command of a human sovereign.[102] Nevertheless, the text also makes an implicit association between the king's authority and divine authority. The rationale for obedience—"he will do whatever he pleases" (8:3)—is used elsewhere in the Bible only in reference to divine supremacy (see Pss 115:3, 135:6; Isa 46:10; Jon 1:14; cf. Aramaic equivalent in Dan 4:14, 22, 29, 32), and the author may be alluding to the absolute nature of divine commands.[103] Indeed, Qohelet's reflections subsequently move into the issue of divine judgment (8:10ff.). The sage may not directly advocate obedience to divine commandments in 4:17—5:6 and 8:5, but neither is he opposed to or unconcerned with the commandments. Qohelet's vision of piety can by no means be narrowly identified with "legal" or "nomistic" piety, but it does encompass obedience to the commandments.

More remarkable about the postscript, however, are the striking echoes of the familiar theme of enjoyment. After issuing the dual imperatives to fear God and keep the commandments, the author provides two rationales. First, he states succinctly, *zeh kol-hā'ādām*.[104]

---

102 The *miṣwâ* in 8:5 refers to the same thing as *pî-melek* in 8:2 and *dĕbar-melek* in 8:3.

103 Choon Leong Seow, "'Beyond These, My Son, Beware!': The Epilogue of Qohelet Revisited," in *Wisdom, You are My Sister* (ed. M. L. Barré; CBQMS 29; Washington, D.C.: Catholic Biblical Association, 1997), 139 n. 55; idem, *Ecclesiastes*, 281.

104 This phrase has posed difficulties for interpreters, as far back as the Talmudic teachers (b. *Ber.* 6b). Rabbi Eleazar proposes that it means that the commands to fear and obey God are the most important things in life. In line with that interpretation, Whitley suggests original *zh kl<l> 'dm* with the final lamed in *kelal* ("general rule" or "principle") lost by haplography, "this is the principle of humanity." Whitley, *Koheleth: His Language and Thought*, 105. Others suggest that the phrase is a pregnant expression indicating "the entire duty of humanity," or the like. Gordis, *Kohelet*, 355; Crenshaw, *Ecclesiastes*, 189, 192; Murphy, *Ecclesiastes*; Longman, *Ecclesiastes*, 282. However, the phrase *kol-hā'ādām* means "everyone" throughout the Old Testament,

The concise formulation is probably elliptical for "this should characterize everyone" or "thus should everyone be."[105] Apart from prefixed particles and prepositions, *kol/kōl* is the most frequently used word in Ecclesiastes. The ubiquity of this word reflects the comprehensive nature of Qohelet's inquiry, epitomized in his claim that he applied his intelligence to "all that is done under heaven" (1:13). This sweeping word appropriately punctuates the final two verses four times, as the book is drawn to a close. The word *ʾādām* is another frequently used word, indicating Qohelet's primary concern with the existential dilemmas of humanity and the question of "what is good for humanity (*běnê hāʾ ādām*) to do under heaven" (2:3). The full expression *kol-hāʾ ādām*, however, occurs only three other times in Ecclesiastes (3:13; 5:18; 7:2), and notably, each time in the context of Qohelet's reflections on the vitality—and fragility—of joy. In the first two instances, Qohelet asserts that enjoyment is God's gift for "every human being," but that the gift is a contingent one. The third occurrence speaks of the universality of death ("it is better to go to the house of mourning than to the house of feasting, for that is the end of every human being"), the ultimate contingency that gives such urgency to Qohelet's call to enjoyment.[106] Qohelet's use of the phrase *kol-hāʾ ādām* thus highlights these two things to be true for everyone: the possibility of enjoyment and the tragic certainty of death. Now, the postscript remarks that the fear of God and obedience to the commandments likewise applies to "every human being." While the postscript does not explicitly identify enjoyment as a component of religious duty, there is an echo of Qohelet's theology of enjoyment in the rhetoric of what is universally true for all humanity.

The resonance is even more pronounced in the subsequent rationale: "God will bring every deed to judgment for every hidden thing, whether good or bad." Qohelet speaks about judgment in a number of places (3:17; 8:6; 11:9), but the correspondence between 12:14a and 11:9c is especially striking. As others have already noted, there is a remarkable similarity in phraseology between these verses:

---

and elsewhere in Ecclesiastes as well. It never represents a construct chain signifying "all of the human."

105 Compare *ʿammēkā nědābôt* "your people are willing" (Ps 110:3); *waʾănî těpillâ* "I am a person of prayer" (Ps 109:4); *ʾănî šālôm* "I am a peaceful person" (Ps 120:7); *těmôl ʾanaḥnû* "we are fleeting" (Job 8:9). Similarly, Seow, "for every mortal is to be so" (*Ecclesiastes*, 390); Fox, "this is [the substance of] every man," or "this rule applies to everyone" (*A Time to Tear Down*, 349, 362f); Whybray, "these admonitions apply to all ..." (*Ecclesiastes*, 173); Christianson, "for this [applies to] everyone" (*A Time to Tell*, 114).

106 See discussion of these texts in chapter 2.

11:9c   *kî ʿal-kol-ʾēlleh yĕbîʾĕkā hāʾĕlōhîm*   *bammišpāṭ*
12:14a   *kî ʾet-kol-maʿăśeh*   *hāʾĕlōhîm yābîʾ bĕmišpāṭ ʿal kol-neʿlām.*

The first of these motive clauses occurs in the joy passage that concludes Qohelet's discourse (11:7—12:7). In its immediate context, the phrase *kol-ʾēlleh* (the basis of judgment, introduced by the preposition *ʿal*) refers to the imperatives "enjoy," "let your heart cheer you," and "follow the way of your heart" in 11:9. In other words, Qohelet urges the youth to enjoy life because God will hold humanity accountable for it.[107] When scholars compare this text with 12:14a, they generally do so in order to highlight the differences between the two: the former is narrowly concerned with the imperative of enjoyment, while the latter is both more universal in scope (*kol-maʿăśeh, ʿal kol-neʿlām*) and more specific in its association with the commandments.[108] Yet the language in the postscript is so reminiscent of Qohelet's imperative of enjoyment in 11:9, it can hardly be incidental. As demonstrated above, life-centered joy is an important dimension of Qohelet's piety. So, even while the postscript "thematizes" along the lines of legal piety and divine judgment, it does so with language that recalls Qohelet's own teachings on piety with its emphasis on joy. Furthermore, it may not be amiss to note the possible hint of eschatological judgment in the claim that "everything hidden" will be revealed (12:14b). [109] Interpreters usually note this possible nuance, again, as evidence of the postscript's dissimilar orientation: it opens up an interpretive trajectory not envisioned by Qohelet. Yet, the intertextual resonances with 11:9 direct the reader to Qohelet's final commendation of enjoyment, which too evokes the specter of the end of the world in order to heighten the urgency of his ethic of enjoyment (12:1—7).[110]

Another important aspect of Qohelet's fear of God is its close association with a theology of divine inscrutability. God is to be feared because God is wholly Other, utterly beyond mortal comprehension. Qohelet reinforces this essential point in various ways: God's ways are "eternal," mortals are bound to the moment (3:11—14); God is in heaven, humanity upon the earth (5:1); God's ways are

---

107 Contra Murphy who asserts, "[Qohelet] recognizes God as judge but nowhere does he attempt to ... motivate human action on the basis of divine judgment" (*Ecclesiastes*, 126).

108 Seow, "The Epilogue of Qohelet Revisited," 139; idem, *Ecclesiastes*, 395.

109 Ginsburg, *The Song of Songs and Cohleleth*, 478; Gordis, *Koheleth—the Man and His World*, 283; Childs, *Introduction to the Old Testament as Scripture*, 588—90.

110 See discussion of this text in chapter 2.

incomprehensible and illogical (3:14; 7:13, 14; 8:17); divine judgment is sure, but entirely enigmatic in its timing and way (3:17; 8:6—7). The postscript may catch something of this mystery in the phrase "all that is hidden."[111] Moreover, just as Qohelet speaks of the opaqueness of divine activity in terms of the unpredictable alternation of good and bad, the postscript now suggests that God will somehow be accountable for every deed, *'im-ṭôb wĕ'im rā'*. The one who "seeks out that which is pursued" (3:15) will bring every deed—every incomprehensible, absurd, mysterious deed—into judgment.

In recent scholarship, Qohelet has been heralded as a courageous iconoclast who subverts rigid theological systems and casts doubt on any attempt to establish absolute meaning. Many discover in him an ancient kindred spirit to the postmodern deconstructive critic, and the surge of interest in Ecclesiastes in the past few decades attests to its profound relevance for the present context. Those who relish his irreverence, however, may too readily dismiss the constructive aspect of its theological discourse. The literary shape of the book militates against this. The final words of the book affirm the central tenets of Israel's faith in its call to fear and obey God, and they must not be dismissed as an irrelevant or misguided appendage. But neither must they be allowed to overwrite or blunt the subversive edge of Qohelet's message. Their placement suggests, first, that Qohelet's vision of piety—with all its probing and unresolved questions—is not antithetical to obedience. Indeed, it is a genuine and legitimate form of piety that can coexist with obedience to the commandments. The postscript's affirmation of the fear of God is not a nostalgic reversion to the secure world of conventional wisdom, or an overeager adaptation to a future wisdom.[112] It comes through the vehicle of Qohelet's tortuous journey through the contingencies of human experience to his discovery of what is possible, what is good, what is right for mortals to do in this world. The final articulation of the meaning of piety, through its subtle hints and echoes, valorizes Qohelet's inquiry and discovery. In doing so, it insists that any notion of piety that is rigidly associated with a prescribed set of norms is insufficient for addressing the pressing concerns of humanity. Existential integrity is indispensable to piety, even if that means raising questions that challenge the

---

111 Murphy, *Ecclesiastes*, 126.

112 Sheppard points out a similar conjoining of the fear of God and divine commandments (and wisdom//Torah) throughout Ben Sirah (see, for example, Sir 1:26—30) and suggests that the postscript belongs to Ben Sirah's period or later. But as noted by Seow, the association between wisdom and the Torah is attested in the Old Testament long before Ben Sirah's generation (cf. Ezra; Neh; Deut 4:6).

fundamentals of doctrine. There is an earthiness about Qohelet that demands that genuine faith be grounded in the realities of human experience. One must confront life head on, with all its inequities and messy contradictions, even while flinching in pain and bewilderment. One must also accept these same contradictions—a mix of the good and the bad—in every human life, including one's own.

3.7 Conclusion

"That is the eternal, as distinct from the temporal gospel: one can love God but one must fear him."[113] Crenshaw begins his discussion of Eccl 3:11 with this quote concerning the universal experience of fear in the presence of the divine. This dictum he believes to be epitomized in Qohelet's theology, a theology in which no trace of divine love remains and fear of God stands entirely alone. The theory that fear, in fact, gave birth to religion was articulated as early as the fourth century B.C.E. by the Greek philosopher Democritus, and later captured by Statius in the oft-quoted line *primus in orbe deos fecit timor* ("at the beginning on earth, fear created the gods").[114] A similar premise lies behind the theory that in the earliest stages of Israelite religion, fear dominated and determined the forms of worship, leading to acts of propitiation or flight before the deity. This sense of terror, however, was accompanied by a simultaneous longing for the presence of the deity, a trust in the benevolence of the deity. As articulated by Otto, the numinous is encountered as both *tremendum* and *fascinans*.[115] This inner polarity and dynamic eventually led to a semantic development in the concept of sacred fear, in which the element of literal fear receded and "fear of God" became tantamount to "religion" or "piety."[116] Pfeiffer articulates

---

113 C. J. Jung, *Answer to Job* (1969), 169; cited by Crenshaw, "The Eternal Gospel," 25.

114 *Thebais* iii.661. Epicurus and Lucretius were also proponents of this notion. It should be noted that although these philosophers believed that awe, dread and fear were the sources of religious behavior, they demanded that the philosopher must put aside such irrational fears and instead follow the gods in their beatific, calm and rational way of life. Lucretius's full exposition of the theory is found in *De rerum natura* v.1161—1240. See W. Jaeger, *The Theology of the Early Greek Philosophers* (Oxford, 1947), 182—83, 250; M. P. Nilsson, *Geschichte der griechischen Religion* (Munich, 1941), 39; H. F. Fuhs, "*yārē'*" *TDOT* 6:290—92.

115 Rudolf Otto, *The Idea of the Holy: An Inquiry into the Non-Rational Factor in the Idea of the Divine and Its Relation to the Rational* (London: Oxford, 1957). See also Derousseaux, *La crainte de Dieu*, 13—20.

116 Bamberger, "Fear and Love of God in the Old Testament," 39—53; P. J. Becker, *Gottesfurcht im Alten Testament* (AnBib 95; Rome: Pontifico Instituto Biblico, 1965), 75; Fuhs, "*yārē'*" *TDOT* 6:290—91.

the general consensus when he says, that fear of God is "the earliest term for religion in biblical Hebrew, and indeed in Semitic languages in general."[117]

Fear of God is an important concept in Old Testament religion. The expression in its various permutations is frequently attested (approximately 250 times), and is particularly important in wisdom literature. One scholar suggests that perhaps here is the elusive "key" to an Old Testament theology that can integrate the "problematic" wisdom corpus.[118] But the concept is an elusive one, with a wide range of connotations and nuances that are not always sharply distinguished.[119] In a number of Old Testament passages, the primary sense of numinous awe persists.[120] More often, however, the subjective element of fear seems largely attenuated and fear of God indicates instead one of various expressions of religious duty.[121] Indeed, the verb *yr'* often appears parallel to other verbs that indicate devotion to God: "to love" (*'hb*), "to cleave" (*dbq*), "to serve" (*'bd*), "to keep commandments" (*šmr*), "to listen" (*šm'*), "to walk in God's ways" (*hlk bidrākāyw*), etc. This suggests that the antithesis between love and fear in Crenshaw's citation above is significantly attenuated for Old Testament writings. Indeed, the two terms "are practically synonymous and interchangeable," both having the general meaning of "religion."[122]

---

117 R. H. Pfeiffer, "The Fear of God," *IEJ* 5 (1955): 41. See also Bamberger, "Fear and Love of God in the Old Testament," 39−53; C. J. de Catanzaro, "Fear, Knowledge, and Love," 166−73. See Derousseaux, *La crainte de Dieu*, 21−66, for a survey of Egyptian, Mesopotamian, and Ugaritic literature that addresses the notion of sacred fear.

118 Walter C. Kaiser, "Integrating Wisdom Theology into Old Testament Theology: Ecclesiastes 3:10−15," in *A Tribute to Gleason Archer* (ed. W. C. Kaiser and R. F. Youngblood; Chicago: Moody, 1986), 197−209. See also Henri Blocher, "The Fear of the Lord as the 'Principle' of Wisdom," *TB* 28 (1977): 23.

119 Moreover, even within the same context, fear of God may take on different connotations. Note, for example, Exod 20:18, where in the context of theophany Moses says to the people, "Do not be afraid; for God has come only to test you and to put the fear of him upon so that you do not sin."

120 Gen 3:10; 28:17; Exod 15:11; Deut 7:21; 10:17, 21; 1 Sam 12:19f; 2 Sam 6:9; 7:23; Is 64:3; Zeph 2:11; Pss 47:2; 65:5; 66:3; 66:5; 76:7, 8, 12; 89:7; 105:22; 111:9; 1 Chr 13:12; 1 Chr 17:21.

121 In Deuteronom(ist)ic literature, the vocabulary of fear is used to express loyalty to the covenant God, devotion to the Torah, and adherence to the cult. In the Elohist narratives of the Pentateuch, fear of God commonly signifies commitment to God, or a moral sensitivity cultivated by the knowledge of God (Wolff). An ethical sense is present in the Holiness Code as well, where the command to fear God concludes various injunctions concerning humanitarian conduct (see Lev. 19:14, 30, 32; 25:17, 36, 43; 26:2). In the Psalter, the verb typically appears in the participial form, and "those who fear God" constitute the community of devout YHWH worshippers.

122 Bamberger, "Fear and Love of God in the Old Testament," 50.

When literal fear is intended, the Old Testament often employs other verbs (*pḥd, gwr, ḥwl, ḥrd, ḥtt,* etc.) but even these verbs may be used as literary variants for *yr*'.

Barré has argued that the fear of God lies at the heart of wisdom's worldview.[123] According to this worldview, a pervasive orderliness is built into creation by a sovereign God, and a wise person finds meaningful existence by living in integrity within that order. The first step to such an existence is the fear of God. Concerning its fundamental importance von Rad says: "[Israel] was, in all seriousness, of the opinion that effective knowledge about God is the only thing that puts a man into a right relationship with the objects of his perception, that it enables him to ask questions more pertinently, to take stock of relationships more effectively and generally to have a better awareness of circumstances."[124] In other words, true knowledge of the self and knowledge of the world flowed first and foremost from knowledge of God. Or, as the sages put it, "the fear of the Lord is the beginning of wisdom." Hence, fear of God essentially represents the basic and proper stance of mortals before the divine. From this stance, humanity can discern the proper interrelatedness of things, including their own place in the order of creation, with both its potentials and limitations. And although fear of God is often closely associated with the doctrine of retribution and the blessings of a long and secure life (particularly in Prov 10–22; see also Prov 23:18; 24:14), or with moral and upright character (parallel with *tam, yāšār, ṣaddîq, sûr mēra*' in Prov 3:7; 8:13; Job 1:1, 8), the sages also acknowledges the limits of human wisdom to master life.

Yet Ecclesiastes is often singled out as the one book that thoroughly preserves the primitive notion of enervating terror, without tempering it in any way with a belief in the deity's beneficence. Its skeptical theology, it is argued, intentionally overturns the traditional wisdom understanding of fear of God, and identifies it once again with its original sense of terror before the numinous. The deity's terrifying and pervasive presence demands that the mortal remain ever vigilant against the deity, so as not to incite divine displeasure. As E. Pfeiffer concludes, "If 'fear of God' is of any avail, it cannot be ordinary fear, but only the fear that makes people tremble in the presence of the holy God."[125]

---

123 Barré, "Fear of God and the World View of Wisdom," 42. See also Derousseaux, *La crainte de Dieu*, 301–357.

124 von Rad, *Wisdom in Israel*, 67–68.

125 Egon Pfeiffer, "Die Gottesfurcht im Buche Kohelet," 151. Similarly, Fuhs, "*yārē*'" 312–13.

To be sure, Qohelet's notion of fearing God is most insistently associated with a theology of divine transcendence. The emphasis is on the deity's essential Otherness: God is eternal while humanity is confined to individual times and moments; God dwells in heaven but mortals are forever earthbound; God's ways are utterly inscrutable, uncontrollable, and inescapable. Qohelet's God is the *deus absconditus*, and humanity—for good or ill—encounters this hidden and mysterious God everywhere in the universe. Hence, fearing God involves a coming to terms with humanity's place "on earth," inescapably marked by *hebel*. There is nothing in this life that humans can grasp and hold on to forever: no possession, no knowledge, no theology, no experience, no joy. Any attempt to strain for the impossible or master the mysterious is destined to lead only to frustration and failure. Those who fear God, instead, must acknowledge their creaturely status and cope with the tragic limitations of the human condition. But Qohelet's explication of the fear of God does not end there, but goes on to speak at length about its positive dimension. Fearing God also means recognizing and embracing the possibilities that are happily a part of humanity's lot. Fearing God means recognizing and living with *both* the impossibilities and possibilities of being human. According to Qohelet's earthy realism, a recognition of human limitations can lead to a profound freedom. The one who fears God becomes free to embrace life all the more fully and enjoy the gift of each moment of goodness present to them. It means knowing that life is beyond one's control, but each moment is for the taking, by the gift of God.

Fear of God, properly understood, is more than a "stance" or "attitude." It has a behavioral component as well, a full range of humanity's response to the deity.[126] As elsewhere in the Old Testament, the command to fear God in Ecclesiastes appears together with other verbs that signify religious duty: watch your conduct while engaging in the activities of the cult (4:17); exercise appropriate thoughtfulness and restraint in your speech to the deity (5:1); fulfill your vows (5:3—5); go forth in life with "both" (7:18); indeed, keep the commandments (12:13b). All these things are important aspects of piety for Qohelet. But remarkably, the most emphatic of his associations is the vital relationship between fearing God and enjoying life. If fear and joy represent the two poles of the human experience of the divine (Otto's categories of *tremendum* and *fascinans*), then Qohelet's portrait of piety puts a surprising twist on the practice of religion. As noted above, his

---

126 Barré, "Fear of God and the World View of Wisdom," 43; Bamberger, "Fear and Love of God in the Old Testament," 39.

theological discourse underscores the distance between the divine and human. Nevertheless, the mortal is not entirely bereft of some means of experiencing and enjoying the divine presence. Qohelet points to the world of the profane, and directs his audience to enjoy the simple pleasures of daily life as the gifts of God. This, he claims, is a genuine expression of the fear of God, humanity's religious duty. All of life — even the seemingly mundane activities of eating, drinking, sleeping, working — is the arena in which God's presence is to be experienced. Life can thus become "sacramental," in the broad sense of the word. Food and drink, work and play become the tangible and sustaining means by which God's grace is communicated to the human being. Engaging in the traditional forms of religion is, of course, a legitimate expression of piety, and Qohelet gives that aspect of religion its rightful due. But of greater importance to the sage is the piety that extends beyond sacred times and sacred places, and expresses itself in the enjoyment and sharing of life's mundane pleasures.

Qohelet's exposition of fearing God, in the end, is an exposition of humanity's religious duty that is guided by traditional wisdom and time-honored theological truths. But the piety that he espouses is forged out of an unflagging engagement with existential realities. It demands a realistic assessment of the human condition with all its ambiguities and contradictions, both on a personal level and a systemic one. It recognizes that the deity dispenses justice (and injustice!) in an incalculable manner. Moral agents are free to face and reflect upon the inequities of the world and shake their heads in astonishment and dismay; they are free to ponder the viability of traditional theological claims in light of existential dilemmas. Qohelet insists that genuine piety requires an on-going negotiation of the tensions between theological principles and the messiness of real life. For it is only through an authentic knowledge of the self and of the world that one may arrive at a form of piety that is therapeutic and life-giving, in short, "good" for humanity.

Conclusion

Qohelet's Theology of Enjoyment

4.1 Introduction

Until only a couple of decades ago, the wisdom books suffered neglect in the theological expositions of the Old Testament, and in the preaching and teaching ministry of the church. Ecclesiastes, in particular, was regarded as a strange, even dangerous, book that stands at the periphery of the canon, a shrill voice of protest from "the farthest frontiers of Yahwistic faith."[1] In recent years, much headway has been made to reappropriate this much neglected body of scripture by both the academy and the church. Indeed, the current turning to the wisdom books is a far cry from Preuss's warning that ministers ought never to preach from this illegitimate expression of Israel's religion![2] However, concerning the interpretation of Ecclesiastes, there are some things that remain unchanged. Von Rad's assessment of the book cited above still persists today, as evident in Brueggemann's recent characterization of the book as "the very edge of the Old Testament."[3] Most interpreters still emphasize the book's profound skepticism and stark negativity as its defining feature. What is different, however, is that this dimension of the book is no longer viewed as a threat to biblical theology and faith, but as a critical witness from within—if only the "very edge"— that opens up alternative ways of engaging in theological discourse. Indeed, the book is often heralded as an early embodiment of the deconstructive spirit and therefore eminently relevant for the postmodern age. This approach to Ecclesiastes has opened up promising lines of investigation and has been a boon for biblical

---

1   Gerhard von Rad, *Old Testament Theology* (trans. D. M. G. Stalker; 2 vols.; New York/Evanston/San Francisco/London: Harper & Row, 1962-65), 2:458; translation of *Theologie des Alten Testaments* (Munich: Kaiser, 1957—1960).

2   Horst Dietrich Preuss, "Erwägungen zum theologischen Ort alttestamentlicher Weisheitsliteratur," *EvT* 30 (1970): 393—417.

3   Walter Brueggemann, *Theology of the Old Testament: Testimony, Dispute, Advocacy* (Minneapolis: Fortress Press, 1997), 393.

studies. Such readings, however, have offered little in the way of constructive theology and ethics.

Others still question whether the book can even be considered to be a theological work.[4] More often than not, Ecclesiastes is characterized as "a book about ideas," and "not a book about God."[5] To be sure, Ecclesiastes does not offer a systematic or sustained exposition about God. Yet the author speaks about God throughout his discourse. Indeed, the word *'ĕlōhîm* is among his most frequently used words, occurring some forty times—even more frequently than the much touted *hebel*. The book repeatedly examines and expounds on the activity of God, and the inscrutable logic behind divine acting, giving, and judging. Moreover, the fear of God, the ancient Near Eastern idiom for religious duty, appears prominently in the book. Along with the other wisdom books, Ecclesiastes acknowledges that the moral life begins with a fundamental orientation around God and the activity of God. Indeed, this book, too, has much to say about the ways of God in this world, and how moral beings are to live in response.

Happily, in recent years, a number of scholars have sought to recover the theological message of the book.[6] Qohelet's theology has appropriately been described as life-centered theology, that is, a theology grounded in and stemming from the life experiences of ordinary people. In this regard, Ecclesiastes is true to the legacy of the wisdom tradition, with its empirical, contextual, and practical approach to theological reflection. This study has sought to make a further contribution in this direction. More specifically, it has argued that the book's theological and ethical claims are largely communicated through Qohelet's conception of enjoyment as religious duty. Through this unique vision of piety, Ecclesiastes addresses the most pressing concerns of daily human existence and gives effective guidance for navigating one's way in a world beyond human control. But his theology of joy offers more than a means of merely coping or just getting by, as is commonly argued. It provides practical and

---

4   Note the interrogative mood in Murphy's, "Qoheleth and Theology?" 30—33.

5   Towner, "The Book of Ecclesiastes," in *New Interpreter's Bible*, 5:283. The book has been likened to the random musings of a philosopher in the style of Pascal's *Pensées* (Roland E. Murphy, "The Pensées of Coheleth," *CBQ* 17 [1955]: 304—14) or Marcus Aurelius's *Meditations* (Rudolph, 1959). Others have classified the book as a "philosophical essay" (Glasser, 1970) or diatribe (Lohfink, 1980).

6   See, for example, Choon-Leong Seow, "Rehabilitating 'the Preacher': Qohelet's Theological Reflections in Context," 90—116; idem, "Theology When Everything is Out of Control," *Int* (July 2001): 237—49; Whybray, "Qoheleth as a Theologian," 239—65.

compassionate instructions on how a person may achieve the greatest human flourishing in such a world.

Although scholars have long noted the importance of joy and fear of God in Ecclesiastes, there has not yet been an extended analysis of these two motifs in relationship to one another. More commonly, fear and joy have been understood to be antithetical to one another. Jerome's comments cited at the end of chapter 3 reflect an interpretive assumption that has been operative for many readers of Ecclesiastes through the ages: Qohelet's commendation of enjoyment is a hedonistic impulse that is fundamentally at odds with genuine piety. For other interpreters who regard joy more positively, enjoyment of life is the *summum bonum* over against the fear of God. According to Lohfink, for example, joy has "revelatory" status in Qohelet's theology because it temporarily enables a person to forget the fear of God (i.e. their own finitude).[7] In one way or another, then, fear of God and joy have been pitted against each other.[8] This study, by contrast, has argued that these two important themes are not antithetical to one another, but rather positively correlated in Qohelet's theological rhetoric. In claiming that the enjoyment of life is a matter of religious duty, the sage redefines the meaning of both enjoyment and piety. This concluding chapter will offer a synthesis of Qohelet's theology of enjoyment and some important ethical implications that derive from it.

4.2 The Normativity of Enjoyment

I have argued that Qohelet's theology of enjoyment addresses the most basic and most urgent questions regarding human existence: What does it mean to be human? What is the norm for a meaningful and complete human life? And how does one live such a life in a world beyond human control? For this sage, the answers to these fundamental questions of the wisdom enterprise lie in his conception of joy as divine gift and divine imperative: it is in the regular practice of joy that a person experiences the authentic and complete life intended by God for humanity. In other words, Qohelet's theology of enjoyment affirms that enjoyment is the mark and measure of genuine humanity.

---

7   So, Lohfink, "Qoheleth 5:17–19–Revelation by Joy," 632.

8   Others have suggested a positive relationship between joy and fear; but since their primary interests lay elsewhere, their comments concerning this relationship are made only in passing, without being grounded in exegetical and rhetorical analysis. Even so, their observations are an important reflection of how emphatically the two are related in Qohelet's rhetoric.

This theological claim is both descriptive and prescriptive. Qohelet not only presents a portrayal of the authentic human life, he also urgently commends a life according to this norm. The purpose of his admonitions is ultimately to motivate people to forsake what is harmful to their well-being and embrace a way of life that will enable them not only to cope with perplexing realities, but also flourish as human beings.

On the one hand, Qohelet's conception of normative humanity is undergirded by a theology of God's inscrutable activity. True humanity is discerned in relationship to God and God's activity in the world. The sage believes that the world as a whole is ordered by the deity, and that norms for human life are a part of this divine design. At the same time, however, he is forced to acknowledge that the logic of this design is inaccessible to the human mind. God is wholly Other, utterly beyond space and time, while mortals are confined to their ephemeral days under the sun. Yet humanity's place before this mysterious God is marked not only by its troublesome limitations and boundaries, but also its invigorating possibilities for good. Enjoyment as religious duty is a matter of acknowledging and embracing both. It encounters both of these dimensions of the human condition and fully engages both. Those who deny or evade either are not truly enjoying life.

On the other hand, Qohelet derives the normativity of enjoyment from what he "sees" in the world. The sage knows that if his teachings are to be compelling and life-changing, they must resonate with human experience. So he engages in a rigorous and sustained examination of the human condition. Again and again he registers what he observes of life under the sun, employing the verb $r'h$ twenty-six times to speak of his personal observations. He then communicates his findings through literary vehicles that capture the imagination of his audience and ingrain his teachings in their minds: gripping anecdotes of particular individuals who failed to enjoy to their detriment; memorable proverbs concerning the folly of greed and the wisdom of contentment; an autobiographical narrative of the wise king *par excellence* who discovers that everything in this life lies in the hands of a mysterious God; an enigmatic and evocative poem concerning the tragic end of all creation. In short, the sage effectively draws from the resources of the wisdom tradition—both its method and its various forms of instruction—to lend weight to his own reflections, and to communicate his ethic of joy in a most compelling way. He repeatedly draws the conclusion that enjoyment is humanity's most urgent responsibility because it both reflects the divine will and addresses the deepest human needs.

Qohelet's theology of enjoyment is, first, a positive affirmation of what humans *can*—indeed, *must*—have in order to thrive as human beings. These necessary ingredients are identified in terms of the basic pleasures that sustain life: daily bread, meaningful work, rejuvenating rest, and companionship of loved ones. Enjoyment is located resolutely in the fulfillment of these most fundamental needs. In the language of ethicist Paul Lehman, these things are what God provides in order to make and keep human life human.[9] They describe in concrete terms the desirable goal of life. By contrast, Qohelet suggests that without the capacity to enjoy these things, life becomes severely impoverished (see 6:3—6). So, he urges his audience to take up every opportunity for enjoyment and enjoy to the full. Even a certain measure of indulgence is validated. Enjoyment is a grateful acceptance of God's gifts, indeed, a celebration of divine generosity whenever it is displayed. Hence, if and when God gives much, people ought to enjoy much in grateful acceptance (see 5:17—19; 9:7—10; 11:7—10).

One may protest that in a culture driven by consumerism and hedonism (as is generally the case in contemporary North American society), there is scarcely a need to tell people to enjoy themselves. The objection is a legitimate and important one. Yet it is precisely because of the prevalent consumerist ethos that a biblical theology of enjoyment must be articulated anew. Qohelet's theology, characterized as the "philosophy of an acquisitive society,"[10] addresses a culture that is fixated on commercial gains beyond healthy boundaries. Qohelet speaks directly to the dangers of such impulses through his explication of what enjoyment is, more precisely, through his insistence on what enjoyment is *not*. By correlating enjoyment with the fear of God, he not only affirms what humans may have by the grace of God, he also establishes what they *cannot* appropriately have. By divine design, human beings are incapable of possessing anything inalienably in this unpredictable and fleeting life. Yet Qohelet observes people toiling away and rushing about to grab hold of more—more goods, more power, more knowledge, more wisdom and righteousness—all in an obsessed attempt to find some advantage in life. They are "demented with the mania of owning things,"[11] as it were, and perpetually dissatisfied. The seductive lure of something more and something better only robs them of the joys that are present here and now. This

---

9   Paul Lehman, *Ethics in a Christian Context* (New York/Evanston: Harper & Row, 1963). See especially the chapter entitled "What God is Doing in the World," 99—101.

10   Bickerman, *Four Strange Books of the Bible*, 139—167.

11   The expression comes from Walt Whitman's "Song of Myself" (in *Leaves of Grass*).

"mania" is antithetical to the contentment that is the hallmark of Qohelet's ethic of enjoyment. Such efforts only impede genuine flourishing, leading only to frustration and despair, and Qohelet repeatedly declares them to be *hebel*.

Qohelet's commentary on his social world, then, is precisely what contemporary society needs to hear. The disease of dissatisfaction that Qohelet observes in his world in fact takes on a heightened virulence in today's culture, shaped by its sophisticated technology of mass communication in service to a consumerist ethos. The dominant culture constantly bombards the public with the message that to be human is to be a consumer. A full life is a life filled with more, and more is always accessible and attainable. Qohelet's ethic of enjoyment opposes precisely these excesses. It issues the warning that this cultural ideology is a tragic deformation of appropriate human longings; it denounces the inflated expectations and inordinate desires that plague and threaten human society. Qohelet's ethic of enjoyment, then, is a recuperation of the norm. Enjoyment is emphatically not about the pursuit of more — not even the pursuit of joy — but the glad appreciation of what is already in one's possession by the gift of God. It means that the human becomes free *not* to grasp, *not* to possess, *not* to know.

Another observation must be made, however. Qohelet's theology of enjoyment addresses not only the secular culture at large, but also a potentially harmful attitude toward enjoyment more specific to Christian circles. One finds in various Christian traditions a long-standing tendency to regard material joys and natural human desires with an attitude of suspicion, if not disdain. Whether it is traced to an Augustinian anthropology or an austere Protestant work ethic, the church has often stigmatized pleasurable experiences as fundamentally sinful. This tendency is evident in the history of the book's interpretation as well. The trend in patristic and medieval interpretation is particularly telling. Uneasy with Qohelet's exuberant commendation of this-worldly joys, interpreters appealed to the verdict of "vanity" to contend that "contempt of the world" — not enjoyment of its gifts — is the primary ethic propounded by the book. Indeed, the book came to be an endorsement of the ascetic life.[12] This reading

---

12   See Roland E. Murphy, "Qoheleth Interpreted: The Bearing of the Past on the Present," *VT* 32 (1982): 331 – 37; idem, *Ecclesiastes*, xlix – lii; Beryl Smalley, *Medieval Exegesis of Wisdom Literature* (ed. R. E. Murphy; Atlanta: Scholars Press, 1986), 40; Svend Holm-Nielsen, "On the Interpretation of Qoheleth in Early Christianity," *VT* 24 (1974): 168 – 77. This interpretation of the book is found even earlier in the commentary of Gregory Thaumaturgus, who says that the purpose of the book is "to show that all the affairs and pursuits of men are vain and useless, in order to lead us to the contemplation of heavenly things."

strategy is not confined to this early period of Christianity, however. One of the better-known comments on Ecclesiastes in the Christian tradition comes from Thomas à Kempis, who offers the following interpretation in his *Imitation of Christ*: "'Vanity of Vanities, all is vanity,' unless we serve God and love him with our whole heart (*Eccles* 1, 2). Oh, this is the highest and safest wisdom, that by contempt of the world we endeavor to please God."[13] To be sure, these interpreters caught something of the spirit of the book—Qohelet does indeed declare all things in this world to be fleeting. But the recognition of life's transience does not lead him to despise the things of the world, but to prize them all the more and see in them humanity's realm for moral living.

The long-standing misgivings concerning material joys persist even today, albeit in more tempered and subtle forms. For communities of faith that are bound to this religious ethos, Qohelet's theology of enjoyment may come as a restorative and liberating word. It declares that the whole-hearted and full-blooded enjoyment of God's provisions in this world is sanctioned, even commanded, by God. Qohelet thereby gives a profound value to *this world* and *this moment*. He allows no world beyond *this* to justify a flight from the responsibility of the present. Following the lead of Qohelet who speaks of enjoyment as an expression of piety, one may even venture to call this-worldly joy a spiritual discipline. The life of piety is cultivated not only by prayer, meditation, worship, and other "religious" observances, but also by concentrating on the responsibility of what is at hand, and engaging joyously in the ordinary activities of daily life with gratitude and contentment. When these activities are recognized and taken up as God-given possibilities for the benefit of humanity, even the profane becomes a channel of divine grace.

4.3 The Ethic of Joy and Social Responsibility

Ecclesiastes is often charged with neglecting the important dimension of community in its search for a meaningful existence. The moral life is discerned and practiced in relationship to the neighbor; Qohelet, however, is said to dwell in utter isolation, with social concerns being largely absent in his self-referential monologue. When communal institutions are depicted at all, they are "on the verge of collapse or

---

13   Thomas à Kempis, *The Following of Christ* (ed. J. van Ginneken; New York: America Press, 1937), 14.

plagued with the withering effects of indifference."[14] Here in
Ecclesiastes, "the selfishness of wisdom literature in general finds full
expression ... [Qohelet] assesses friendship in terms of protection from
robbers and warmth on cold nights. He evaluates the world in terms of
his own safety and comfort."[15] If social concerns were indeed absent
from the book, or oriented only to meet self-serving needs, one would
have to be wary about Qohelet's theology of enjoyment. The validation
of enjoyment could easily be misappropriated to rationalize a self-
indulgent materialism at the expense of neighbor. It is especially vital
to consider the social implications of such a theology in a world where
a large proportion of the human race still must contend daily with
hunger, disease, and oppressive working conditions. All too often,
these tragic and objectionable circumstances are perpetuated—
wittingly or unwittingly—by the privileged members of the global
community who all too readily "enjoy" consuming the world's goods.
A revalidation of enjoyment must keep this larger world in view.

And Qohelet's ethic prompts us to do so with diligence. While an
interest in communal life may not be foregrounded in his reflections, it
is nevertheless clearly in his field of vision. Indeed, a vision of how a
person ought to live in relationship with neighbor undergirds his ethic.
This is evident, first of all, in what the sage decries as *hebel*. The intense
bitterness and pathos with which he laments social injustices betrays
the belief that life ought not to be so. For him, the most tragic scenario
in life is the case of isolated individuals, devoid of community, who
wearily toil away at life in total alienation. Eccl 4 in particular speaks
poignantly about this.[16] First, the sage laments the plight of the
oppressed (4:1−4). What disturbs the sage is not only the fact of
oppression, but also the fact that those who suffer have no
compassionate companion who might allay their suffering and perhaps
embolden them to stand up against their tormentors. Twice he intones
plaintively that they have "no one to comfort them" (4:1b, 1c). He then
describes another absurd state of affairs: a solitary miser works
obsessively to no end, depriving himself of all that is good (4:7−8).
This person is utterly alone (*yēš ʾeḥad*), with no companion, no son, no
brother—absolutely no "other" (*ʾên šēnî*) with whom to share the riches

---

14   William Brown, *Character in Crisis*, 159. But see his more recent article, where he
     asserts instead that Qohelet "places great value on community" (idem, "'Whatever
     Your Hand Finds to Do' Qoheleth's Work Ethic," 283).

15   Crenshaw, *Ecclesiastes*, 25.

16   As noted in chapter 3 above, the motif of "two" or "second" unifies the various
     sayings in chapter 4. This idea is communicated not only by the vocabulary of
     "two," but also by other terms that designate a counterpart (*rēʿēhû*, v. 4; *ḥābērô*, v.
     10).

he has amassed. In both of these cases, the primary focus of Qohelet's lament is the unmitigated isolation of these individuals. By contrast, says the sage, two are better than one (4:9—12). It is impossible to be free of trouble in this precarious world; one is bound to encounter various inconveniences and hazards along the way, whether the cold otherness of the night or some unnamed foe. Yet the solidarity found in companionship makes the critical difference; a life shared with another is a rewarding life.

Qohelet's concern for social responsibility is also evident in his explication of enjoyment. His theology of enjoyment does not exclude but in fact leads directly to a consideration of the good of the larger world. As discussed above, Qohelet commends enjoyment because it is what promotes the well-being of the individual. But the benefits of enjoyment are not limited to the personal level, because the individual's practice of enjoyment also has ramifications for the health of a much wider circle of humanity. The sage makes this point forcefully by describing the terrible state of affairs that ensues in the absence of enjoyment.[17] For Qohelet, enjoyment—and the contentment implied by enjoyment—is what preserves life and moral order in the cosmos. Stated negatively, greed—even discontentment with one's lot—poses a grave threat to the moral structures of society. But the sage does not simply offer a clinical diagnosis of discontentment. In order to heighten the impact of his analysis and press home the urgency of his counsel, Qohelet takes recourse to the mythic language of Death's insatiable appetite to illustrate the insidious effects of greed (6:7—9). In doing so, he suggests rather shockingly that the health of the entire created order is at stake in the practice of enjoyment. In other words, an individual's commitment to contentment has a dramatic and far-reaching impact in the social arena; it is what preserves the good order of creation that is constantly under threat. Ultimately, for Qohelet, a world devoid of enjoyment is a less ethical world.

Some interpreters have faulted Qohelet for displaying an indifferent resignation to unjust social structures. He observes, and indeed bemoans, the oppressive conditions that prevail in the world (3:16; 4:1—3; 5:7; 8:9—11) but never goes on to cry for justice or reform. Instead, he only remarks, "do not be amazed at the matter" (5:7). For those of us who are enamored with the prophetic model for social change and its bold critique of systemic maladies, the sage's focus on the individual's capacity to enjoy may seem to be a flight from social responsibility. But such a view is a misunderstanding of Qohelet's

---

17   See especially the discussion of 5:7—6:9 in chapter 2.

theological program. The sage's approach to social change may differ
from the prophetic model, but it has the same goal of effecting positive
societal changes, albeit from a different angle. Qohelet's teachings
combat social injustices, not by calling his audience to political or social
activism, but rather by addressing the fundamental human vices that
lie at the root of societal maladies. This emphasis on inculcating
appropriate attitudes in the individual, in the end, is just as crucial for
the formation of a just human community.

Finally, Qohelet's social vision is also implicit in his most common
and most characteristic metaphor for enjoyment: the metaphor of
eating and drinking. Eating and drinking commonly occurs in the
context of a shared meal, whether a modest family meal or a festive
communal banquet. At a most basic level, these activities are meant to
sustain human life. By extension, they have a profound effect on the
quality of communal life and therefore bear an important ethical
dimension. One may eat and drink for good or for ill. On the one hand,
eating and drinking may promote health, fellowship, good will, and
gladness. On the other hand, however, the insatiability of the human
appetite may all too easily lead to a destructive kind of *eating up* at
another's expense. It may degenerate into reckless self-indulgence and
debauchery, the kind of feasting that the wisdom tradition denounces
as immoral (Prov 31:5—7; Sir 31:27—31). Such intemperance usually
indicates a character deficiency, and only further compromises the
moral faculties of those who engage in it. Prov 31:5, for example, warns
that those who drink excessively will "forget what has been decreed,
and will pervert the rights of all the afflicted" (cf. Isa 5:11—13, 22—23;
Amos 6:4—6).

In the moral world of the Old Testament, life-giving meals, by
contrast, take place in the context of a caring community.[18] They are a
social matter that produce joy. In a number of Old Testament passages,
the themes of eating, drinking, and rejoicing appear together in a
cluster. The intertextual connections with Qohelet's "joy passages"
suggest that a comparison may be appropriate and fruitful. In the
Deuteronomic injunctions concerning eating the tithe before the Lord,
Israel is commanded to eat and rejoice together, and to be especially
attentive to the Levites, resident aliens, orphans, and widows (Deut
12:7−8, 11−12; 14:22−27; cf. 27:7). Members of the community who
have no portion of their own are to be embraced in the joy of eating;
they too must be invited to come and eat their fill. And in this way,

---

18   Similarly, Brown notes that "The sage's table, despite its modest setting evokes the
     feast of fellowship ...." William Brown, "'Whatever Your Hand Finds to do'
     Qoheleth's Work Ethic," 271−84.

Israel is to learn the fear of the Lord (Deut 14:23). In the book of Nehemiah, when the returned exiles celebrate the public reading of the Law, their eating, drinking, and rejoicing is to be accompanied by "sending portions" (*lĕšallaḥ*) to those who have none (Neh 8:10, 12). Similarly, in Esther's description of the festival of Purim, the rejoicing of the community must spill over to the poor and disenfranchised members of society (9:22; cf. 9:19; 2:18). In all of these passages, joy and inclusiveness are the hallmark of the communal meal. It is in the context of breaking the bread and sharing the cup, giving and caring for the needy, that communities are strengthened and lives are transformed toward greater wholeness. Indeed, these communal feasts of joy may be seen as a foretaste of the eschatological banquet, when there will be plenty for all (cf. Isa 25:6—8).

It must be granted that Qohelet does not speak explicitly of a communal meal or make provisions for inclusiveness the way these festal regulations do. But the rhetoric of his admonitions concerning eating, drinking, and the proper use of food suggests that an individual's enjoyment must never come at the expense of the neighbor, but must instead promote the same possibilities for the neighbor. Qohelet first refers to "bread" in his exuberant call to celebrate life in 9:7: "go, eat your bread with gladness." Each subsequent occurrence then sheds further light on how that bread is to be appropriated. In 10:19, he refers to the "making of bread"[19] in a saying that, at first blush, appears to be a simple affirmation of life's pleasures: food is meant to be enjoyed, and wine makes people happy.[20] However, in its immediate context (10:16—20), the saying appears to be a subtle criticism of the lifestyle of the rich and powerful: "Alas for you, O land, whose king is a juvenile, and whose princes feast in the morning! Happy are you, O land, whose king is a noble, and whose princes feast at the proper time—for strength and not for drunkenness!" (vv. 16—17). Qohelet in effect portrays and condemns irresponsible forms of feasting, which impede a person's capacity to fulfill one's social and moral obligations. He suggests that anyone who has the means of enjoyment must exercise moral stewardship over those means. Those in positions of privilege and power, in particular, must be accountable for the way they eat and drink, because the fate of

---

19 The expression "to make bread" (cf. Ezek 4:15) corresponds to the Aramaic idiom "to prepare food for a feast" (Dan 5:1); it is roughly synonymous with "to prepare a banquet" (Gen 21:8).

20 Some commentators have speculated that the original saying may have come from a drinking song that celebrated life's pleasures. Galling, "Der Prediger"; Lauha, *Kohelet*, 196—97.

the land depends on it (see two-fold reference to "the land" in vv. 16—17).

However, Qohelet does not stop with this denunciation of deviant forms of enjoyment. He offers a constructive ethic as well. In contrast to the reckless self-indulgence of the immoral, the ethical life is characterized by a recklessness of a very different sort—by a spontaneous and lavish generosity toward others. Immediately following his invective against the ruling class, he gives the positive exhortation to "release (*šlḥ*) our bread upon the water" (11:1a) and "give a portion to seven, and even eight." *This* is what one ought to do with one's "bread," and this public dimension of joy is a vital expansion of Qohelet's ethic of enjoyment. One's portion and one's "bread" are God-given provisions. Whenever they are in one's possession, they should be enjoyed with relish; they should also be gladly released for the benefit of others. In other words, the generosity of God must engender a generosity in those who have received of the divine bounty. This derivative generosity then becomes a further investment in joy. According to this ethic, then, any appropriation of joy that stops at the personal level is deficient. Enjoyment is not complete until it is shared. It requires the moral being to manage one's life with proper concern for the needs and rights of others. Indeed, the ethic propounded by Ecclesiastes is even more striking—more demanding—than that of the other Old Testament texts cited above. The sage commends such generosity not only on grand occasions for celebration, but also in the day-to-day routine of living. Moreover, one must do so even in the face of an uncertain future, even when one cannot know what tragic turn of fortunes may strip away one's own resources (11:2b). Indeed, according to Qohelet's theology, no one ever has a secure claim on this basic means of sustenance and enjoyment (9:11). But Qohelet insists that the practice of enjoyment for the sake of the other should never be held in abeyance because of these uncertainties. One should never refrain from "doing good" (cf. 3:12)—indeed, one should even *risk* doing good—as long as it is in one's means.

Qohelet's ethic of enjoyment thus suggests that there must be a salutary balance between personal enjoyment and an open-handed concern for the neighbor. He teaches that every human being must pursue not only one's own flourishing but also that of the other. In the language of Barth, it is impossible to be "merry in isolation." It is a false joy if a person does not also desire "rejoice with me."[21] The principle

---

21   Barth, *CD*, III.4, 380.

aim of Qohelet's instructions, then, is to make his audience capable of enjoyment and of bringing the good life to others as well. Indeed, it is not an overstatement to declare that "[t]he appropriation of joy marks nothing less than a moral triumph."[22]

4.4 Enjoyment and Double Agency

Finally, Qohelet's theology of enjoyment speaks of a double agency in the exercise of joy. On the one hand, Qohelet affirms that joy is entirely God-given. It is God who grants the means of joy, and it is God who enables one person to enjoy the things in one's possession while withholding it from another. At the same time, however, joy is urgently commended, even commanded. Brown captures something of this tension when he writes, "the exhortation [to enjoy life] is given by Qohelet in full awareness that its fulfillment lies solely in God's determination. And yet joy is potentially realized by all: eating and drinking are not activities limited to the 'elect,' as it were."[23] Indeed, Qohelet holds together two conflicting claims of agency in his discourse concerning enjoyment.

Ecclesiastes has been noted for its deterministic worldview, according to which the deity is the ultimate cause behind all that happens in the world. In Qohelet's theology, every event, even events with human causation, are ultimately *ma'ăśeh hā'ĕlōhîm* "the work/activity of God." This determinism is often associated with a denial of human freedom and a loss of trust in life.[24] As one scholar puts it: "God is the first cause, and the doctrine of causality must inevitably lead to determinism and thus to pessimism."[25]

But Qohelet's theology of determinism (and of the Old Testament in general) does not exempt the human agent from responsibility; neither does it engage in a theoretical discussion concerning the reconciliation of these two contraries. It affirms equally both divine determinism and human responsibility. The tension is evident in Qohelet's own remarks concerning the nature of divine activity: in one place, he claims that no one can straighten what the deity has made crooked (7:13); in another, he remarks that "God made human beings straightforward, but they have devised many schemes" (7:29).

---

22   William Brown, *Ecclesiastes*, 107.
23   William Brown, " 'Whatever Your Hand Finds to do' Qoheleth's Work Ethic," 281.
24   See Lohfink's comments in *Kohelet*, 15–16.
25   Charles C. Forman, "The Pessimism of Ecclesiastes," *JSS* 3 (1958): 342.

While Qohelet portrays God as the primary actor behind all that happens, his discourse points to a propitious intersection of divine and human agency in and around the exercise of enjoyment. The appropriation of joy is not attributed to divine activity alone. To be sure, God gives the means. But this divine giving always calls for a taking up on the part of the human beneficiary. Whenever the divine agent gives an occasion for enjoyment, the human recipient must actively and willingly take up that opportunity and enjoy to the full, with all that it entails. Indeed, Qohelet speaks of enjoyment as a God-given responsibility (5:19) for which the human agent will be called to account (11:9). Hence, in Qohelet's ethic of joy, the dual notions of God's gift and human participation are not incompatible, but rather indispensable parts of the whole.

Each side of this duality says something significant about the nature of joy. As already noted, the foundational affirmation is that enjoyment is a divine gift. This is what the sage underscores time and time again (2:24—26; 3:13; 5:19; 8:15; 9:9). Every one of his commendations of enjoyment, without exception, is grounded theologically in the affirmation that this life and all its incumbent joys are a "grant of God," or "in the hand of God." For Qohelet, the fact that the possibility of joy is ultimately located in the hand of a mysterious deity underscores both the serendipitous and tenuous nature of this grant. Whenever the possibility of joy is present before an individual, it is there purely as the gift of God. It cannot be attributed to a person's moral virtues; it cannot be secured through heroic effort. Instead, the gift of joy is given to those who are somehow—mysteriously and graciously—already approved of God (2:24—26; 9:7), for God gives according to God's own economy. By the same token, that grant may be taken away just as inexplicably by some absurd circumstances of life (2:20—21, 26; 5:12—13; 6:1—2). Human beings cannot possess anything inalienably. Neither can they control the perplexing vagaries of life, with its unpredictable alternation between favorable and unfavorable times (3:1—8; 7:13—18). And finally, enjoyment is bounded by death. When the fragile and fleeting existence under the sun comes to its inexorable end, so too will all possibilities of joy.

Enjoyment is thus firmly anchored in the giving of God. Nevertheless, the concomitant affirmation of human agency is not insignificant. For Qohelet, the recognition that the possibility of enjoyment is in the hand of an inscrutable deity does not lead to an attitude of fatalism or bitter resignation, but to an ardent recommendation that each moment of joy be prized all the more dearly, seized all the more diligently. Human beings are recognized as moral agents, and the grant of enjoyment therefore comes to them as a *human* responsibility fraught with implications for the well-being of the human community. In Qohelet's own rhetoric, God not only gives the means of enjoyment, God also *authorizes* (*šlṭ*) the human agent to "take up" and exercise moral stewardship over what has been granted them (5:17–19). Over these things, the human agent has the power of disposal, if only for a given moment.

Moreover, Qohelet's discourse indicates that when human agents in turn give the gift of enjoyment to others, they are in fact emulating the divine giver and become a momentary reflection of the divine agent. In several places, the verb typically used for God's giving (*ntn*) is applied rather ambiguously in reference to people who fail to enjoy for one reason or another. The subject of the verb is not specified and the circumstances are not detailed, but their inability to enjoy is often described in terms of a forfeiture of their portion; the means of enjoyment is simply *given over* (*ntn*) to another (see especially 2:21 and 2:26). In 11:1–2, by contrast, Qohelet explicitly applies the verb to the human agent in the command to voluntarily give up—or, more aptly, *give away*—one's portion for the benefit of others. God's giving sets in motion another wave of generous giving, this time on the part of the human agent. Qohelet's theology of enjoyment, then, is an affirmation of human agency *for the sake of* promoting joy and enhancing the life of both the individual and the broader community.

Indeed, the larger context of this command to give away (11:1–6) is a remarkable exposition of the life-giving potential of the double agency in enjoyment. As elsewhere in the book, Qohelet speaks of the work of God, "who does everything" (11:5). The text acknowledges that the deity does indeed determine everything, and in a mysterious fashion. Here, however, the mystery of divine activity is described almost wondrously, as the creative force behind the miracle of gestation (11:5). Qohelet then suggests that God's work—precisely because of its mystery and unknowability—may be liberating rather than debilitating for the human agent. It may in fact motivate vigorous activity at both morning and evening: "for you do not know which will prosper, this or that, or whether both alike will be good" (11:6). In this scenario, human beings are not hapless victims in an unpredictable and uncontrollable world. The openness of the unknown future stimulates the human agent to be actively involved in the affairs of the world, to be industrious and diligent in the work at hand, to give liberally and spontaneously to the neighbor, all for the possibility of good. The possibilities are stated in surprisingly positive terms: "both" may turn out to be good. When the divine agent and human agent act in concert, as they do in this passage, the possibilities of good and general human flourishing are thereby multiplied.

Finally, enjoyment promotes human agency in yet another way. As discussed above, enjoyment is the desired end and goal of human agency. But it is also the *means*. It is what fuels and sustains the human agent in the enterprise. Indeed, Qohelet's metaphors for joy amply testify to the sustaining power of enjoyment. Eating, drinking, working, playing, and being with one's beloved—these activities provide the nourishment and joy requisite for living life to one's fullest potential. It is important to note, moreover, that the pleasurable aspects of these activities are by no means incidental. It is the experience of delight that fuels the desire to press on with the task of living "well" (*ṭôb*). If it is true that ethics should never be completely independent of what human beings deeply need and desire,[26] then Qohelet has hit upon a salutary point of orientation for his theological ethics. Joy is both the end and the means of human agency. It is both the substance and the driving force of his ethic.

Living in a world beyond human control is not an easy task. The experience of joy, however, can motivate, sustain, and invigorate the human agent to fully engage life for the sake of the self and the other. A sense of this vitality of joy may be captured in Nehemiah's remark to the returned exiles: "Go your way, eat ... drink ... release portions ... do not be grieved, *for the joy of YHWH is your strength*" (8:10; cf. 1 Chr 16:27; Ps 81:1). Similarly, Qohelet's most expansive commendation of joy in 9:7—10 naturally culminates in the counsel: "whatever your hand finds to do, do *with all your strength.*" Here, Simone Weil's comments concerning the joy of learning may be aptly applied to the joy of *living*. She writes: "The intelligence can only be led by desire. For there to be desire, there must be pleasure and joy in the work... The joy ... is as indispensable ... as breathing is in running."[27] The fact that God provides moments of joy to accompany and sustain humanity in the journey is a gift indeed. Qohelet's theology of enjoyment thus speaks practically and compassionately about how one is to live in a world utterly beyond one's control. It is a theology that addresses the deepest

---

26   See, for example, Martha Nussbaum, *Therapy of Desire* (Princeton: Princeton University Press, 1994), where Nussbaum insists that there must be a measure of correspondence between ethics and the deepest of human joys. She explores the philosophical underpinnings of this claim in her study of Hellenistic philosophers and their therapeutic approach to ethics.

27   Simone Weil, *Waiting For God* (New York: Harper & Row, 1973), 110. A similar point is made by proponents of narrative ethics, who emphasize the role of desire in reading and in the formation of moral character. See, for example, Wayne Booth, *The Company We Keep: An Ethics of Fiction* (Berkeley: University of California Press, 1988).

human needs and confronts the most perplexing problems of human life. This seemingly idiosyncratic book, then, offers a profound vision of piety and the moral life.

Bibliography

Abusch, T. "Ishtar's Proposal and Gilgamesh's Refusal: An Interpretation of *The Gilgamesh Epic*, Tablet 6, Lines 1—79." *History of Religions* 26 (1986): 143—87.

Ackroyd, P. R. "Two Hebrew Notes." *Annual of the Swedish Theological Institute* 5 (1966/67): 82—86.

Alonso Schökel, Luis. *A Manual of Hebrew Poetics*. Rome: Pontifical Biblical Institute, 1988.

Anderson, Gary. *A Time to Mourn, a Time to Dance*. University Park: Pennsylvania State University Press, 1991.

Anderson, W. H. U. Qoheleth and Its Pessimistic Theology: Hermeneutical Struggles in Wisdom Literature. Lewiston/ Queenston/Lampeter: Mellen Biblical Press, 1997.

Aranda, Mariano Gómez, ed. El Comentario de Abraham Ibn Ezra Al Libro del Eclesiastes: Introducion, Traduccion y Edicion Critica. Textos y estudios "Cardenal Cisneros" 56. Madrid: Instituto de Filologia del CSIC, 1994.

Armstrong, James. F. "Ecclesiastes in Old Testament Theology." *Princeton Seminary Bulletin* 94 (1983): 16—25.

Auffret, P. " 'Rien de tout de nouveau sous le soleil'. Étude structurelle de Qoh 1, 4—11." *Folia Orientalia* 26 (1989): 145—66.

Backhaus, Franz. J. *"Denn Zeit und Zufall trifft sie alle": Studien zur Komposition und zum Gottesbild im Buch Qohelet*. Bonner biblische Beiträge 83. Frankfurt am Main: Anton Hain, 1993.

————. "Widersprüche und Spannungen im Buch Qohelet. Zu einem neueren Versuch, Spannungen und Widersprüche literarkritisch zu lösen." Pages 123—54 in *Das Buch Kohelet: Studien zur Struktur, Geschichte, Rezeption und Theologie*. Edited by Ludger Schwienhorst-Schönberger. Berlin: de Gruyter, 1997.

Baer, S. and Strack, H.L, editors. *Die Dikduke Ha-Těamim des Ahron ben Moscheh ben Ascher und andere alte grammatischmassorethische Lehrstücke*. Leipzig: Verlag von L. Fernau, 1879.

Bamberger, Bernard J. "Fear and Love of God in the Old Testament." *Hebrew Union College Annual* 6 (1929): 39—53

Barré, Michael L. "Fear of God and the World View of Wisdom." *Biblical Theology Bulletin* 11—13 (1983): 41—43.

Barth, Karl. *Church Dogmatics*. Translated by A. T. Mackay et al. 4 volumes. Edinburgh: T. & T. Clark, 1936—1977.

Barton, George. A. *A Critical and Exegetical Commentary on the Book of Ecclesiastes*. International Critical Commentary. Edinburgh: T. & T. Clark, 1908.

Barucq, André. *Ecclésiaste*. Verbum Salutis 3. Paris: Beauchesne, 1968.

Becker, P. J. *Gottesfurcht im Alten Testament*. Analecta Biblica 95. Rome: Pontifico Instituto Biblico, 1965.

Bell, R. D. "Structure and Themes of Ecclesiastes." *Biblical Viewpoint* 31 (1997): 3—9.

Benoit, P. "L'Inscription Greque du Tombeau de Jason." *Israel Exploration Journal* 17 (1967): 112—13.

Bianchi, R. "The Language of Qohelet: A Bibliographical Survey." *Zeitschrift für die alttestamentliche Wissenschaft* 105 (1993): 210—23.

Bickell, Gustav. *Der Prediger über den Wert des Daseins: Wiederherstellung des Bisher zerstückelten Textes*. Innsbruck: Wagner, 1884.

Bickerman, Elias J. *Four Strange Books of the Bible: Jonah, Daniel, Koheleth, Esther*. New York: Schocken Books, 1967.

Birch, Bruce, and Larry Rasmussen. *Bible and Ethics in the Christian Life*. Minneapolis: Augsburg, 1989.

Blocher, Henri. "The Fear of the Lord as the 'Principle' of Wisdom." *TB* 28 (1977): 23.

Bondi, Richard. "The Elements of Character." *Journal of Religious Ethics* 12 (1984): 201—218.

Booth, Wayne. *The Company We Keep: An Ethics of Fiction*. Berkeley: University of California Press, 1988.

_____. *A Rhetoric of Irony*. Chicago: University of Chicago, 1974.

Braun, R. *Kohelet und die frühhellenistische Popularphilosophie*. Beihefte zur *Zeitschrift für alttestamentliche Wissenschaft* 130. Berlin/New York: de Gruyter, 1973.

Bréton, S. "Qoheleth Studies." *Biblical Theology Bulletin* 3 (1973): 22—50.

Brown, S. G. "The Structure of Ecclesiastes." *Evangelical Review of Theology* 14 (1990):195—208.

Brown, William P., ed. *Character and Scripture: Moral Formation, Community, and Biblical Interpretation*. Grand Rapids, Mich.: Eerdmans, 2002.

_____. *Character in Crisis: A Fresh Approach to the Wisdom Literature of the Old Testament*. Grand Rapids, Mich.: Eerdmans, 1996.

_____. *Ecclesiastes*. Interpretation: A Bible Commentary for Teaching and Preaching. Louisville: John Knox, 2000.

_____. "'Whatever Your Hand Finds to Do': Qoheleth's Work Ethic." *Interpretation: A Journal of Bible and Theology* 55, no. 3 (July 2001): 271–284.

Brueggemann, Walter. *Theology of the Old Testament: Testimony, Dispute, Advocacy.* Minneapolis: Fortress Press, 1997.

Bruns, J. E. "The Imagery of Eccles 12,6a." *Journal of Biblical Literature* 84 (1965): 428–30.

Burkes, Shannon. *Death in Qoheleth and Egyptian Biographies of the Late Period.* SBLDS 170. Atlanta: Society of Biblical Literature, 1999.

Buzy, D. "La notion du bonheur dans l'Ecclésiaste." *Revue biblique* 43 (1934): 494–511.

_____. "Le portrait de la vielliesse (Ecclésiaste XII, 107)." *Revue biblique* 41 (1932): 329–40.

Byargeon, Ricky William. "The Significance of the Enjoy Life Concept in Qoheleth's Challenge of the Wisdom Tradition." Ph. D. diss., Southwestern Baptist Theological Seminary, 1991.

Castellino, George R. "Qohelet and His Wisdom." *Catholic Biblical Quarterly* 30 (1968): 15–28.

Catanzaro, C. J. de. "Fear, Knowledge, and Love: A Study in Old Testament Piety." *Canadian Journal of Theology* 9 (1963): 166–73.

Ceresko, A. R. "The Function of Antanaclasis (*ms̱ʾ* 'to find' // *ms̱ʾ* 'to reach, overtake, grasp') in Hebrew Poetry, Especially in the book of Qoheleth." *Catholic Biblical Quarterly* 44 (1982): 551–69.

Chia, Philip P. Y. "The Thought of Qoheleth: Its Structure, Its Sequential Unfolding, and Its Position in Israel's Theology." Ph.D. diss., Sheffield University, 1988.

Childs, Brevard S. *Introduction to the Old Testament as Scripture.* Philadelphia: Fortress, 1979.

Christianson, Eric S. *A Time to Tell: Narrative Strategies in Ecclesiastes.* Journal for the Study of the Old Testament: Supplement Series 280. Sheffield: Sheffield, 1998.

Clay, Albert T. *Legal Documents from Erech Dated in the Seleucid Era (312–65 B.C.).* Babylonian Records in the Pierpont Morgan Library, pt. 2. New York: Pierpont Morgan Library, 1913.

Clements. Ronald E. "Wisdom and Old Testament Theology." Pages 269–86 in *Wisdom in Ancient Israel.* Edited by J. Day et al. Cambridge: Cambridge University Press, 1995.

_____. *Wisdom in Theology.* Grand Rapids, Mich.: Eerdmans, 1992.

Coppens, J. "La structure de l'Ecclésiaste." Pages 288—92 in *La sagesse de l'Ancien Testament*. Edited by M. Gilbert. Bibliotheca ephemeridum theologicarum lovaniensium 51. Gembloux: Leuven University, 1979.

Crenshaw, James. L. "The Birth of Skepticism." Pages 1—19 in *The Divine Helmsman*. Edited by J. L. Crenshaw and S. Sandmel. New York: KTAV, 1980.

_____. *Ecclesiastes: A Commentary*. Old Testament Library. Philadelphia: Westminster, 1987.

_____. "The Eternal Gospel (Eccl. 3:11)." Pages 23—55 in *Essays in Old Testament Ethics*. Edited by J. L. Crenshaw and J. T. Willis. New York: KTAV, 1974.

_____. "In Search of Divine Presence: Some Remarks Preliminary to a Theology of Wisdom." *Review and Expositor* 74 (1977): 353—69.

_____. "Qohelet in Current Research." *Hebrew Annual Review* 7 (1983): 41—56.

Cross, Frank M. "Papyri of the Fourth Century B.C. from Dâliyeh." Pages 45—69 in *New Directions in Biblical Archaelogy*. Edited by D. N. Freedman and J. C. Greenfield. Garden City, N.Y.: Doubleday, 1969.

Crüsemann, F. "The Unchangeable World: the 'Crisis of Wisdom' in Koheleth." Pages 57—77 in *The God of the Lowly: socio-historical interpretations of the Bible*. Edited by W. Schottroff and W. Stegemann. Translated by M. J. O'Connell. Maryknoll, N.Y.: Orbis, 1984. Translation of *Der Gott der kleinen Leute: sozialgeschichtliche Bibelauslegungen*. München: Kaiser, 1979.

Davis, Ellen. *Proverbs, Ecclesiastes, and the Song of Songs*. Westminster Bible Companion. Louisville: Westminster John Knox, 2000.

DeJong, Stephen. "A Book of Labour: the Structuring Principles and the Main Theme of the Book of Qoheleth." *Journal for the Study of the Old Testament* 54 (1992): 107—116.

_____. "God in the Book of Qohelet: A Reappraisal of Qohelet's Place in Old Testament. " *Vetus Testamentum* 47 (1997): 154—67.

Delitzsch, Franz. *Commentary on the Song of Songs and Ecclesiastes*. Translated by M. G. Easton. Edinburgh: T. & T. Clark, 1877. Translation of *Hoheslied und Koheleth*. Leipzig: Dörffling und Franke, 1875.

Dell, K. J. "Ecclesiastes as Wisdom: Consulting Early Interpreters." *Vetus Testamentum* 44 (1994): 301—29.

Derousseaux, Louis. *La crainte de Dieu dans l'Ancien Testament: royauté, alliance, sagesse dans les royaumes d'Israël et de Juda; recherches d'exégèse et d'histoire sur la racine yārē'*. Paris: Éditions du Cerf, 1970.

Diez, H. F. von. *Denkwürdigkeiten von Asien*. Vol. 1. Berlin: Nicolaischen Buchhandlung, 1811.

Ehlich, K. "Hebel—Metaphern der Nichtigkeit." Pages 49—64 in *"Jedes Ding hat seine Zeit..." Studien zur israelitischen und altorientalischen Weisheit*. Edited by A. A. Diesel et al. BZAW 241. Berlin/New York: de Gruyter, 1996.

Ehrlich, A.B. *Randglossen zur hebräischen Bibel*. Vol. 7. Leipzig: Hinrich's, 1914.

Ellermeier, F. *Qohelet I/1. Untersuchungen zum Buche Qohelet*. Herzberg: Jungfer, 1967.

————. "Das Verbum ḤWŠ in Koh 2,25." *Zeitschrift für die alttestamentliche Wissenschaft* 75 (1963): 197—217.

Elster, Ernst. *Commentar über den Prediger Salomo*. Göttingen: Dieterich, 1855.

Euringer, Sebastian. *Der Masorahtext des Koheleth*. Leipzig: Hinrich's, 1890.

Farmer, Kathleen A. *Who Knows What Is Good? A Commentary on the Books of Proverbs and Ecclesiastes*. International Theological Commentary. Grand Rapids: Eerdmans, 1991.

Fecht, Gerhard. *Metrik des Hebräischen und Phönizischen*. Ägypten und Altes Testament 19. Wiesbaden: Harrassowitz, 1991.

Fichtner, Johannes. *Die altorientalische Weisheit in ihrer israelitischjüdischen Ausprägung: eine Studie zur Nationalisierung der Weisheit in Israel*. Beihefte zur Zeitschrift für die alttestamentliche Wissenschaft 62. Giessen: Töpelmann, 1933.

Fisch, Harold. "Qohelet: A Hebrew Ironist." Pages 158—78 in *Poetry with a Purpose*. Indiana Studies in Biblical Literature. Bloomington: Indiana University Press, 1988.

Fishbane, Michael. *Biblical Interpretation in Ancient Israel*. Oxford: Clarendon, 1985.

Forman, Charles G. "The Pessimism of Ecclesiastes." *Journal of Semitic Studies* 3 (1958): 336—43.

Foster, Benjamin. *Before the Muses: An Anthology of Akkadian Literaure*. Vol. 2. Bethesda, Md.: CDL Press, 1996.

Fox, Michael V. "Aging and Death in Qoheleth 12." *Journal for the Study of the Old Testament* 42 (1988): 55—77.

_____. "Frame-Narrative and Composition in the Book of Qohelet." *Hebrew Union College Annual* 48 (1977): 83—106.

_____. "The Meaning of HEBEL for Qohelet." *Journal of Biblical Literature* 105 (1986): 409—27.

_____. *Qoheleth and His Contradictions.* Journal for the Study of the Old Testament: Supplement Series 71. Sheffield: Almond, 1989.

_____. "Qoheleth's Epistemology." *Hebrew Union College Annual* 58 (1987): 137—55.

_____. "A Study of Antef." *Orientalia* 46 (1977): 393—423.

_____. *A Time to Tear Down & a Time to Build Up: A Rereading of Ecclesiastes.* Grand Rapids, Mich.: Eerdmans, 1999.

_____. "Wisdom in Qoheleth." Pages 115—31 in *In Search of Wisdom: Essays in Memory of John G. Gammie.* Edited by L. G. Perdue et al. Louisville: Westminster/John Knox, 1993.

Fredericks, D. C. "Chiasm and Parallel Structure in Qoheleth 5:6—6:9." *Journal of Biblical Literature* 108 (1989): 17—35.

_____. *Coping with Transience: Ecclesiastes on Brevity in Life.* The Biblical Seminar 18. Sheffield: JSOT Press, 1993.

_____. "Life's Storms and Structural Unity in Qoheleth 11:1—12:8." *Journal for the Study of the Old Testament* 52 (1991): 95—114. Fuhs, H. F. "*yārēʾ*." Pages 290—315 in vol. 6 of *Theological Dictionary of the Old Testament.* Edited by G. J. Botterweck and H. Ringgren. Translated by John T. Willis. 12 vols. Grand Rapids, Mich.: Eerdmans, 1975—2003.

Galling, Kurt. "Koheleth-Studien," *ZAW* 50 (1932): 279—82.

_____. "Der Prediger." In *Die fünf Megilloth.* 2d ed. Handbuch zum Alten Testament 18. Tübingen: Mohr, 1969.

Gammie, John G. "Stoicism and anti-Stoicism in Qoheleth." *Hebrew Annual Review* 9 (1985): 169—87.

Gardiner, Alan H. *The Admonitions of an Egyptian Sage from a Hieratic Papyrus in Leiden (Pap. Leiden 344 recto).* Leipzig: J.C. Hinrichs, 1909.

Genung, J. F. *The Words of Qoheleth.* Boston: Houghton Mifflin, 1904.

Gese, Hartmut. "The Crisis of Wisdom in Koheleth." Pages 141—53 in *Theodicy in the Old Testament.* Issues in Religion and Theology 4. Edited by J. L. Crenshaw. Philadelphia/London: Fortress/SPCK, 1983.

Gianto, Agustinos. "The Theme of Enjoyment in Qohelet [smch]." *Biblica* 73 (1992): 528—532.

Gilbert, Maurice. "La Description de la vieillesse en Qoheleth 12:1−7, est-elle allégorique?" Pages 96−109 in *Congress Volume, Vienna, 1980*. Edited by J. A. Emerton. VTSup 32. Leiden: Brill, 1981.

Ginsberg, H. L. *Koheleth*. Jerusalem: Newman, 1961.

————. "The Quintessence of Koheleth." Pages 47−59 in *Biblical Motifs*. Edited by A. Altmann. Philip W. Lown Institute of Advanced Judaic Studies. Studies and Texts 3. Cambridge, MA: Harvard University, 1966.

————. "The Structure and Contents on the Book of Koheleth." Pages 138−49 in *Wisdom in Israel and in the Ancient Near East*. Edited by M. Noth and D. Winton Thomas. Supplements to Vetus Testamentum 3. Leiden: Brill, 1955.

Ginsburg, Christian D. *Coheleth, Commonly Called the Book of Ecclesiastes: Translated from the Original Hebrew, with a Commentary, Historical and Critical*. London: Longman, 1861. Repr., New York: KTAV, 1970.

Glasser, Étienne. *Le procès du bonheur par Qohelet*. Lectio divina 61. Paris: Cerf, 1970.

Good, Edwin M. *Irony In the Old Testament*. 2d ed. Sheffield: Almond, 1981.

————. "The Unfilled Sea: Style and Meaning in Ecclesiastes 1:2−11." Pages 59−73 in *Israelite Wisdom*. Edited by J. G. Gammie et al. Missoula, Mont.: Scholars Press, 1978.

Gordis, Robert. *Koheleth−the Man and His World*. 3d ed. New York: Schocken, 1968.

————. "Quotations as a Literary Usage in Biblical, Oriental, and Rabbinic Literature." *Hebrew Union College Annual* 22 (1949): 157−219.

————. "Quotations in Wisdom Literature." *Jewish Quarterly Review* 30 (1939/40): 123−47.

Gorsen, L. "La cohérence de la conception de Dieu dans l'Ecclésiaste." *Ephemerides theologicae lovanienses* 46 (1970): 282−324.

Graetz, Heinrich. *Kohelet*. Leipzig: Winter, 1871.

Grapow, Hermann. *Die bildlichen Ausdrückes des Ägyptischen*. Leipzig: Hinrich's, 1924.

Greenfield, Jonas C. "Lexicographical Notes II." *Hebrew Union College Annual* 30 (1959): 141−151.

Gropp, Douglas M. "The Origin and Development of the Aramaic šallîṭ Clause." *Journal of Near Eastern Studies* 52 (1993): 31−36.

————. *Wadi Daliyeh II: The Samaria papyri from Wadi Daliyeh*. Discoveries in the Judean Desert 28. Oxford: Clarendon, 2001.

Gustafson, James M. *Ethics From a Theocentric Perspective*. Vol. 1 of *Theology and Ethics*. Chicago: University of Chicago Press, 1981.

Hertzberg, Hans Wilhelm. *Der Prediger*. Kommentar zum Alten Testament 17/4. Gütersloh: Mohn, 1963.

Holm-Nielsen, Svend. "The Book of Ecclesiastes and the Interpretation of it in Jewish and Christian Theology." *ASTI* 10 (1975/76): 38—96.

_____. "On the Interpretation of Qoheleth in Early Christianity." *Vetus Testamentum* 24 (1974): 168—77.

Hoomisen, G. van "'Et je fais l'éloge de la joie?' (Qoh 8,15)." *Lumen Vitae* 43 (1988): 37—46.

Humbert, Paul. "'Laetari et exultare' dans le vocabulaire religieux de l'ancien Testament." *Revue d'histoire et de philosophie religieuses* 22 (1942): 185—214.

_____. *Recherché sur les sources égyptiennes de la literature sapientiale d'Israël*. Neuchâtel: Paul Attinger, 1929.

Isaksson, B. *Studies in the Language of Qoheleth: With Special Emphasis on the Verbal System*. Studia Semitica Upsaliensia 10. Stockholm: Almqvist & Wiksell, 1987.

Jaeggli, J. R. "Seven Reasons in Ecclesiastes for Enjoying Life." *Biblical Viewpoint* 31 (1997): 25—33.

Japhet, S., and Robin B. Salters. *The Commentary of R. Samuel ben Meir Rashbam on Qoheleth*. Jerusalem: Magnes, 1985.

Jastrow, Marcus. *Dictionary of the Targumim*. New York: Pardes, 1950.

Jastrow, Morris. *A Gentle Cynic: Being a Translation of the Book of Koheleth, Commonly Known as Ecclesiastes, Its origin, Growth, and Interpretation*. Philadelphia: J. B.\Lippincott, 1919.

Jenni, Ernst. "Das Wort ʿōlām im Alten Testament." *Zeitschrift für die alttestamentliche Wissenschaft* 64 (1952): 197—248.

Johnson, R. E. "The Rhetorical Question as a Literary Device in Ecclesiastes." Ph.D. diss., Southern Baptist Theological Seminary, 1986.

Johnston, Robert K. "Confessions of a Workaholic: A Reappraisal of Qoheleth." *Catholic Biblical Quarterly* 38 (1976): 14—28.

Jones, Brian W. "From Gilgamesh to Qoheleth." Pages 349—79 in *The Bible in the Light of Cuneiform Literature: Scripture in Context III*. Edited by W.W. Hallo et al. Lewiston, NY: Edwin Mellen, 1990.

Joüon, P. *A Grammar of Biblical Hebrew*. Translated and revised by T. Muraoka. 2 vols. Rome: Editrice Pontificio Instituto Biblico, 1996.

Kaiser, Walter C. "Integrating Wisdom Theology into Old Testament Theology: Ecclesiastes 3:10—15." Pages 197—209 in *A Tribute to Gleason Archer*. Edited by W. C. Kaiser and R. F. Youngblood. Chicago: Moody, 1986.

Kempis, Thomas à. *The Following of Christ*. Edited by J. van Ginneken. New York: America Press, 1937.

Klopfenstein, Martin A. "Die Skepsis des Qohelet." *Theologische Zeitschrift* 28 (1972): 97—109.

Knobel, P. S. "Targum Qoheleth: A Linguistic and Exegetical Inquiry." Ph.D. diss., Yale University, 1976.

Knoph, C. S. "The Optimism of Koheleth." *Journal of Biblical Literature* 49 (1930): 195—99.

Krüger, Thomas. *Kohelet (Prediger)*. Biblischer Kommentar: Altes Testament 19 Sonderband. Neukirchener-Vluyn: Neukirchener, 2000.

Lambert, W. G., ed. *Babylonian Wisdom Literature*. Oxford: Clarendon, 1960.

Lang, Bernhard. "Ist der Mensch hilflos? Das biblische Buch Kohelet, neu und kritisch gelesen." *Theologische Quartalschrift* 159 (1979): 109—24.

Lauha, Aarre. *Kohelet*. Biblischer Kommentar: Altes Testament 19. Neukirchen-Vluyn: Neukirchener, 1978.

Laurent, Françoise. *Les biens pour rien en Qohéleth 5,9—6,6 ou La traversée d'un contraste*. BZAW 323. Berlin/New York: de Gruyter, 2002.

Leahy, M. "The Meaning of Ecclesiastes (12:2—5)." *Irish Theological Quarterly* 19 (1952): 297—300.

Lehman, Paul. *Ethics in a Christian Context*. New York/Evanston: Harper & Row, 1963.

Levy, Ludwig. *Das Buch Qoheleth*. Leipzig: Hinrich's, 1912.

Lichtheim, Miriam. *Ancient Egyptian Literature: A Book of Readings*. 3 vols. Berkeley: University of California Press, 1973, 1976, 1980.

_____. *Late Egyptian Wisdom Literature in the International Contex: A Study of Demotic Instructionst*. Freibourg Schweiz: Universitätsverlag, 1983.

_____. "The Song of the Harpers." *Journal of Near Eastern Studies* 4 (1945): 178—212.

Loader, J. A. *Ecclesiastes: A Practical Commentary*. Grand Rapids, Mich.: Eerdmans, 1986.

150   Bibliography

_____. *Polar Structures in the Book of Qohelet*. Beihefte zur Zeitschrift für die alttestamentliche Wissenschaft 152. Berlin/New York: de Gruyter, 1979.

_____. "Qohelet 3:2—8—A 'Sonnet' in the Old Testament." *Zeitschrift für die alttestamentliche Wissenschaft* 81 (1969): 240—42.

Lohfink, Norbert. *Christian Meaning of the Old Testament*. Translated by R. A. Wilson. Milwaukee: Bruce, 1968. Translation of *Das Siegeslied am Schilfmeer*. Frankfurt am Main: Knecht, 1965.

_____. *Kohelet*. Die Neue Echter Bibel. Würzburg: Echter, 1980.

_____. "Koh 1,2 'alles ist Windhauch'—universale oder anthropologische Aussage?" Pages 201—16 in *Der Weg zum Menschen*. Edited by R. Mosis and L. Ruppert. Freiberg: Herder, 1989.

_____. "Das Koheletbuch: Strukturen und Struktur." Pages 39—121 in *Das Buch Kohelet: Studien zur Struktur, Geschichte, Rezeption und Theologie*. Edited by Ludger Schwienhorst-Schönberger. Beihefte zur Zeitschrift für die alttestamentliche Wissenschaft 254. Berlin/New York: de Gruyter, 1997.

_____. *Qoheleth: A Continental Commentary*. Translate by Sean McEvenue. Minneapolis: Fortress, 2003. Translation of *Kohelet*. Die Neue Echter Bibel. Würzburg: Echter, 1980.

_____. "Qoheleth 5:17—19—Revelation by Joy." *Catholic Biblical Quarterly* 52 (1990): 625—35.

_____. "Von Windhauch, Gottesfurcht und Gottes Antwort in der Freude." *Bibel und Kirche* 45 (1990): 26—32.

_____. "Warum is der Tor unfähig, böse zu handeln? (Koh 4:17)." Pages 113—20 in *Augewählte Vorträge*. ZDMG Supplement 5. Edited by F. Steppat. Wiesbaden: Steiner, 1983.

Longman, Tremper. *The Book of Ecclesiastes*. New International Commentary on the Old Testament. Grand Rapids, Mich.: Eerdmans, 1998.

_____. *Fictional Akkadian Autobiography: A Generic and Comparative Study*. Winona Lake, Ind.: Eisenbrauns, 1991.

Loretz, Oswald. *Qoheleth und der alte Orient: Untersuchungen zu Stil und theologischer Thematik des Buches Qohelet*. Freiburg/Basel/Wien: Herder, 1964.

Luther, Martin. "Notes on Ecclesiastes." Pages 3—187 in *Luther's Works*. Vol. 15. Edited by J. Pelikan. St. Louis: Concordia, 1972.

Lux, Rüdiger. "Der 'Lebenskompromiss'—ein Wesenzung im Denken Kohelets? Zur Auslegung von Koh 7,15—18." Pages 268—78 in *Alttestamentlicher Glaube und Biblische Theologie*. Edited by J. Hausmann and H.-J. Zobel. Stuttgart: Kohlhammer, 1992.

Lys, Daniel. *L'Ecclésiastes ou que vaut la vie?* Paris: Letouzey at Ané, 1977.

MacDonald, D. B. *The Hebrew Philosophical Genius: A Vindication.* Princeton: Princeton University Press, 1936.

Machinist, Peter. "Fate, *miqreh*, and reason: some reflections on Qohelet and Biblical thought." Pages 159−75 in *Solving Riddles and Untying Knots.* Edited by Z. Zevit et al. Winona Lakes, Ind.: Eisenbrauns, 1995.

McKenna, J. E. "The Concept of *Hebel* in the Book of Ecclesiastes." *Scottish Journal of Theology* 45/1 (1992): 19−28.

McNeile, A. H. *An Introduction to Ecclesiastes.* Cambridge: Cambridge University Press, 1904.

Meier, Samuel A. *The Messenger in the Ancient Semitic World.* Harvard Semitic Monograph Series 45. Atlanta: Scholars Press, 1988.

Michel, Diethelm. "Gott bei Kohelet: Anmerkungen zu Kohelets Reden von Gott." *Bibel und Kirche* 45 (1990): 32−36.

————. *Qohelet.* Erträge der Forschung 258. Darmstadt: Wissenschaftliche Buchgesellschaft, 1988.

————. *Untersuchungen zur Eigenart des Buches Qohelet.* Beihefte zur Zeitschrift für die alttestamentliche Wissenschaft 183. Berlin/New York: de Gruyter, 1989.

————. "Vom Gott, der im Himmel ist (Reden von Gott bei Qohelet)." *Theologia Viatorum* 12 (1973/74): 87−100.

Miller, A. "Aufbau und Grundproblem des Predigers." *Miscellanea Biblica* 2 (1934): 104−22.

Miller, Douglas. "Qohelet's Symbolic Use of *lbh*." *Journal of Biblical Literature* 117 (1998): 437−54.

————. *Symbol and Rhetoric in Ecclesiastes: The Place of Hebel in Qohelet's Work.* Studia Academica. Leiden/Boston: Brill, 2002.

Miskotte, Kornelis H. *When the Gods Are Silent.* New York: Harper & Row, 1967.

Mitchell, H. G. "'Work' in Ecclesiastes." *Journal of Biblical Literature* 32 (1913): 123−38.

Moran, William L. "The Ancient Near Eastern Background of the Love of God in Deuteronomy." *Catholic Biblical Quarterly* 25 (1963): 77−87.

Muffs, Yochanan. *Love and Joy: Law, Language Religion in Ancient Israel.* New York: The Jewish Theological Seminary of America, 1992.

Mulder, J. S. M. "Qoheleth's Division and Also Its Main Points." Pages 341—65 in *Von Kanaan bis Kerala*. Edited by W C. Delsman et al. Neukirchen-Vluyn: Kevelaer/Neukirchener, 1982.

Müller, H.-P. "Der unheimliche Gast. Zum Denken Kohelets." *Zeitschrift für Theologie und Kirche* 84 (1987): 440—64.

————. "Wie sprach Qohälät von Gott?" *Vetus Testamentum* 18 (1968): 507—21.

Muntingh, L. J. "Fear of Yahweh and Fear of the Gods According to the Books of Qohelet and Isaiah." Pages 143—158 in *Studies in Isaiah*. Edited by W. C. van Wyk. OTWSA 22/23. Pretoria: NHW Press, 1979—80.

Murphy, Roland E. *Ecclesiastes*. Word Biblical Commentary 23A. Dallas: Word Books, 1992.

————. "The Faith of Qoheleth." *Word & World* 7 (1987): 253—60.

————. "The Pensées of Coheleth." *Catholic Biblical Quarterly* 17 (1955): 304—14.

————. "Qoheleth and Theology?" *Biblical Theology Bulletin* 21 (1991): 30—33.

————. "Qoheleth Interpreted: the Bearing of the Past on the Present." *Vetus Testamentum* 32 (1982): 331—37.

————. "Qoheleth's 'Quarrel' With the Fathers." Pages 235—54 in *From Faith to Faith*. Edited by D. Y. Hadidian. Pittsburgh: Pickwick Press, 1979.

Nishimura, Toshiaki. "Quelques réflexions sémiologues à propos de la crainte de dieu de Qohelet." *Annual of the Japanese Biblical Institute* 5 (1979): 67—87.

Newsom, Carol A. "Job and Ecclesiastes." Pages 177—94 in *Old Testament Interpretation: Past, Present, and Future*. Edited by J. L. Mays et al. Nashville: Abingdon, 1995.

Nussbaum, Martha. *Therapy of Desire*. Princeton: Princeton University Press, 1994.

Ogden, Graham. "The 'Better'-Proverb (Tôb-Spruch), Rhetorical Criticism, and Qoheleth." *Journal of Biblical Literature* 96 (1977): 489—505.

————. "Qoheleth's Use of the 'Nothing is Better'-Form." *Journal of Biblical Literature* 98 (1979): 339—50.

————. *Qoheleth*. Readings—A New Bible Commentary. Sheffield: JSOT Press, 1987.

_____. "Qoheleth XI 7−XII 8: Qoheleth's Summons to Enjoyment and Reflection." *Vetus Testamentum* 34, no. 1 (1984): 27−38.

_____. "'Vanity' It Certainly is Not." *The Bible Translator* 38 (1987): 301−307.

Oppenheim, A. Leo *The Interpretation of Dreams in the Ancient Near East, with a Translation of an Assyrian Dream-book.* Philadelphia: American Philosophical Society, 1956.

Otto, Rudolf *The Idea of the Holy: An Inquiry into the Non-Rational Factor in the Idea of the Divine and Its Relation to the Rational.* London: Oxford, 1957.

Pedersen, Johannes. *Scepticisme Israélite.* Paris: Alcan, 1931.

Pennacchini, B. "Qohelet ovvero il libro degli assurdi." *Euntes Docete* 30 (1977): 491−510.

Perdue, Leo. G. *Wisdom and Creation: The Theology of Wisdom Literature.* Nashville: Abingdon, 1994.

_____. *Wisdom and Cult: A Critical Analysis of the Views of Cult in the Wisdom Literature of Israel and the Ancient Near East.* Society of Biblical Literature Dissertation Series 30. Missoula: Scholars Press, 1977.

Perry, T. A. *Dialogues with Kohelet.* University Park, Pa.: Pennsylvania State University, 1993. Pfeiffer, Egon. "Die Gottesfurcht im Buche Kohelet." Pages 133−58 in *Gottes Wort und Gottes Land.* Edited by H. Reventlow. Göttingen: Vandenhoeck & Ruprecht, 1965.

Pfeiffer, R. H. "The Fear of God." *IEJ* 5 (1955): 41.

_____. "The Peculiar Skepticism of Ecclesiastes." *Journal of Biblical Literature* 53 (1934): 100−9.

Pick, B. "Ecclesiastes or the Sphinx of Hebrew Literature." *Open Court* 17 (1903): 361−71.

Plath, Siegfried. *Furcht Gottes: der Begriff yārēʾ im Alten Testament.* Arbeiten zur Theologie 2, pt.2. Stuttgart: Calwer, 1963.

Plumptre, E. H. *Ecclesiastes, or, the Preacher.* Cambridge: Cambridge University Press, 1887.

Podechard, Emmanuel. "La composition du livre de l'Ecclésiaste." *Revue biblique* 21 (1912): 161−91.

_____. *L'Ecclésiastes.* Études bibliques. Paris: Gabalda, 1912.

Polk, Timothy. "The Wisdom of Irony: A Study of *Hebel* and Its Relation to Joy and the Fear of God in Ecclesiastes." *Studia Biblica et Theologica* 6, no. 1 (1976): 3−17.

Preuss, Horst Dietrich. "Erwägungen zum theologischen Ort Alttestamentlicher Weisheitsliteratur." *EvangelischeTheologie* 30 (1970): 393—417.

Priest, J. F. "Humanism, Skepticism, and Pessimism in Israel." *Journal of the American Academy of Religion* 36 (1968): 311—26.

Rad, Gerhard von. *Old Testament Theology.* Translated by D. M. G. Stalker. 2 vols. New York/Evanston/San Francisco/London: Harper & Row, 1962—65. Translation of *Theologie des Alten Testaments.* Munich: Kaiser, 1957—1960.

_____. *Wisdom in Israel.* Translated by James D. Marton. London: SCM Press, 1972. Translation of *Weisheit in Israel.* Neukirchen Vluyn: Neukirchener, 1970.

Rainey, A. F. "A Study of Ecclesiastes." *Concordia Theological Monthly* 35 (1964): 148—57.

_____. "A Second Look at Amal in Qoheleth." *Concordia Theological Monthly* 36 (1965): 805.

Rashbam. *The Commentary of R. Samuel Ben Meir Rashbam on Qoheleth.* Edited by S. Japhet and R. Salters. Jerusalem/Leiden: Magnes/Brill, 1985.

Reitman, J. S. "The Structure and Unity of Ecclesiastes." *Bibliotheca Sacra* 154 (1997): 297—319.

Rendtorff, R. *The Old Testament: An Introduction.* Translated by John Bowden. Philadelphia: Fortress, 1986.

Robinson, H. Wheeler. *The Old Testament: Its Making and Meaning.* New York: Abingdon, 1937.

Rose, Martin. *Riev de nouveau: Nouvelles approches du livre de Qohéleth.* Orbis biblicus et orientalis 168. Göttingen: Vandenhoeck & Ruprecht, 1999.

Rousseau, F. "Structure de Qohélet 1 4—11 et plan du livre." *Vetus Testamentum* 31 (1981): 200—17.

Rude, T. "The Alleged Epicurean Passages." *Biblical Viewpoint* 31 (1997): 19—24.

Rudman, D. "The Anatomy of the Wise Man: Wisdom, Sorrow and Joy in the book of Ecclesiastes." Pages 465—71 in *Qohelet in the Context of Wisdom.* Bibliotheca ephemeridum theologicarum lovaniensium 136. Edited by A. Schoors. Leuven: Leuven University Press, 1998.

Salyer, Gary D. *Vain Rhetoric: Private Insight and Public Debate in Ecclesiastes.* Journal for the Study of the Old Testament: Supplement Series 327. Sheffield: Sheffield Academic Press, 2001.

Sawyer, J. F. A. "The Ruined House in Ecclesiastes 12: A Reconstruction of the Original Parable." *Journal of Biblical Literature* 94 (1976): 519—31.

Scheffler, E. H. "Qohelet's Positive Advice." *Oud Testamentiese Werkgemeenschap in Suid-Afrika* 6 (1993): 248—71.

Schoors, Antoon. *The Preacher Sought to Find Pleasing Words: A Study of the Language of Qoheleth.* Orientalia Lovaniensia Analecta 41. Leuven: Peeters, 1992.

_____. "La structure littéraire de Qoheleth." *Orientalia lovaniensia periodica* 13 (1982): 91—116.

_____. "The Verb *r'h* in the book of Qoheleth." Pages 227—41 in *"Jedes Ding hat seine Zeit ...": Studien zur israelitischen und altorientalischen Weisheit.* Beihefte zur Zeitschrift für die alttestamentliche Wissenschaft 241. Edited by A. A. Diesel et al. Berlin/New York: W. de Gruyter, 1996.

_____. "Words Typical of Qohelet." Pages 33—40 in *Qohelet in the Context of Wisdom.* Bibliotheca ephemeridum theologicarum lovaniensium 136. Edited by A. Schoors. Leuven: Leuven University Press, 1998.

Scott, R. B. Y. *Proverbs. Ecclesiastes.* Anchor Bible Commentary 18. Garden City, N.Y.: Doubleday, 1965.

Seow, Choon Leong. "Beyond Mortal Grasp: The Usage of *Hebel* in Ecclesiastes." *Australian Biblical Review* 48 (2000): 1—16.

_____. "'Beyond These, My Son, Beware!': The Epilogue of Qohelet Revisited." Pages 125—41 in *Wisdom, You are My Sister.* Edited by M. L. Barré. Catholic Biblical Quarterly Monograph Series 29. Washington, D.C.: Catholic Biblical Association, 1997.

_____. *Ecclesiastes: A New Translation with Introduction and Commentary.* Anchor Bible Commentary 18c. New York: Doubleday, 1997.

_____. "The Epilogue of Qohelet Revisited." Pages 125—141 in *Wisdom, You Are My Sister.* Edited by M. L. Barré. Catholic Biblical Quarterly Monograph Series 29. Washington, D. C.: Catholic Biblical Association, 1997.

_____. "Linguistic Evidence and the Dating of Qohelet." *Journal of Biblical Literature* 115 (1996): 643—66.

_____. "Qohelet's Autobiography." Pages 257—82 in *Fortunate the Eyes that See.* Edited by A. Beck et al. Grand Rapids, Mich.: Eerdman, 1995.

_____. "Qohelet's Eschatological Poem." *Journal of Biblical Literature* 118, no. 2 (1999): 209–34.

_____. "Rehabilitating 'the Preacher': Qohelet's Theology in Context." Pages 90–116 in *Papers of the 1997 Henry Winters Luce III Fellows in Theology.* ATS Series in Theological Scholarship and Research 7. Edited by M. Zienowitcz. Pittsburgh: The Association of Theological Schools, 2000).

_____. "The Socioeconomic Context of 'the Preacher's' Hermeneutic," *Princeton Seminary Bulletin,* n.s., 17, no. 2 (1996): 168–195.

_____. "Theology When Everything is Out of Control." *Interpretation* (July 2001): 237–49.

Shank, H. C. "Qohelet's World and Lifeview as Seen in His Recurring Phrases." *Westminster Theological Journal* 37 (1974): 57–73.

Sheppard, Gerald T. "The Epilogue to Qoheleth as Theological Commentary." *Catholic Biblical Quarterly* 39 (1977): 182–89.

_____. *Wisdom as a Hermeneutical Construct: A Study in the Sapientializing of the Old Testament.* Beihefte zur Zeitschrift für die alttestamentliche Wissenschaft 151. Berlin: de Gruyter, 1980.

Siegfried, Carl G. A. *Prediger und Hoheslied.* Handkommentar zum Alten Testament 2:3, 2. Gottingen: Vandenhoeck & Ruprecht, 1898.

Smalley, Beryl. *Medieval Exegesis of Wisdom Literature.* Edited by R. E. Murphy. Atlanta: Scholars Press, 1986.

Smend, Rudolf. "Essen und Trinken—Ein Stück Weltlichkeit des Alten Testaments." Pages 446–59 in *Beiträge zur alttestamentlichen Theologie.* Edited by R. Hanhard and R. Smend. Göttingen: Vandenhoeck & Ruprecht, 1977.

Sneed, Mark. "Qohelet as 'Deconstructionist'." *OT Essays* 10 (1997): 303–11.

Spangenberg, I. J. J. "A Century of Wrestling with Qohelet: The Research History of the Book Illustrated with a Discussion of Qoh 4,17–5,6." Pages 61–91 in *Qoheleth in the Context of Wisdom.* Edited by A. Schoors. Leuven: Leuven University Press, 1998.

_____. "Irony in the Book of Qohelet." *Journal for the Study of the Old Testament* 72 (1996): 57–69.

_____. "Quotations in Ecclesiastes: An Appraisal." *Old Testament Essays* 4 (1991): 19–35.

Spolsky, Ellen. *The Uses of Adversity: Failure and Accomodation in Reader Response.* London: Associated University Press, 1990.

Staples, William Ewart. "'Profit' in Ecclesiastes." *Journal of Near Eastern Studies* 4 (1945): 87–96.

_____. "The 'Vanity' of Ecclesiastes." *Journal of Near Eastern Studies* 4 (1943): 95—104.

_____. "Vanity of Vanities." *Canadian Journal of Theology* 1 (1955): 141—56.

Strassmaier, J. N. *Inschriften von Nabuchodnosor, König von Babylon (605—561 v. Chr.).* Leipzig: Pfeiffer, 1889.

Szubin, H. Z., and B. Porten, "Royal Grants in Egypt: A New Interpretation of Driver 2." *Journal of Near Eastern Studies* 46 (1987): 39—48.

Taylor, C. *The Dirge of Coheleth in Ecclesiastes XII.* London: Williams & Norgate, 1874.

Thompson, J. A. "Ointment." Pages 593—96 in vol. 3 of *The Interpreter's Dictionary of the Bible.* Edited by G. A. Buttrick. 4 vols. Nashville: Abingdon, 1962.

Tigay, Jeffrey H. *The Evolution of the Gilgamesh Epic.* Philadelphia: University of Pennsylvania Press, 1982.

Towner, W. Sibley. "The Book of Ecclesiastes." Pages 265—360 in vol. 5 of *The New Interpreter's Bible.* Nashville: Abingdon, 1994.

Ungnad, A. *Vorderasiatische Schriftdenkmäler des Berliner Museums, herausgeben von der Generalverwaltung.* Vol. 6. Leipzig: Pfeiffer, 1908.

Waard, J. de. "The Structure of Qoheleth." Pages 57—64 in *Proceedings of the Eighth World Congress of Jewish Studies, Division A: The Bible and Its World.* Jerusalem, 1982.

Walsh, J. T. "Despair as a Theological Virtue in the Spirituality of Ecclesiastes." *Biblical Theology Bulletin* 12 (1982): 46—49.

Weil, Simone. *Waiting For God.* New York: Harper & Row, 1973.

Whitley, Charles Francis. *Koheleth: His Language and Thought.* Beihefte zur Zeitschrift für die alttestamentliche Wissenschaft 148. Berlin/New York: de Gruyter, 1979.

Whybray, R. N. *Ecclesiastes.* New Century Bible Commentary. Grand Rapids, Mich.: Eerdmans, 1989.

_____. "The Identification and Use of Quotations in Ecclesiastes." Pages 435—51 in *Congress Volume, Vienna, 1980.* Supplements to Vetus Testamentum 32. Edited by J. A. Emerton. Leiden: Brill, 1981.

_____. "Qohelet the Immoralist? (Qoh 7:6—17)." Pages 191—204 in *Israelite Wisdom* Edited by J. G. Grammie et al. Missoula, Mont.: Scholars Press, 1978.

_____. "Qohelet as a Theologian." Pages 239—266 in *Qohelet in the Context of Wisdom*. Edited by A. Schoors. Leuven: Leuven University Press, 1998.

_____. "Qoheleth, Preacher of Joy." *Journal for the Study of the Old Testament* 23 (1982): 87—98.

Wilson, G. H. "'The Words of the Wise': The Intent and Significance of Qoheleth 12:9—14." *Journal of Biblical Literature* 103/2 (1984): 175—92.

Witzenrath, Hagia Hildegard. *Süss ist das Licht: eine literaturwissenschaftliche Untersuchung zu Koh 11,7—12,7.* St. Ottiliten: EOS Verlag, 1979.

Wolff, Hans Walter. *Anthropology of the Old Testament.* Philadelphia: Fortress, 1974.

Wright, Addison G. "Additional Numerical Patterns in Qoheleth." *Catholic Biblical Quarterly* 45 (1983): 32—43.

_____. "'For Everything There Is a Season': The Structure and Meaning of the Fourteen Opposites (Ecclesiastes 3,2—8)." Pages 321—28 in *De La Tôrah au Messie: Mélanges Henri Cazelles.* Edited by J. Dore et al. Paris: Desclée, 1981.

_____. "The Riddle of the Sphinx Revisited: Numerical Patterns in the Book of Qoheleth." *Catholic Biblical Quarterly* 42 (1980): 38—51.

_____. "The Riddle of the Sphinx: The Structure of the Book of Qoheleth." *Catholic Biblical Quarterly* 30 (1968): 313—34.

Zapletal, V. *Das Buch Kohelet.* Freiburg: Gschwend, 1905.

Zimmerli, Walther. *Das Buch des Predigers Salomo.* Das Alte Testament Deutsch 16/1. Gottingen: Vandenhoeck & Ruprecht, 1962.

Zimmermann, Frank. *The Inner World of Qohelet.* New York: KTAV, 1973.

Index of Ancient Texts

Old Testament

Genesis

3:10 119
3:17—19 60
6:3 77
11:7 .... 87 n. 11
12:2 .... 53 n. 69
13:16 .... 87 n. 11
14:18 .... 63 n. 86
14:24 .... 69 n. 105
17:1 .... 53 n. 69
21:8 133
22:14 .... 87 n. 11
26:29 41
28:17 119
29:34 60
30:4 .... 63 n. 87
30:9 .... 63 n. 87
42:6 46
47:22 37

Exodus

15:11 119
18:19 .... 53 n. 69
20:18 119
34:2 .... 53 n. 69

Leviticus

4:2 ....95, 114
4:22 ....95, 114
4:27—30 ....96, 114
10:3 .... 97 n. 38

19:14 .... 119 n. 117
19:30 .... 119 n. 117
19:32 .... 119 n. 117
25:17 .... 119 n. 117
25:36 .... 119 n. 117
25:43 .... 119 n. 117
26:2 .... 119 n. 117

Numbers

11:15 38
15:22—31 .... 95, 114
15:39 75
15:40 76
16:22 98

Deuteronomy

1:34 98
4:2 89
4:6 .... 117 n. 108
4:10 .... 87 n. 11
4:39 96
6:18 41
7:21 119
9:19 98
10:17 119
10:21 119
11:2 .... 54 n. 72
12:7—8 132
12:11—12 132
13:1 89
14:22—27 132
14:23 133
18:8 .... 69 n. 105

20:5—7 .... 64 n. 90
22:22 .... 63 n. 87
23:22—24 ....95, 115
24:5 .... 64 n. 90
27:7 132
27:24 103
28:30 .... 64 n. 90
29:5 .... 63 n. 86
33:9 .... 54 n. 72

Joshua
2:11 96
22:18 98

Judges
9:16 41
17:10 .... 53 n. 69
18:19 .... 53 n. 69
19:19 .... 63 n. 86

Ruth
2:14 .... 63 n. 86

1 Samuel
10:3 .... 63 n. 86
12:19 119
15:22 ....95, 96
16:20 .... 63 n. 86
18:17 .... 53 n. 69
24:18 41
25:18 .... 63 n. 86
25:43 .... 63 n. 87
30:24 .... 69 n. 105

2 Samuel
6:9 119
2:23 119
13:5 .... 102 n. 61

1 Kings
8:59 .... 95 n. 38
12:21 .... 75 n. 119

2 Kings
17:24—28 93
18:32 .... 63 n. 86
22:20 38

1 Chronicles
13:12 .... 119 n. 116
16:27 138
17:21 .... 119 n. 116
29:9 .... 49 n. 58
29:17 .... 49 n. , 69

2 Chronicles
15:12—15 .... 49 n. 58
24:10 .... 49 n. 58
25:5 .... 75 n. 119
32:8 .... 77 n. 126

Nehemiah
5:5 45
8:10 .... 70, 133
8:12 .... 70, 133

Esther
4:16 22
9:1 45
9:22 70

Job
1:1 .... 5, 84, 120
1:4—5 92
1:8—9 .... 5, 84
1:8 120
2:3 84

2:10 37
3:4—5 .... 73 n. 117
3:16 73
7:7 38
8:5—6 93
8:9 .... 115 n. 101
9:5 38
10:4 .... 77 n. 126
11:13—15 92
15:8 95
15:23 .... 73 n. 117
20:2 .... 38 n. 22
21:3 95
21:13 52
22:27 .... 92, 95
23:11 95
28:24 96
28:28 5
31:5 95
32:3 49
32:5 49
33:28 73
33:30 73
34:14 77
42:8—10 92

Psalms
14:1 41
23:5 64
25:13 .... 52 n. 65
26:12 95
27:13 38
30:11 .... 53 n. 69
30:12 63
31:3 .... 53 n. 69
33:12 96
34:13 38
34:15 41

34:19 .... 95 n. 38
36:10 73
37:3 41
45:7 .... 64 n. 89
47:2 .... 119 n. 116
53:2 41
56:24 73
63:4 59
65:5 .... 119 n. 116
66:3 .... 119 n. 116
66:5 .... 119 n. 116
71:3 .... 53 n. 69
73:9 50
76:7 .... 119 n. 116
76:8 .... 119 n. 116
76:12 .... 119 n. 116
78:39 77
81:1 138
85:10 .... 95 n. 38
89:7 .... 119 n. 116
89:49 38
90:15 57
92:11 .... 64 n. 89
102:20 96
104:15 .... 38, 63, 64
105:22 .... 119 n. 116
109:4 .... 115 n. 101
110:3 ...... 78 n. 126, 115 n. 101
111:9 .... 119 n. 116
111:10 5
113:6 96
115:3—7 96
115:3 .... 97, 114
115:12—13 96
115:16 99
117:1 59
119:59 95
119:101 95

119:133 45
119:151 .... 95 n. 38
120:7 .... 115 n. 101
128:2 — 3 38
128:5 38
133:2 64
135:6 114
143:4 102
145:4 59
147:11 68
147:12 59
148:14 .... 95 n. 38

Proverbs
1:7 .... 5, 83
1:15 — 16 95
2:5 5
3:1 — 18 104
3:7 120
4:10 — 27 104
4:27 95
5:5 95
5:18 — 19 .... 64 n. 90
6:18 95
8:13 120
9:5 — 6 63
9:10 .... 5, 83
10:14 97
10:19 97
10:27 106
14:13 57
14:27 106
15:1 49
15:8 92
15:23 49
15:33 5
16:1 49
17:1 92

19:2 95
20:25 92
21:3 96
21:23 97
21:27 92
23:18 120
24:14 120
26:5 — 6 .... 55 n. 77
27:20 50
28:29 92
29:19 49
30:6 89
30:16 50
30:23 .... 69 n. 106
31:5 132
31:30 83

Ecclesiastes
1:1 .... 11, 18
1:2 ....1, 16, 19, 21, 113
1:3 .....19, 25, 37, 41, 59, 60, 93
1:3 — 4 27
1:3 — 7 26
1:3 — 11 ....16, 18 — 19, 26, 72
1:4 42
1:5 — 7 27
1:7 19
1:8 .... 19, 77
1:9 ....19, 27, 40, 89
1:10 .... 42 n. 34, 91 n. 22
1:12 — 2:26 ....19, 27, 34, 35, 51
1:13 — 14 40
1:13 — 2:3 .... 19, 35
1:13 .... 15, 19, 23 n. 42, 26,
.... 35, 40, 42, 75, 89,
.... 96 n. 39, 97, 115
1:14 .... 16, 27
1:16 .... 19, 24, 25

1:17 .... 19, 23 n. 42, 27, 107
2:1 ......3, 19, 24, 25, 27, 33, 38,
.... 52, 54, 91 n. 22
2:1 – 2 ....34, 35, 39
2:1 – 3 39
2:2 40
2:3 ....19, 36, 40, 48, 61, 75,
.... 110 n. 83, 115
2:4 – 11 19
2:5 40
2:6 40
2:8 40
2:10 41
2:10 – 11 35
2:11 ....16, 19, 27, 40
2:12 41
2:12 – 17 19
2:14 .... 62 n. 85, 107
2:15 .... 25, 27, 62 n. 85
2:16 42
2:17 ....16, 19, 27, 40, 89, 90
2:18 19
2:18 – 2:23 19
2:19 ....27, 46
2:20 – 21 136
2:21 27
2:22 41
2:23 ....27, 77, 93
2:24 .....3, 17, 33, 41, 59, 60, 97
2:24 – 26 ....3, 9, 19, 34, 35,
.... 35 – 39, 44, 136
2:25 16
2:26 ....27, 35, 40, 47, 93, 96
3:1 – 8 ....19, 27, 40, 42, 87,
.....................................90, 136
3:1 – 15 ....19 – 20
3:9 – 15 ....19, 105
3:9 – 22 ....86 – 87

3:9.........28, 40 – 41, 42, 59, 60
3:10 ... 20, 26, 35 n. 14, 42, 93,
.... 96 n. 39, 97
3:10 – 15.................. 20, 39, 40
3:11 – 14...................... 85, 116
3:11..............26, 28, 42, 45, 67,
.... 89 – 90, 96
3:12............ 3, 33, 36 n. 16, 59,
.... 82, 107
3:12 – 13............... 3, 9, 35, 37,
.................40 – 44, 67, 90, 134
3:13............ 3, 36 n. 15, 38, 42,
.....................45, 60, 115, 136
3:14..............10, 26, 40, 43, 57,
.................81, 83, 86 – 91, 94,
.....................99, 105, 107, 117
3:15......................... 87, 89, 117
3:15 – 22............................. 43
3:16............19, 20, 90, 99, 131
3:16 – 22............................. 20
3:17.............12, 13, 20, 24, 25,
......................77, 87, 100, 107,
.... 108, 115
3:18.................24, 25, 87, 100
3:19...................... 27, 62 n. 85
3:19 – 22............................. 56
3:20......................................77
3:22.............. 3, 9, 20, 35, 36 n.
.... 16, 41 n. 32 , 60,
.........................43 – 44, 59, 91
4:1.. 20
4:1 – 3..... 20, 20 n. 32, 90, 131
4:1 – 4................................. 130
4:1 – 16................. 20, 28 n. 68
4:2.. 59
4:3.................. 20, 38 n. 26, 89
4:4................................. 16, 20
4:5.. 60

4:6 20
4:7 ....20, 81
4:7−8 130
4:7−16 .... 20 n. 33
4:8 .... 35 n. 14, 36 n.
..................................15, 50, 93
4:9 20
4:9−12 131
4:10 .... 20 n. 33, 89
4:13 20
4:14 106
4:16 ....16, 106
4:17 ....98, 114, 121
4:17−5:6 ....86, 91−99,
.........................107, 113−114
5:1 ....85, 94, 96, 116, 121
5:2 .... 35 n. 14, 93, 97
5:3−5 ....95, 121
5:4 94
5:4−7 77
5:5 ....36, 94, 108
5:6 ....10, 12, 83, 86, 93
.... n. 29, 113−114
5:7 131
5:7−6:2 37
5:7−6:9 ....44, 49, 82
5:9 49
5:10 .... 38 n. 27, 49
5:11 ....49, 73
5:12 97
5:12−13 136
5:13 ....35, 91
5:14 74
5:14−19 56
5:15 59
5:16 ....38, 49, 60, 73, 77
5:17−19 ....3, 9, 35, 37, 44−
........................50, 74, 127, 137

5:17.........3, 36 n. 15, 38, 41 n.
.... 32, 60, 61, 110 n. 83
5:18.............41 n. 32, 46 n. 46,
............................96 n. 39, 115
5:19..................25, 53, 66, 136
5:29........................ 89 n. 19
6:1−2.............44, 46−47, 136
6:1−9................................. 20
6:2................... 49, 50, 89 n. 19,
.... 96 n. 39
6:2−5...................... 89 n. 19
6:3........................... 49, 50
6:5....................................... 73
6:6...................... 36 n. 15, 39
6:7... 50
6:7−9............................... 131
6:8... 21
6:9.........16, 20−21, 38, 50, 76
6:10.............................. 16, 51
6:10−12.................. 20, 21, 51
6:10−7:14...................... 51, 57
6:11...............20, 41, 59, 93, 97
6:12.......... 21, 28, 48 n. 53, 55,
.... 61, 106, 110 n. 83
6:13............................ 89 n. 19
6:24............................ 89 n. 19
7:1....................................... 56
7:1−12.....21, 28, 54−56, 107
7:2....................................... 115
7:2−4............................... 35
7:4....................................... 56
7:8................................ 54, 83
7:9.............................. 55 n. 77
7:10..................................... 54
7:11..................................... 73
7:13...................... 67, 104, 135
7:13−14............... 28, 50−57,
.... 99, 101, 117

7:13−18 136
7:14 .... 3, 9, 33, 35, 36 n.
.... 15, 39, 67, 87 n. 11,
.... 101 n. 53, 105
7:15 ....22, 61, 99, 101−102
7:15−18 ....105, 108
7:16−17 ....100−102
7:17 108
7:18 ....6, 10, 12, 14, 86,
...........................99−105, 121
7:19 46
7:20 ....35, 41, 102
7:22 106
7:23−24 99
7:23−29 21
7:24−28 67
7:25 75
7:26 ....36, 41
7:27 11
7:29 ....21, 135
8:1 ....21, 22
8:1−17 105
8:2 .... 21, 114 n. 98
8:3 114
8:3−5 21
8:4 22
8:5 ....108, 114
8:5−6 22
8:5−7 91
8:6 .... 77, 89 n. 19, 115
8:6−7 117
8:7 21
8:8 ....22, 47
8:9 .... 21, 22, 23 n. 42,
....................................46, 89, 90
8:9−11 131
8:9−15 104
8:9−17 ....58−59

8:10...................... 58, 114, 138
8:10−17.............................. 22
8:11.................................... 103
8:11−12.............................. 58
8:12........................... 10, 36, 86
8:12−13............. 6, 12, 14, 83,
.... 105−110
8:14.............................. 90, 104
8:15............ 1, 3, 9, 35, 36 n. 5,
...................37, 58−62, 67, 96
.... n. 39, 109−110
8:16...................... 23, 35 n. 14,
.....................89, 93, 106, 110
8:16−17...................... 22 n. 41
8:17...................21, 23, 67, 85,
.... 89, 110, 117
8:18................................... 104
9:1............................... 22−23
9:1−10...................... 66−67
9:2........................... 36, 62, 92
9:3........................... 62, 89−90
9:5−10............................... 56
9:6.................. 42 n. 34, 72, 89
9:7........................... 36, 68, 133
9:7−10.............3, 9, 17, 35, 37,
...............62−72, 74, 127, 138
9:7−12:7 98
9:9................3, 33, 38, 54, 60,
.... 61, 96 n. 39, 136
9:10...................................... 61
9:11................................... 134
9:12................................... 106
9:18...................................... 36
10:4....................................... 36
10:8−20............................ 107
10:12.........................89 n. 19
10:13−14...................... 93, 97
10:16−19............................ 82

10:16—20 133
10:19 ....25, 63, 133
10:20 .... 89 n. 19
11:1 ....68, 69, 134
11:1—2 137
11:1—6 ....82, 137
11:2 ....69, 91, 134
11:5 ....85, 91, 137
11:6 ....62, 92
11:7 74
11:7—12:1 .... 3, 36
11:7—12:7 ....9, 17, 57,
.....................73—81, 87, 117,
11:9 .... 12, 17, 39, 76 n.
...................121, 77, 81, 109,
.........................116—117, 137
11:9—10 29
11:10 ....78, 79
12:1 ....26, 29, 74, 79, 80, 81
12:1—7 ....19, 26, 28—29,
....................................79, 117
12:2 74
12:2—5 80
12:3—7 16
12:4 116
12:5 .... 43 n. 34
12:6—7 80
12:7 .... 29, 78, 97 n. 39
12:8 ....1, 16, 19, 73, 80,
.....................................111, 114
12:9 111
12:9—11 25
12:9—14 117
12:13 ....5, 10, 84, 87, 94
12:13b—14 .....8, 14, 111—119
12:14 ....11, 117
13:4 .... 90 n. 19
13:5 90

Song of Songs
1:4................................65 n. 90

Isaiah
1:12—17...................... 106
5:11—13...................... 133
5:14............................... 51
5:22—23...................... 133
25:6—8........................ 134
28:28........................70 n. 106
33:2............................54 n. 69
36:17..........................64 n. 86
40:6............................78 n. 126
46:10.............................. 115
47:6................................ 99
55:8—9............................ 98
56:3................................ 61
56:6................................ 61
57:16................................ 99
59:7................................ 96
59:16.............................. 103
61:3................................ 65
63:5.............................. 103
64:3.............................. 120

Jeremiah
26:2.................................... 90

Lamentations
2:12............................64 n. 86
5:22................................ 99

Ezekiel
4:15................................. 134
13:17........................103 n. 16
16:20............................. 47
21:15..........................54 n. 69
43:19..........................96 n. 38

Daniel
2:23 60
2:39 46
3:27 46
4:14 115
4:22 115
4:29 115
4:31 60
4:32 115
4:34 60
5:1 134
5:4 60
5:7 46
5:16 46
5:23 60
6:25 46
8:27 103

Hosea
6:6 97

Amos
5:18 .... 74 n. 117
5:22—24 97
6:4—6 133

Jonah
1:14 115

Habakkuk
1:13 .... 39 n. 26
1:16 .... 70 n. 105
2:5 51
2:20 97

Zechariah
1:2 99
1:15 99

2:11 120
2:15 61

Apocrypha

Sirach
1:26—30 .... 118, 118 n. 108
5:2 .... 76 n. 121
13:7 22
14:5 72
14:11—14 72
15:11—20 .... 48 n. 48
31:27 .... 64 n. 86
31:27—31 133
34:5 .... 98 n. 41
39:26 .... 64 n. 86
41:12 61
43:24 103

New Testament

Matthew
6:16—17 .... 65 n. 89

Other Extra-Biblical
Ancient Sources

Akkadian
Descent of Ishtar ...... 74 n. 116
Gilgamesh Epic .... 49 n. 53,
..... 64 n. 87, 65—68, 74 n. 116

Egyptian

Admonitions of Ipuwer 39
.... n. 21, 65 n. 88
Complaints of Khakheppere-Sonb .... 24 n. 46, 25
Dialogue of Pessimism 67
Dispute Between a Man and his Ba .... 24 n. 46, 25
Eloquent Peasant ...... 72 n. 113
Instruction Addressed to King Merikare .... 96 n. 37
Instruction of Anii 71
Instruction of Onchsheshonqy 71

Instruction of Ptahhotep .... 77 n. 123
Song of Antef ...... 49, 77 n. 123
Tale of Sinuhe .... 65 n. 88

Rabbinic

b. Shab. 30b 1, 112
b. Pesahim 71a 65
Lev. Rabb. section 18 ..... 26, 79
Qoh. Rabb. on 12:1 .... 26, 79

Ugaritic

KTU 1.23.61−64 .... 51 n. 60
KTU 1.5.2.2−4 .... 51 n. 60